D0951944

# FINDING

# GEORGE ORWELL

*in*

# BURMA

# FINDING
# GEORGE ORWELL
*in*
# BURMA

## EMMA LARKIN

*The Penguin Press*
*New York*
*2005*

THE PENGUIN PRESS
Published by the Penguin Group
Penguin Group (USA) Inc., 375 Hudson Street, New York, New York 10014, U.S.A. • Penguin
Group (Canada), 10 Alcorn Avenue, Toronto, Ontario, Canada M4V 3B2 (a division of Pearson
Penguin Canada Inc.) • Penguin Books Ltd, 80 Strand, London WC2R 0RL, England • Penguin
Ireland, 25 St. Stephens's Green, Dublin 2, Ireland (a division of Penguin Books Ltd) • Penguin
Books Australia Ltd, 250 Camberwell Road, Camberwell, Victoria 3124, Australia (a division of
Pearson Australia Group Pty Ltd) • Penguin Books India Pvt Ltd, 11 Community Centre,
Panchsheel Park, New Delhi – 110 017, India • Penguin Group (NZ), Cnr Airborne and Rosedale
Roads, Albany, Auckland 1310, New Zealand (a division of Pearson New Zealand Ltd) • Penguin
Books (South Africa) (Pty) Ltd, 24 Sturdee Avenue, Rosebank, Johannesburg 2196, South Africa

Penguin Books Ltd, Registered Offices:
80 Strand, London WC2R 0RL England

First American edition
Published in 2005 by The Penguin Press,
a member of Penguin Group (USA) Inc.

Originally published in Great Britain as *Secret Histories* by John Murray.

LIBRARY OF CONGRESS CATALOGING IN PUBLICATION DATA

Larkin, Emma.
Finding George Orwell in Burma / Emma Larkin.
p. cm.
Originally published under title: Secret histories : a journey through Burma today in the
company of George Orwell; London : John Murray, 2004.
ISBN 1-59420-052-1
1. Larkin, Emma—Travel—Burma.   2. Orwell, George, 1903–1950—Travel—Burma.
3. Burma—Description and travel.   4. Burma—Political conditions—20th Century.   I. Title.
DS527.7.L37 2005 2004065786
915.9104'53—dc22

This book is printed on acid-free paper. ∞

Printed in the United States of America
1   3   5   7   9   10   8   6   4   2

Designed by Stephanie Huntwork

*For my friends in Burma*

# Contents

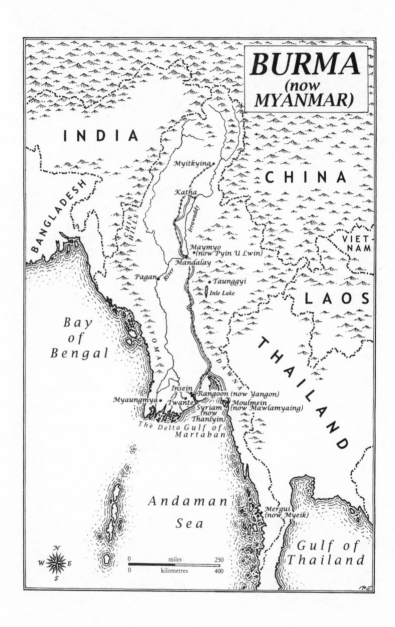

# PROLOGUE

**G**EORGE ORWELL,' I said slowly. 'G-e-o-r-g-e O-r-w-e-l-l.' But the old Burmese man just kept shaking his head.

We were sitting in the baking-hot front room of his house in a sleepy port town in Lower Burma. The air was oppressive and muggy. I could hear mosquitoes whining impatiently around my head, and I was about to give up. The man was a well-known scholar in Burma, and I knew he was familiar with Orwell. But he was elderly; cataracts had turned his eyes an oystery blue, and his hands trembled as he readjusted his sarong. I wondered if he was losing his memory but, after several failed attempts, I made one final stab.

'George Orwell,' I repeated—'the author of *Nineteen Eighty-Four.*' The old man's eyes suddenly lit up. He looked at me with a brilliant flash of recognition, slapped his forehead gleefully, and said, 'You mean the prophet!'

**A** YEAR BEFORE GEORGE ORWELL died in 1950, his typewriter was confiscated. Orwell lay tucked under an electric blanket in a small wooden chalet in the green and pleasant heart of the Cotswolds, dying of pulmonary tuberculosis. Piled around his sickbed were a variety of books: tomes on Stalin and on German atrocities in the Second World War, a study of English labourers in the nineteenth century, a few Thomas Hardy novels, some early Evelyn Waugh. Under the bed was a secret stash of rum.

The doctors at the sanatorium where Orwell was being treated had advised him to stop writing. Any kind of writing, they said, would tire him out. What he needed was total rest. Both his lungs were clogged with lesions, and he was coughing up blood. The disease had now reached a critical stage, and doctors were not hopeful of his chances of recovery. Even if he did survive, he might never be able to write again—or at least not with the same intensity he was used to. Orwell, however, continued to write. He scribbled letters, composed essays, reviewed books, and corrected proofs of his soon-to-be-published novel *Nineteen Eighty-Four*. And, simmering in his fevered mind, was an idea for another book: a novella entitled 'A Smoking Room Story', which would revisit Burma, a place he had not been to since his youth.

Orwell had lived in Burma in the 1920s as an officer of the Imperial Police Force. For five years he dressed in khaki jodhpurs and shining black boots. Armed with guns and a sense of moral superiority, the Imperial Police Force patrolled the countryside and kept this far-flung corner of the British Empire in line. Then, suddenly and without warning, he returned to England and handed in his notice. Just as abruptly, he began his career as a writer. Exchanging his real name, 'Eric Arthur Blair', for the pen-name 'George Orwell', he donned the rags of a tramp and marched off into the dank London nights to collect the stories of the down-at-heel. Orwell based his first novel, *Burmese Days*, on his experiences in the Far East, but it was his later novels such as *Animal Farm* and *Nineteen Eighty-Four* that would turn him into one of the most respected and visionary writers of the twentieth century.

It is a particularly uncanny twist of fate that these three novels effectively tell the story of Burma's recent history. The link begins with *Burmese Days,* which chronicles the country's period under British colonialism. Not long after Burma became independent from Britain in 1948, a military dictator sealed off the country from the outside world, launched 'The Burmese Way to Socialism', and turned Burma into one of the poorest countries in Asia. The same story is told in Orwell's *Animal Farm,* an allegorical tale about a socialist revolution gone wrong in which a group of pigs overthrow the human farmers and run the farm into ruin. Finally, in *Nineteen Eighty-Four* Orwell's description of a horrifying and soulless dystopia paints a chillingly accurate picture of Burma today, a country ruled by one of the world's most brutal and tenacious dictatorships.

In Burma there is a joke that Orwell wrote not just one novel about the country, but three: a trilogy comprised of *Burmese Days, Animal Farm* and *Nineteen Eighty-Four.*

A S I WALKED down a busy street in Mandalay on my first visit to Burma, in 1995, a Burmese man strode purposefully towards me twirling a black umbrella. He smiled brightly and said, 'Spread our need of democracy to the rest of the world—

the people are so tired.' Then he turned around and walked briskly away. And that was it: one of the few, fleeting glimpses I had that all is not as it seems in Burma.

During the three weeks I spent wandering through postcard-perfect scenes of bustling markets, glittering pagodas and faded British hill stations I found it hard to believe I was travelling through a country that has one of the worst records for human-rights abuse in the world. To me, this is the most staggering thing about Burma: that the oppression of an entire nation of some 50 million people can be completely hidden from view. A vast network of Military Intelligence spies and their informers ensures that no one can do or say anything that might threaten the regime. The Burmese media—books, magazines, movies and music—are controlled by a strict censorship board and government propaganda is churned out not only through newspapers and television, but also in schools and universities. These methods of reality-control are kept firmly in place by the invisible, though ever present, threat of torture and imprisonment.

For an outsider like myself, unable to see beyond the façade the generals have created, it was impossible to imagine the daily fear and precariousness of living in such a state. It was during my efforts to understand this aspect of Burmese life that I became fascinated by Orwell. All his novels explore the idea of individuals being trapped within their environment, controlled by their family, the society around them or an all-powerful government. In *Nineteen Eighty-Four* he conjured up the ultimate vision of oppression, even giving us the language with which to describe it: 'Big Brother', 'Room 101', 'Newspeak'.

As I reread Orwell's novels—books I had not read since my schooldays—I became curious about his personal connection with Burma. What was it that had made him trade his career in the colonies for that of a writer? And why, after nearly a quarter of a century away from Burma, did he look to the country for inspiration while he lay on his deathbed? I began to imagine that Orwell had seen something in Burma, had had some thread of an idea, that had worked its way into all his writing. I looked through the various biographies that have been written about Orwell, but their authors seemed to underplay the significance of Burma and, as far I could gather, none of them had ever conducted any research in the places where Orwell spent five life-changing years. The towns and cities where Orwell was posted span the geographical heart of the country and, in a sense, it is still possible to experience Burma as Orwell knew it—almost half a century of military dictatorship has given it the air of a country frozen in time. But a journey through Orwell's Burma would lead through an even eerier and much more terrifying landscape: that of a real-life *Nineteen Eighty-Four* where Orwell's nightmare visions are being played out with a gruelling certainty.

FOREIGN WRITERS and journalists are denied entry to Burma. Occasionally some are able to slip into the country posing as tourists, but if they are discovered their notebooks and photographic film are confiscated and they are swiftly deported. For the Burmese people they interview, the repercussions are infinitely greater. Under the country's 1950 Emergency Provisions Act, providing foreigners with information that the regime considers inimical is punishable with a seven-year prison sentence. Though I worked as a journalist, I rarely wrote about Burma and so it was still possible for me to blend in among tourists or the small expatriate community of business people who are granted long-stay visas. In basing a book on my experiences there were concessions to be made: I would have to change the names of the Burmese people I spoke with and, in some cases, their locations. But, if I was careful, it would be possible to forge a pathway through this seemingly impenetrable country.

Before I left for Burma, I went to the George Orwell Archive in London to look at Orwell's final manuscript. When Orwell died, in 1950, he had only just begun the project. 'A Smoking Room Story' was planned as a novella of thirty to forty thousand words which told how a fresh-faced young British man was irrevocably changed after living in the humid tropical jungles of colonial Burma. In an inky scrawl on the first three pages of a notebook bound in marbled paper Orwell had written an outline for the tale and a short vignette. I flicked through the rest of the book and found the pages blank. The rest of the story, I realized, lay waiting in Burma.

## One

# MANDALAY

Who controls the past controls the future:
who controls the present controls the past.

*Nineteen Eighty-Four*

THE KNEE-HIGH TABLES at a busy Mandalay tea shop are packed close together. Around them, men in peacock-bright sarongs perch on footstools. The large room is noisy with the babble of hundreds of different conversations. Grubby serving boys weave through the crowd bellowing orders to the kitchen staff. Swirls of steam waft from the cups of tea they carry aloft, and the air is thick with the incense-like smell of cheroots.

'Have you read Charles Dickens?' the Burmese man sitting next to me asks.

'Yes, of course,' I yell above the clamour.

'Maupassant?'

'One or two stories.'

'Sidney Sheldon?'

'Um, yes.'

'Robert Louis Stevenson?'

'Yes.'

'Ah-ha! *Dr Jekyll and Mr Hyde!*'

'Yes.'

'Tell me! What is *Dr Jekyll and Mr Hyde* about?'

A Burmese friend had introduced me to Aye Myint because of his passion for books. He is a tall man with overly long arms and a stooped posture more suited to the well-worn reclining chair where he does his reading than to standing upright. He quizzes me endlessly about books, posing queries I am ill-equipped to answer. It has been a long time since I read *Dr Jekyll and Mr Hyde,* but I hazard a reply to his question.

'I think it's about the dark side that every person keeps hidden. It explores the idea that we are all of us both good and bad.'

'I agree!' he shouts and, pausing briefly to adjust his milk-bottle glasses, he continues with his quiz: 'Henry James? . . . Franz Kafka?'

Aye Myint's love of books is not unusual in Burma. Everywhere you go you see people reading. The trishaw drivers parked by the corner of my hotel in Mandalay were always draped across the tattered seats of their vehicles, poring over magazines or books. Sometimes three of them would be hunched hungrily over a single volume. New and second-hand books are sold off tarpaulin mats spread across the pavements of Rangoon and at the night-time book bazaar in Mandalay. Magazines can be bought from fold-up wooden tables on every street or from vendors who carry large stacks under their arms, yelling out the titles as they wander through tea shops and train stations.

One elderly lady told me how she lost her house and everything in it to one of the fires that periodically rage through the parched streets of Mandalay. It is her book collection she misses most: 'I lost all my books—every single one,' she told me. She cited a Dickens novel as if she were murmuring the name of a long-lost lover. *'Great Expectations,'* she said mournfully.

A Burmese man once tried to chat me up using a scene from Emily Brontë's novel which he endearingly referred to as *Woothering Heights*. He suggested I help him with his English-language studies as the young Catherine had taught Hareton, each correct answer receiving a kiss. Undeterred by my doubtful expression, he told me to check the reference: 'Penguin edition, page 338.'

After Aye Myint had thoroughly quizzed me about which authors I had read and what I thought about them, he decided to show me his book collection. It is not easy to get English-language books in Burma, but his collection numbers over a thousand volumes, the result of decades spent scouring second-hand bookshops. As he puts it, he 'retired from the world' in his early twenties and for the past forty years has lived a hermit-like existence in Mandalay, sequestered with his library and one spinster sister in a two-storey wooden house that they inherited from their parents. The interior of the house was dark and cool. The front room was crammed with sagging wooden furniture. An empty teacup sat on the arm of an old planter's chair, and the glass-fronted book cabinets were filled with old newspapers, their corners orange and crackling with age. Two grandfather clocks stood in opposite corners of the room, each telling a different time.

Aye Myint led me upstairs to where his books were kept. A thick carpet of dust lay across the wooden floor, and a narrow trail of footprints marked a pathway from the staircase to the bookshelf to a reading chair and back to the staircase again—a map of Aye Myint's entire world. His books were stored in trunks, and he opened one up for me. Each book was carefully wrapped in a plastic bag to protect it from the white ants and mould that destroy so many manuscripts in the humid, tropical climate of Burma. He started pulling out volumes.

'Hans Christian Andersen!' he shouted as he tossed me a beautifully illustrated collection of children's stories. 'O. Henry! Somerset Maugham! James Herbert!' A well-thumbed edition of *Rats* came flying towards me. Aye Myint reached deeper inside his trunk. 'Ernest Hemingway!' he bellowed as he pulled out a copy of *For Whom the Bell Tolls* folded up inside a used coffee-powder bag. 'Ah-ha! Hemingway!' he said. 'Now, do you know why he committed suicide?'

I was saved from having to answer when Aye Myint stuck his head deep inside his trunk and emerged with a triumphant cry: 'Ha! George Orwell!' He uncovered an old Penguin copy of *Animal Farm*. It had the familiar orange and white stripes on the cover, and yellowed pages that felt very slightly damp. He told me it was the first novel he had read in English. 'It is a very brilliant book. And it is a very Burmese book. Do you know why?' he asked, poking a finger enthusiastically in my general direction. 'Because it is about pigs and dogs ruling the country! That is what has been happening here in Burma for many years now.'

I had already told Aye Myint that I was interested in George Orwell, and he soon unearthed a worm-eaten copy of *Nineteen*

*Eighty-Four* from the growing piles of books on the floor. 'Another very brilliant book,' he said. 'It is a particularly wonderful book because it is without "-isms". It is not about socialism or communism or authoritarianism. It is about power and the abuse of power. Plain and simple.' He said that *Nineteen Eighty-Four* is banned in Burma because it can be read as a criticism of how the country is being run and the ruling generals do not like criticism. As a result, he told me, I would be unlikely to meet many people in Burma who had actually read the novel. 'Why do they need to read it?' he said. 'They are already living inside *Nineteen Eighty-Four* in their daily lives.'

I HAD COME to Mandalay carrying a dog-eared copy of Orwell's *Burmese Days*, the margins of its pages filled with messy notes and scrawls. As I saw it, this novel was the beginning of Orwell's uncanny and prophetic trilogy which told the history of present-day Burma. Orwell was just nineteen years old when he arrived in Mandalay to join the British government's Police Training School. It was there that he began the colonial career which would mark the beginning of his journey towards becoming a writer. And it was the British administration in Burma, of which Orwell was a part, which laid the foundations for the ruthless powers that have controlled the country for the past half-century. The British colonized Burma in stages, gradually taking over large chunks of what they called Lower Burma, and it was not until they captured the royal capital of Mandalay, in 1885, that

Burma as a whole could be declared part of the British Empire. Here in Mandalay, then, the imprint was laid both for Orwell and for Burma.

Mandalay, located in the flat, dry plains of what the British called Upper Burma, is the country's second largest city. In *Burmese Days* Orwell described it as 'rather a disagreeable town' that was 'dusty and intolerably hot'. Though the description remains true today, little remains of the wooden houses and dirt streets of Orwell's time. Fierce battles between Allied forces and Japanese soldiers during the Second World War destroyed large swathes of the city. And what wasn't later consumed by fires has been demolished to make way for an influx of Chinese merchants. The city's strategic position on the banks of the great Irrawaddy river makes it a key trading centre for commerce with China. As flashy Chinese buildings with mirrored windows and gilded Corinthian columns take over the city centre, Burmese families are forced into squatter towns outside the town. It is a common Burmese complaint that Mandalay is becoming little more than a satellite of China, and that the romance of old Mandalay is long gone. Mandalay's streets are numerically ordered and run north–south and east–west in a mathematically precise grid. Though the massive walls of the Burmese king's former palace are still standing, draped in bougainvillea, the regime has stationed a large military garrison inside the compound. From here the city fans out in an orderly maze of shop-houses, pagodas and tea shops.

I always find it impossible to say the name 'Mandalay' out loud without having at least a small flutter of excitement. For many foreigners the name conjures up irresistible images of lost oriental kingdoms and tropical splendour. The unofficial Poet Laureate of British colonialism, Rudyard Kipling, is partly responsible for this, through his well-loved poem 'Mandalay'. But the name also tugs at Burmese heartstrings. The city was the seat of power in Burma, and it was here that the last Burmese monarch, King Thibaw, reigned. Many of the families who lived here then were artisans responsible for the pleasures and rituals of the royal court. They were silk-weavers, gold-beaters, puppeteers and dancers, and Mandalay was considered the cultural and artistic capital of the country. Somerset Maugham, who passed through the city in the 1920s, wrote that the name 'Mandalay' had 'an independent magic' all its own. Wise men, he speculated, probably stayed away from the city, for they knew it could never live up to the expectations aroused by those lilting syllables.

'Mandalay' is one of the few place names in Burma that has not been changed by the Burmese military government. In 1989 the regime renamed streets, towns and cities across Burma. Maymyo, the old British hill station that Orwell visited, became Pyin-Oo-Lwin, and Fraser Street in Rangoon became Anawyatha Lan in Yangon. Most of the old names were Anglicized Burmese names that had been used by the British colonial government, and the regime claimed that the changes were a long-overdue move to discard these colonial tags. But there was a deeper-rooted motive. The generals were rewriting history. When a place is renamed, the old name disappears from maps and, eventually, from human memory. If that is possible, then perhaps the memory of past events can also be erased. By renaming cities, towns and streets, the regime seized control of the very space within which people lived; home and business addresses had to be rewritten and relearned. And, when the regime changed the name of the country, maps and encyclopedias all over the world had to be corrected. The country known as Burma was erased and replaced with a new one: Myanmar.

The crucial event which triggered this rewriting of the past was the people's uprising of 1988. At eight minutes past eight in the morning on the eighth day of the eighth month of that year, students launched a countrywide demonstration against almost three decades of poverty and oppression under military rule. Thousands of people flooded into the streets of cities and towns all over Burma shouting, 'Dee-mo-ka-ra-see! Dee-mo-ka-ra-see!' The government response was brutal: that evening, soldiers marched into the streets and strafed the crowds with machine-gun fire. In Rangoon, doctors and nurses, overwhelmed by the wounded, hung a sign outside the general hospital begging the soldiers to stop killing people. The sign was written with the blood of the wounded and dead. When a column of nurses joined the protest in the streets, wearing their white uniforms, they too were shot. Among those who died during the days of chaos that followed were high-school children, teachers and monks. Smoke billowed from crematoriums as the authorities rapidly disposed of their corpses. The uprising did not end until more than 3,000 people had been shot or bludgeoned to death by government soldiers.

Around that time a Burmese woman called Aung San Suu Kyi, who lived in Oxford, England, happened to be back in Rangoon nursing her sick mother. Aung San Suu Kyi is the daughter of Aung San, the much-loved Burmese military hero who led negotiations for Burma's independence from Britain and who was assassinated just months before independence came into effect in 1948, when his daughter was two years old. A week after the worst of the violence, Aung San Suu Kyi left her mother's sickbed to stand beneath a giant portrait of her father and speak to the crowd of half a million people who had turned up to see her. 'I could not as my father's daughter remain indifferent to all that was going on,' she said, and she compared the uprising to the country's fight against British colonialism: 'This national crisis could in fact be called the second struggle for national independence.'

The struggle is not yet over. As soon as the military regained control of the country, it began systematically to erase the bloody events of 1988. It renamed itself the State Law and Order Restoration Council (SLORC), and announced a new line-up of ruling generals. Soldiers mopped up the streets, repainted public buildings, and forced people to paint their own houses in what was a literal whitewashing of history. In Mandalay and Rangoon, whole neighbourhoods were swept away as people were forcibly relocated from areas where anti-government sentiment had been particularly strong. Demonstration leaders were hunted down, tortured and imprisoned. Some 10,000 people were forced to flee central Burma, taking refuge in jungle areas on the border or in neighbouring countries. SLORC promised to let the people choose their own government and organized a general election. But, when Aung San Suu Kyi formed an immensely popular party called the

National League for Democracy (NLD), the generals tried to prevent the NLD from winning the elections by arresting thousands of its supporters and placing Aung San Suu Kyi under house arrest. Nevertheless, the NLD won a landslide victory, securing over 80 per cent of the parliamentary seats. SLORC ignored the results and continued to rule.

The military—now called the State Peace and Development Council (SPDC)—still controls Burma today. The army has more than doubled in size and now has almost half a million soldiers. Aung San Suu Kyi has spent most of the intervening years locked up in her run-down family home in Rangoon. The date of the uprising, 8–8–88, or *shiq lay-lone* ('four eights'), has become a whispered mantra in Burma, denoting a tragic turning point in the history of the country which can only be remembered secretly, behind closed doors. It is as if the events of 1988 never happened. A year after the uprising, a spokesman for the regime summed up what had taken place: 'Truth is true only within a certain period of time,' he announced. 'What was truth once may no longer be truth after many months or years.'

I SPENT MY FIRST few days in Mandalay visiting old friends and telling them about my plans to follow Orwell's path through Burma. My friends introduced me to Burmese writers and historians—people who were also interested in Orwell—and it was not long before I had gathered around myself an unofficial Orwell Book Club.

It was a small group—of necessity, so as not to attract the attention of the authorities. Unauthorized gatherings of people are technically illegal, and a gathering that included a foreigner would attract more attention than most. Our first meeting took place in a busy tea shop with bright blue awnings. We chose a corner table beside a noisy television—the screech and wail of soap operas would drown out the sound of our voices for any unwanted listeners. There were four of us altogether. Za Za Win, a university graduate in her early twenties, was eager to improve her English; she reads anything she can get her hands on, and has a particular passion for *Reader's Digest* magazine ('Because the stories always have happy endings,' she told me). The two men in the group were Maung Oo, a young writer and poet, and Tun Lin, a retired teacher, whose favourite hobbies are telling jokes and reading George Orwell.

For our first meeting we planned to talk about Orwell's *Burmese Days*. It would have been a fairly innocuous topic in the eyes of the government: though *Animal Farm* and *Nineteen Eighty-Four* are banned, you can buy a pirated English-language copy of *Burmese Days* in Burma for roughly one US dollar. But, before we could begin, we had to order tea.

Tea is an integral part of Burmese cultural life, and Mandalay is renowned for having some of the best tea shops in the country. They are mostly open-air affairs of low wooden tables and tiny stools that spill out on to the pavements beneath high awnings or umbrellas. Each tea shop has its own specialty. Everyone admires the mutton curry puffs at the Minthiha Tea Shop chain in Mandalay, for instance, and I favoured a corner tea shop near my hotel where the baked-to-order *naan* bread and split-pea dip became my breakfast staple. There is a pleasing rhythm to the life of the Mandalay tea shops, and whole days can be lost inside them. In the morning, bicycles and motorbikes crowd around them in congested rows as customers down their first cup of the day before going to work. At lunchtime, the peak of the day's heat, the tea shops are lazy and quiet; the young waiting boys doze on the tables, while flies hover above them in sultry slow motion. In the late afternoon and early evenings the pace picks up as the boys become busy with orders for tea and snacks, and the shops are again noisy with chatter.

Yet Burmese tea shops are not as innocent as they first appear. The conversations can range from the exorbitant price of this year's pineapples or the quality of the shop's tea to love, literature and, of course, politics. The events which led to the 1988 uprising were triggered by a brawl in a tea shop, and tea shops are treated by the military regime as potential breeding grounds for anti-government activities. Government spies collect intelligence by eavesdropping on conversations or, as the gossip wafting around the tables has been more atmospherically dubbed, 'tea-shop vapours'. As a result, you have to choose your seat carefully, and when a Burmese person enters a tea shop he or she must perform an instant and invisible scan of the clientele.

Orwell understood the magical powers of tea. A well-brewed cup, he wrote, can make you feel wiser, braver and more optimistic. He preached that the only way to drink tea was strong and sugarless, and preferably brewed with Typhoo Tips tea bags. The Burmese are also extremely fussy about tea, and a tea shop's reputation is built on its ability to cater to each person's individual requirements. Tea is served honey-thick with condensed milk, and is washed down with Oolong tea. In the centre of every table is a flask of this clear brew, which Orwell's anti-heroine in *Burmese Days*, Elizabeth, complains tastes exactly like earth. To aid our *Burmese Days* debate, Tun Lin and I ordered *lepet-yay paw kya* ('tea, strong and not too sweet'). Maung Oo had his tea *cho hseint* ('milky and sweet'), while Za Za Win preferred hers *paw hseint* ('milky and not overly sweet').

I was anxious to hear what the members of this impromptu Orwell Book Club had to say about his first novel. To my mind, *Burmese Days* is a bleak and wonderful book. It tells the story of John Flory, a British timber merchant living in the remote hills of Upper Burma during the 1920s. Flory is torn between upholding the code of the pukka sahib, the social requirements of the British administration in which he lives, and the beguilingly exotic nature of the Burmese around him. He visits *pwe,* the colourful Burmese street theatre performed by travelling troupes. He wanders around bazaars pungent with 'garlic, dried fish, sweat, dust, anise, cloves and turmeric'. And he spends his evenings at the club downing tepid gin-and-tonics (because the ice hasn't yet arrived from the ice factories in Mandalay), listening to dated records on a scratchy gramophone, playing bridge and complaining about the insufferable heat and the equally insufferable insolence of the natives.

The writer Maung Oo stirred his tea thoughtfully and announced that he found *Burmese Days* insulting. 'Orwell looks down on the Burmese people. He did not like us,' he said as he poured clear tea from the central flask into four miniature ceramic bowls, one for each of us. Indeed, the Burmese characters are repellent. Flory's Burmese mistress is sluttish and desperate, his servant is obsequious, and a corrupt Burmese magistrate attempts to scheme and blackmail his way into the British-only club. Maung Oo showed us an article written recently by a Burmese academic about Orwell's novel. The article takes Edward Said's book *Orientalism* as its point of departure, and puts forward the theory that a Western person can only see the East and Eastern peoples not as cultures and peoples in their own right, but as a creation of the West. If the East is seen and interpreted only through the prism of Western ideals, it is destined to be portrayed as primitive and brutal, lacking in law and order. Maung Oo said that Orwell fell into this trap with *Burmese Days*. He chose to come to the East so that he could be someone respectable and civilized among the uncivilized natives. There are only two kinds of men in Orwell's *Burmese Days,* said Maung Oo: masters and slaves. The white men are always the masters.

Za Za Win, the recent graduate, agreed. The fact that the novel ends with the suicide of the main character, Flory, who is the one British person to sympathize with the Burmese people, illustrates that those who did not buy into the mainstream beliefs of the time could not survive. As she summed it up, 'Orwell upholds that the British way was the only way.'

A flurry of activity erupted around the open kitchen area as a giant kettle came to the boil above the charcoal fire. Two young serving boys held the kettle with damp rags and poured the tea into a tin vat. The tea-master, an older man with a large pot-belly filling out his lemon-yellow singlet, mixed individual helpings of tea with condensed milk, expertly pouring the creamy concoction back and forth between two dented tin cans. The tea-shop boys shouted customer preferences to him (*'Cho hseint* two!' or *'Paw kya* one!'), and he decanted the mixture into waiting cups which were swiftly distributed around the shop. As the boys rushed past me with their orders, I could smell the comforting toffee-like smell of the fresh brew.

I put in a plea in Orwell's defence. Orwell once wrote that one of the attributes which qualified him to be a writer was his ability to face unpleasant facts: he felt he was able to voice what he saw as the truth no matter how painful or awkward it might be. In *Burmese Days,* Orwell was simply painting a picture of how he saw things in Burma. It is not that Orwell disliked Burma or the Burmese, I said: it was the system he disliked. He was condemning a political framework that made good men—both Burmese and British—do bad things.

The retired teacher and self-confessed Orwell aficionado Tun Lin, however, would not hear a word said against the British. He was sixty-four years old, and had been born in British Burma. He was educated at a mission school in Mandalay, and can still remember the names of all his teachers. He once showed me sepia-tinted photographs of his female instructors—sensible ladies in flat shoes, with hair pulled back into taut buns. He even remembers the titles of the essays he had to write at school ('Compose 500 words with the title "Under the Banyan Tree"'). In his eyes, the British can do, and did, no wrong. 'Under the British we were able to live peacefully,' he once told me. 'A sixteen-year-old girl could travel on her own from the southern tip of the train system in Moulmein all the way to the northern tip in Myitkyina and no harm would come to her. The British looked after the people. We had a secure life. We could go to sleep each night confident that tomorrow would come.'

There was an uncomfortable few moments as we all gazed into our teacups, unhappy to be disagreeing with each other. Something in the street attracted my attention; a rude quack-quacking noise. I looked out towards the entrance of the tea shop, into the unforgiving glare of the sun and saw a hawker walking past blowing a toy horn. Slung over his back was a large fishnet sack of bright pink footballs, wobbling gently in the heat haze.

Over a few more cups of tea our conversation turned, inexplicably, to dogs. At the end of *Burmese Days* just before Flory commits suicide, he drags his terrified black cocker spaniel, Flo, into his bedroom and blows her head to pieces with his pistol. Tun Lin fondly remembered how much the British loved their dogs. During the Second World War, he said, many British people shot their dogs before the Japanese soldiers took over, because they could not bear to leave them with the enemy. He described a documentary about England's dog shows that he had seen on a friend's satellite television. 'On Discovery Channel I saw many, many dogs having their fur washed and combed and eating wonderful food,' he said, chuckling at the absurdity of it all. 'In England you can have a better life as a dog than you can have as a human being here in Burma.'

---

THE POLICE TRAINING SCHOOL where George Orwell studied and the Police Officers' Mess where he first lived when he came to Burma are still standing. They are located in a quiet neighbourhood just off the south-eastern corner of the palace walls. The streets here are peaceful and pleasantly dusty. A few people on bicycles glide along beneath the shade of tamarind trees, and the occasional car or pick-up truck grinds its way over the bumpy tarmac. A handful of old British houses survive here, lived in by today's government officials. The buildings are chunky structures made of cream-coloured cement and wooden beams, their lawns cluttered with banana trees and makeshift shacks. The Police Training School—a long row of airy red-brick buildings with whitewashed colonnades—is still used to house policemen. They overlook the old parade grounds, today busy with police fitness drills and impromptu football games. At the intersections of the grid-plan streets there are fresh-water wells, green with moss, where the policemen bathe with their *longyi* tied slick around their waists.

I cycled past Orwell's former residence, the Police Officers' Mess, a few times before I could muster up the courage to go inside. From the seat of my bicycle, I saw the building at dawn, when a soft mist still skulked in the corners of the garden, and again at dusk, when the streets around it took on a dreamlike quality as the feathery branches of the tamarind trees were silhouetted purple-black against a moody lilac sky. An imposing two-storey, red-brick building the mess was always, rather spookily, devoid of people. I asked a number of Burmese friends if they would accompany me inside, but, since no one wanted to wander into an official building with a foreigner, I had to go alone.

Late one morning I walked down the semicircular driveway, past a neatly mowed lawn with flamboyant fountains of white bougainvillea. The oppressive midday heat was about to descend and the compound was completely silent and empty. At one end of the ground floor a makeshift room had been built with bamboo-matting walls. I peered inside and saw a man ironing clothes. He did not seem pleased to see a foreigner. '*Doukkha yauppi,*' he mumbled under his breath (literally, 'Trouble has arrived'). The caretaker wouldn't let me look inside the mess building. It is a guest house for high-ranking police officers, he told me, and he was not allowed to let anyone but police officers enter. After some coercing he allowed me to walk around the outside, as long as I promised not to take any photographs.

Orwell arrived here in November 1922 and spent a year living in this building with two other British candidates who were also training for the position of assistant district superintendent. The Police Training School in the next block was attended by some seventy Burmese constables and overseen by the school principal, Clyne Stewart, who was described by one of Orwell's contemporaries as 'a gigantic Scotsman with a character of oak and muscles to match'. Stewart sits in the centre of a photograph depicting Orwell's year at the police school. He has a dark, bushy moustache, and looks rather like the Soviet leader Joseph Stalin, on whom Orwell is said to have based the image of Big Brother, the omnipotent ruler depicted in *Nineteen Eighty-Four*.

In an old copy of the *Burma Police Journal* I once found a report of the rigorous daily routine at the training school. A typical day began at dawn with ablutions and a cup of coffee with bread. Then came physical jerks on the parade grounds (in *Nineteen Eighty-Four* the main character, Winston Smith, drags his wasted body through the compulsory early-morning exercise routine 'wearing on his face the look of grim enjoyment which was considered proper during the Physical Jerks'). At 6.30 A.M. officers began an hour and a half of military-style parades and musketry drills. The rest of the day was filled with classes in law and police procedure, based on dreary tomes such as the *Indian Penal Code,* the *Finger Print Bureau Manual,* the *Manual of Map Reading and Field Sketching,* and the *Indian Manual of First Aid.* There were also daily language lessons in Hindustani and Burmese (in which Orwell did particularly well, even studying an optional third language belonging to one of Burma's many ethnic groups, the Karen). In the late afternoon there was another hour-long parade, after which officers returned to the mess for the evening.

When Orwell was living here, the police mess building was regarded as the finest regimental mess in Mandalay and provided grand lodgings for a probationary officer undergoing training. The three British officers were tended to by a small army of servants: a butler and his assistant, a cook and his mate, a punkah-wallah (fan-puller), several gardeners, a billiard-marker and a lamp-trimmer. In addition, each officer had his own personal servant. On the ground floor there were three spacious, well-furnished rooms: one for dining, one for sitting and reading, and one for billiards. Officers usually dressed in dinner jackets for evening meals, but once a month they wore full mess kit with spurs and boiled shirts for guest nights at which the popular police band played. The rooms are now empty. I managed to stick my head through an open door and feel the cool gloom of the interior before the caretaker hurried me on.

The premises were in impeccable condition, the walkways had been swept clean, the doorways were newly painted, yet something was amiss. Upstairs, a broad verandah with shining white balusters connected a row of bedrooms. Each bedroom had been built with a private bathroom and a narrow staircase at the back to allow access for servants. In contrast to those around it, the bedroom at the western end of the building looked derelict. The window panes were cracked, and rotting wooden planks had been placed across the window frame. As I looked up, a sparrow balancing delicately on a piece of broken glass ducked inside. This, then, must be the haunted room.

A British police officer called William Tydd, who lived in the mess in the 1920s, recalled that this end bedroom had always been kept empty. In his memoir, *Peacock Dreams,* Tydd wrote that a few years before he himself moved into the mess (before Orwell had arrived) a young British probationer, 'unable to bear the homesickness which assailed us all at times, shot himself after his first four months. He stretched out on the rug beside his bed, placed the barrel of his shotgun in his mouth and then pulled the trigger.' Later, an unwitting Irish officer was sent to the training school for tuition in Burmese. He came to stay at the mess, and was housed in this end bedroom. On his first morning, he turned up groggy for breakfast after a sleepless night. Just as he had fallen asleep, he told the other officers, he had been awoken by a nightmare in which a man lay down on the floor beside the bed, put a shotgun to his mouth, and pulled the trigger.

Before I went to the mess, I had shown a photograph of it to a Burmese friend who lived in Mandalay. 'Oh, that's the haunted place, isn't it?' she asked. She didn't know anything about the British officer's suicide, but she told me that every ten years or so a person died in that ill-fated end bedroom. The most recent incident, she recalled, was about five years ago, when a policeman was stabbed to death.

I later repeated these ghost stories to an elderly Burmese pastor I knew. Though Theravada Buddhism is the predominant religion in Burma, it is a Buddhism mixed with strong animistic beliefs, and the pastor told me about the Burmese belief in *leippya* (the soul of a dead person—or, literally, the butterfly). If improperly escorted from its home in the human body, the *leippya* remains to haunt the living. The pastor attributed the murders in the empty bedroom to the tortured soul of the British probationer. 'That place is evil,' he said shaking his head solemnly. 'It ought to be burned down to the ground.'

The caretaker walked me around the back of the compound, where a lonely outhouse sat amid a sea of crackling bamboo leaves. The servants' stairways leading up to the bedrooms had rotted away, leaving ungainly doorways-to-nowhere peering out from the first floor. I made one last attempt to talk my way inside, and was refused. I walked slowly back down the driveway, thinking about a colonial memoir I had recently read which warned that the past always comes back to haunt us. It stated, with absolute certainty, that anyone who spent time in Burma would sooner or later start seeing ghosts.

When Orwell went to Burma he was fascinated by ghost stories. Indeed, one of his childhood friends, Jacintha Buddicom, who wrote a book called *Eric and Us* about her early friendship with Orwell, suggests a very different picture from the pragmatic, down-to-earth Orwell of later years. Orwell's favourite tales were ghostly ones, she claimed, and she was surprised that he never wrote a book of ghost stories during his writing career. He favoured the bony-fingered, soulless-eyed ghouls of M. R. James, and once gave her a copy of Bram Stoker's *Dracula* for Christmas, accompanied by a crucifix and a clove of garlic (safeguards against vampires, so she need not be as scared as he had been when he read it). The suicide and the empty bedroom in the mess where Orwell lived in Burma may have haunted him. In *Burmese Days,* John Flory dies a strikingly similar death. He locks himself in his bedroom, puts the muzzle of a pistol against his chest, and blasts himself on to the floor beside his bed, where he is later found by his servant.

THE GIANT-SIZED FACE of Burma's favourite comic actor beamed down at me from a movie billboard. His stage name is Zagana, and he is rarely depicted without a cheeky grin and a star-shaped twinkle painted in the corner of his eye. A few days after my first meeting with the Orwell Book Club, the young writer Maung Oo and his girlfriend invited me to go and see Zagana's latest film.

We met in the early evening in front of a cinema in central Mandalay. The cinema was a square cement block, its entranceway choked with vendors and with people impatiently queuing for tickets. One stall sold countless plastic bags containing soggy concoctions of pickled fruits, dried meats, oily potato crisps and the national number-one favourite snack, roasted sunflower seeds. I could hear the steady clank-clank of a sugar-cane-juice vendor squeezing fresh cane through a mangle. I saw Maung Oo and his girlfriend standing on the steps of the cinema, and pushed my way through the crowd towards them. Inside, the auditorium was noisy with the sound of viewers settling into their mildewed red-velvet seats, giggling, rustling bags of snacks, and cracking open sunflower-seed shells. Next to me, Maung Oo opened a bag of betel nut neatly wrapped in fresh green leaves, and slipped a quid into his mouth. Despite the air-conditioning, the air was hot and humid, laced with the spicy smell of betel and an inescapable feeling of anticipation.

We all stood up briefly as the red-and-blue Burmese flag appeared on the screen and a croaking rendition of the national anthem was played. Everyone sat down long before it was over, and the cracking of sunflower seeds resumed. Maung Oo's girlfriend forced an unidentifiable pickled and pungent piece of fruit into my hand, and the movie began. Zagana played the overpossessive guardian of a young and beautiful woman. In a string of predictable slapstick vignettes, he wore a bad wig to meet a childhood sweetheart (Zagana himself is bald), was caught eavesdropping on the young beauty's conversations with a lover, and so on. The audience loved it. Maung Oo chortled all the way through, sometimes clapping his hands with joy.

Zagana, however, is no ordinary comedian. He is a former political prisoner, having been arrested for his anti-government activities during the people's uprising of 1988. He was sentenced to ten years' imprisonment, but was released before he completed his sentence. Like most other political prisoners granted an amnesty, on his release from prison he must have signed a legally binding agreement not to talk about politics or take part in any more political activities. The Burmese film industry is heavily controlled by the regime, and no one who openly holds anti-government views is allowed to succeed within its limited confines. All films are subjected to censorship, and directors are encouraged to promote a strong nationalistic sentiment in their movies. The military bullies high-profile actors, actresses and musicians into toeing the government line in public: they are coerced into promoting the regime, or are bribed with material goods such as a coveted cellphone licence, a car or a house. As a result, you can see starlets demurely posing for, say, the Ministry of Defense's yearly calendar, and a former political prisoner like Zagana reinventing himself as the country's lovable comedic uncle.

The authoritarian rule of the Burmese generals is well-hidden behind a curtain that is held tightly closed by strict control of the country's movies, music, books and newspapers. Indeed, I often knew more about what was going on in Burma when I was away from it. Outside the country you can read inch-thick human-rights reports recording in encyclopedic detail atrocities perpetrated by the current regime, such as the arcane torture methods used on political prisoners or the estimated number of people who have died in forced-labour projects. The authorities keep a stranglehold on news that enters the country from the outside world. Government censors deal with imported magazines and newspapers by simply tearing out the bits they don't like. I once flipped through a copy of *Time* magazine in a hotel lobby and found pages 63–6 missing. On the contents page, which had not been ripped out, I saw that the missing pages had contained a piece about an exiled doctor treating Burmese refugees who had fled to refugee camps in Thailand.

Events taking place inside Burma are also carefully controlled. I was given an example of this when I passed an evening in my hotel room watching a televised football match between Burma and Malaysia. The coverage was somewhat irregular, and every so often the camera settled, for no discernible reason, on an empty goal. The next day a friend asked me if I had heard about the scuffles that took place at the football stadium between football fans and riot-control police in which one policeman had been killed and a handful of people had been injured. I replied confidently that nothing had happened, explaining that I had watched the whole match from start to finish. 'Yes,' said my friend, 'but who do you think controls the television channel?' He told me he had listened to the match on his radio and knew that something was up when the programme fell silent as the commentary was temporarily taken off the air.

Maung Oo's girlfriend nudged me. The movie was over. Zagana was freeze-framed on the screen, winking merrily at the audience. Happy after an hour and a half of snacking and mindless humour, we gathered up our belongings and filed messily out of the cinema, discarded sunflower-seed shells crunching loudly beneath our feet.

I HAD A LETTER of introduction to a bookseller in Zay Kyo, Mandalay's main market, and one afternoon I went there to find him. The street in front of the market was chaotic with traffic. Over the sound of blaring vehicle horns, conductors shouted out their destinations as passengers squeezed on to the overcrowded buses. A traffic policeman dressed in smart blue trousers and wearing a dented white helmet blew his whistle and waved his hands, frantically trying to control the bicycles, mopeds and buses that thundered past him. On top of a pick-up truck I saw a group of monks sitting in a messy pile of brick-coloured robes and shaved heads. They waved at me, yelling out joyous hellos and grinning widely through betel-stained lips. A steady stream of women walked out of the market carrying baskets laden with produce. One woman had a sack of vegetables in each hand and a bundle of runner beans balanced rakishly on her head.

The market's claustrophobic alleyways are always stacked high with multicoloured *longyi* and silks, terracotta pots and tin trunks. You can buy anything here, from Chinese fig biscuits to Burmese school textbooks. The market used to be housed in a building designed by an Italian count at the start of the twentieth century ('It was as beautiful as Buckingham Palace,' remembered one Mandalay resident). But ten years ago the government knocked it down and replaced it with the modern concrete blocks in which it is housed today. Mandalay's frequent power cuts have rendered the smart new escalators useless, and Burma's heavy annual rains have left stains of damp on the walls and stagnant puddles in the corners.

I found the bookshop I was looking for on a quieter upper storey of the market. It consisted of little more than a piece of tarpaulin spread on the floor. On top of this sat a pile of books that looked as if they had been unceremoniously dumped from a giant sack. Most of them were in English—biochemistry textbooks from the 1950s, old library books, a few pocket-sized classics published by Oxford University Press and bound in dark-blue cloth. Behind this small literary mountain, Hla Htut sat reading a collection of Tolstoy's short stories in a faded deckchair. I gave him my letter of introduction, from a mutual friend in Rangoon. He read it carefully, folded it up, and handed it back to me. With great solemnity he pulled a plastic stool from behind some boxes and offered me a seat. Then he leaned back in his chair, lit a slender cheroot, and confessed that he hates books.

Hla Htut is in his early thirties. He has placid, sculpted features and an easy, slow manner. Since his schooling was disrupted by the government's frequent and haphazard closure of Burma's universities, he never finished the bachelor's degree he started in English literature. Instead, he began dealing in books. It isn't that he hates *all* books, he clarified: he just hates Burmese books. In fact Hla Htut has no time for any contemporary Burmese writing, be it in novels, newspapers or magazines. 'I don't trust them. They always lie,' he said. 'I understand it is not the same in your country. Your books and newspapers never lie, isn't that so?' I thought about it for a moment, and was preparing to launch into a long and complicated answer about the warped images of world affairs painted by tabloid newspapers and about mainstream international news channels simplifying stories for mass consumption, but Hla Htut took my hesitation for agreement and summed up his theory on reading. 'I trust only old books,' he said.

Burma has always had a high literacy rate, thanks to a strong tradition of education instilled by the country's Buddhist monasteries, and reading for pleasure became a widespread pastime under the British. After a few generations under the colonial education system and with the introduction of printing presses, Burmese writers began to write more for the masses rather than for the palace elite. An adventure story inspired by *The Count of Monte Cristo* was published in 1904 and is considered the first example of the novel in Burma. It was an instant hit, and a few years later novels and short stories written by Burmese writers were everywhere.

The Burmese, explained Hla Htut, had always been primed to love stories. All Burmese children were weaned on the Jataka stories, a collection of some 550 moral tales which describe the many reincarnations of Prince Siddhārtha before he achieved enlightenment as the Buddha. Prince Siddhārtha appears in human and animal form wandering through the Buddhist cosmological landscape—a wonderland of celestial beings and forests filled with mythical beasts. Among other early favourites were H. Rider Haggard and Arthur Conan Doyle (the translator of the latter transformed Sherlock Holmes into the *longyi*-clad Sone Dauk

Maung San Sha, or Detective Maung San Sha, and the sleuth's famous Baker Street address became Bogalay Zay Street in Rangoon). A hundred years later, both Rider Haggard and Conan Doyle are still big sellers. Hla Htut puts it down to the oppressive political environment in which people live. 'We Burmese, we need to escape. We don't want to read non-fiction. We want only fiction and fantasy. We want to read about heroes—strong men, clever men.'

As we were talking, one of Hla Htut's friends, a plump elderly man who was browsing through the disorganized pile of books, looked up at me. After listening to us for some time, he interrupted our conversation and, to my surprise, said in perfect English, 'Please allow me to introduce myself.' Kyaw Thein presented himself as a poet and a lover of words. He was one of those courtly old Burmese gentlemen I met from time to time in Burma who spoke a quaint old-world English and had an air of sadness that lingered around them like cigarette smoke. Kyaw Thein recited a few of his poems to me there in the dingy upper reaches of the market, within the stench of an overflowing rubbish bin. They were beautiful and simple verses about love and loss and loneliness. 'I can only write love poems,' he said with some embarrassment. 'The censors warned me away from writing about anything else. They told me, *"Bawa akyaung m'yay neh"* ("Don't write about life").'

By the time we had finished our conversation it was late afternoon and the market was closing down. The hallways had darkened and now echoed with the bangs and shouts of stall-holders packing up their unsold wares. The overhead fluorescent lights

flickered on and off again, eventually settling for a subdued, un-
earthly light that was accompanied by a nerve-tingling buzzing
sound. As Hla Htut shovelled his books into burlap sacks, he invited me to join him for what he called a 'tea party' taking place
the next day, and I happily accepted.

I walked out into the street and hailed a trishaw to take me
back to my hotel. The night air was sticky and humid. The trishaw driver wore only a *longyi,* and the sinewy muscles of his
arms and back glistened with sweat. As we left the market area,
the streets dissolved into darkness. There are few street lights in
Mandalay, and the roads are pitch-black at night. The trishaw rattled haphazardly along the pot-holed roads, and mysterious shapes
hurtled towards us. Every so often the headlights of a passing car
gave me brief glimpses of lone pedestrians, stray dogs and other
trishaws.

The next afternoon I went to the address that Hla Htut had
given me. The tea shop was on a street corner, surrounded by
low-rise buildings. Under the shade of a large tree outside the
shop, a group of eight men were huddled together, girlish and secretive, around a long wooden table. Hla Htut uncoiled himself
from what I had come to know as the characteristic 'tea-shop
hunch' (sitting on a doll-sized wooden stool, back rounded over
tea and conversation), shook my hand vigorously, and introduced
me to the *waing,* literally 'circle', as it is called in Burmese. There
were a few writers, another poet, a couple of former professors,
and a retired psychologist. Hla Htut ordered me a cup of tea and
handed me a doughy slice of *sanwinmakin* (sweetened sticky rice
cake) from a central platter.

The *waing* was a jolly affair, full of jokes and literary allusions. When Hla Htut announced that I was interested in George Orwell's writings and how they applied to Burma, everyone had something to say. 'Russia no longer has its Big Brother, but we still do,' said the psychologist, a distinguished-looking gentleman wearing a crisp white shirt and a shimmering silvery *longyi*. 'Orwell's predictions are still quite true for us.' 'Yes, yes,' everyone agreed. 'We are a country of 50 million hostages,' said the psychologist. 'They have kept fifty million hostages for almost fifty years!' There was laughter, and some sporadic clapping.

'Quite so!' said one of the retired professors from behind a cloud of cheroot smoke. 'My Western friends always ask me, "Why are the Burmese intelligentsia so cynical?" I reply that there isn't any *single* reason to be cynical. But in these prevailing conditions there is absolutely *no* reason for optimism.'

Again, everyone agreed. But Burma had not reached the nightmare all-encompassing totalitarianism portrayed in *Nineteen Eighty-Four,* insisted the psychologist. 'Mind control on a mass scale like that is not possible any more,' he said. 'Diversity is ever present. Even in Burma there are channels for other viewpoints to seep in. Here you cannot have absolute control of people's minds.'

'Well, not yet,' Hla Htut murmured.

'Of course,' continued the psychologist, 'that *is* exactly what they want. That's why the education system is so poor: they don't want to train thinkers. They don't want us to think at all.' (Almost everyone I spoke to in Burma referred to the regime simply as 'they', although one poetic English-literature student called the generals 'the green sleeves', referring to their olive-coloured army uniforms.)

One of the professors brought up the new government initiative to raise the number of Ph.D. candidates from the current 40 students per year to 800. Everyone laughed heartily. Hla Htut turned to me and said, 'In Burma, "Ph.D." stands for "Phoney Doctorate".'

'They are simply opening up more and more schools so the system will look good on paper. It's all bluff,' said one of the professors. 'It's only education on paper. They build the building. They put up the sign. And that's it. After that they go away. They don't care about quality. They don't care if the teachers are properly trained, or if the school is fully equipped.'

'Quantitatively we have progress,' said the psychologist. 'Qualitatively we are going down the drain.'

It is true that, on paper, the country is progressing splendidly. The government's Ministry of Information keeps itself busy producing books and articles which detail the country's ever accelerating rate of development. The cover of one of its recent publications, entitled *Myanmar Facts and Figures 2002*, shows the ornate teak gateways of Mandalay Palace. Beneath them, a satellite dish hovers in the clouds, and beneath that are students bending over a row of computers. This cover is somewhat deceptive, given that few people outside the urban areas can afford satellite dishes and, even if they could, an unregistered dish is punishable with a prison sentence. Though many schools are equipped with computers, few have been given the expertise, let alone the access to electricity, required to run them. Many pupils in Burma are still using slates and chalk to do their homework. The book is full of equally fanciful statistics about the country, such as the number of universities (many of which are closed to prevent political agitation) and hospitals (few of which can provide ailing people with medicines or adequately trained doctors). I showed the book to a writer friend who had formerly worked in the Ministry of Information. 'Lies!' she said. 'We used to have to pluck these numbers out from somewhere inside our heads.'

She added a popular Burmese joke: 'When I pick up a newspaper, the first thing I turn to is the back page to read the only reliable news in the whole paper—the obituaries.' In fact, if you do pick up a copy of a Burmese newspaper, you will see that its pages contain only good news. New roads have been constructed in underdeveloped areas; leprosy has been totally eradicated; the school enrolment rate is now 93.07 per cent—the highest it has ever been.

Good news from government sources also pours into the world of *Nineteen Eighty-Four*: 'As compared with last year there was more food, more clothes, more houses, more furniture, more cooking-pots, more fuel, more ships, more helicopters, more books, more babies—more of everything except disease, crime, and insanity.' In Orwell's novel, Winston Smith spends his dreary days rewriting snippets of the past and present so that they correspond to what the authorities—the Party—want to be true at any given time. The material he has to rewrite is delivered to his desk in the Records Department of the Ministry of Truth through pneumatic tubes. He might receive an article from an issue of *The Times* that is a few months old, reporting Ministry of Plenty promises that there will be no reduction of individual chocolate rations during the year 1984. The chocolate ration, however, has just been reduced from thirty grams to twenty grams. Smith's job is to rewrite the article so that it appears that the Party had issued warnings of an upcoming chocolate shortage. The original article is dropped into an oblong slit nicknamed the 'memory hole'. The past is whisked away through a vent to be burned in furnaces hidden in the bowels of the Records Department. The past and present rapidly disappear down Smith's memory hole as he rewrites other articles, erasing wars that took place, creating Party heroes that never were, and doctoring statistics.

'We cannot speak or write about what is really going on in Burma,' one of the writers at the tea party said. Authors and journalists who present views or information that the government deems to be reactionary are blacklisted. In its mildest form, being blacklisted means you are prohibited from having your work published; at its worst it can mean years in a Burmese jail.

The writer told me about one of the most respected and prolific historians living in Burma, who had made some outspoken comments during an international radio interview. 'We can no longer write his name in magazines or newspapers and he cannot be mentioned any more,' the writer said. The historian's articles have been banned, and his books have been taken out of bookshops. People disappeared like this in *Nineteen Eighty-Four*: 'Your name was removed from the registers, every record of everything you had ever done was wiped out, your one-time existence was denied and then forgotten. You were abolished, annihilated: *vaporized* was the usual word.'

In the cubicle next to Winston Smith in the Records Department, a woman was responsible for tracking down the names of those who had been vaporized and deleting them from any written records: 'Whatever happened you vanished, and neither you nor your actions were ever heard of again. You were lifted clean out of the stream of history.'

The writer laughed as he told me that so many writers have been blacklisted in Burma that it is no longer even possible to write the history of the country's modern literary movement.

There are currently a number of well-known poets, writers, journalists and editors in prison. Writer Kyaw San was sentenced to seven years in jail for composing poems and articles in support of demonstrations against the government. He was so badly beaten during his interrogation in 1997 that he is now partially deaf. Aung Tun, a young student who compiled a history of the student movement in Burma, was imprisoned along with the historians who helped him. When another journalist, Thaung Tun, was found collating data on human-rights violations he was tortured at a government interrogation centre for three weeks and given an eight-year prison sentence.

The psychologist sighed heavily. 'Arthur Koestler, who was, I believe, a predecessor of Orwell, wrote a book called *Darkness at Noon* set in the totalitarian state in Russia,' he said. 'Here in Burma we have darkness in the morning, darkness at noon, darkness all day long.' He paused before adding, 'And this, now, is our darkest time.' It was easy to imagine how that might seem true.

The military regime has been in place in Burma for over forty years, making it one of the most tenacious dictatorships in the world. Whole generations have grown up knowing nothing but authoritarian rule, and many Burmese I spoke to have lost hope that the situation will ever change for the better.

I decided to try my hand at making the literary allusions that everyone else was producing so well. 'You know what they say,' I ventured hesitantly: '"The darkest hour comes just before dawn."'

There was much laughter, slapping of thighs, clapping of hands. When the noise died down the psychologist said in a hushed voice, 'Thank you.' 'Yes,' said someone else, 'thank you.' Everyone nodded silently, including me.

FOR FIVE DOLLARS tourists can buy a ticket to Mandalay Palace with an accompanying glossy brochure. The only area that you are allowed to see within the vast 1,000-acre complex inside the palace walls is the palace itself, which occupies the centre. The rest of the grounds is used by the junta as a military base, and the area is treated as a high-security zone. Tourists must write down their names and passport numbers before entering the grounds, registering and paying extra fees to take in any cameras and video recorders. And the palace that they pay to see is not the original palace, which began construction in 1857, but a recently built facsimile. It is a garish ensemble: the walls and pillars are painted betel-spit red, and the multi-tiered wedding-cake roofs are drenched in thick gold paint. Inside one of the enormous empty rooms are statues of Burma's last king and queen,

King Thibaw and Queen Supayalat, seated upon a replica of their joint throne, staring blindly out from behind a glass case.

When the British annexed Upper Burma, in 1885, they exiled this royal couple to India and took control of the palace and its grounds, renaming it Fort Dufferin after the viceroy of India. They transformed the grounds into a British military base, building a railroad, barracks and mess houses, a polo field, a nine-hole golf course, tennis courts and a chapel. In the early years of British rule in Mandalay, the social centre of colonial life—the club—was housed in the exiled queen's abandoned quarters. The Lily Throne Room, where ladies of the court once paid homage to her, sported a billiard table, and instead of gongs and cymbals and the whispers of the royal harem there was, as one British official fondly wrote, 'the swish of soda water bottles, the crack of ice, the click of billiard balls'. During the Second World War, when the Japanese marched into Burma, they too stationed a military garrison within the palace walls, and the palace was destroyed when it caught fire during fighting between Japanese and British troops.

A paragraph in the government's tourist brochure states that the current regime rebuilt the palace to 'uplift the national prestige and integrity of the entire nation' and 'to revive and maintain of [sic] the national patriotism'. The palace has been reinvented so many times that it is now impossible to hear the echo of history within its well-lacquered walls. Today it is one of the key tourist attractions in Mandalay.

The Burmese government promotes tourism to garner much-needed revenue, but it wants foreign visitors to experience Burma only on its terms—as what the tourist brochures call 'A Golden

Land' of pagodas and smiling people. When the government launched Burma as a tourist destination, in 1996, it tidied up the country, repainting buildings and moving slums out of city centres. Strict controls were placed on workers in the tourism industry. A hotel manager working in a government-run hotel explained to me that if she was too friendly with foreigners she was given a warning. She was transferred every two years, to prevent her from cementing friendships with returning tourists. Burmese tour guides are trained in a government programme that teaches them not to talk about politics with visitors. As one former guide explained, 'It doesn't matter what the tourists ask us or what is happening around us: we must only tell them about the good things. It doesn't matter if there is a demonstration going on right next to us: we just have to keep on telling them about the history of the pagoda they are looking at.' A book published in Burma called *Discussing Myanmar Culture* provides an English-language vocabulary and sentences for explaining all the 'safe' aspects of Burmese culture, like the glittering Mahamuni Pagoda in Mandalay, or *mohingha,* the famous fish noodles eaten for breakfast. Tour guides are warned that the government's eyes and ears are everywhere. 'They told us that if we talk about politics they will know—they can find out. They have people watching us always, they say,' the guide told me.

I know a tour guide who does refuse to speak about politics. I've known him for a few years now, but whenever I ask him anything vaguely political—about a protest that was rumoured to have taken place in his neighbourhood, say, or his meeting with the Minister of Hotels and Tourism—he always has the same response: he laughs loudly and says nothing. It is as if I haven't even asked a question. Other tour guides, however, make a point of talking. One young guide in Mandalay told me he made it his mission to tell foreigners what was happening in Burma: 'We tell them everything we can. We try and act as messengers to the outside world. We tell them about the student demonstrations in 1988 when many of our friends were killed. We tell them about our true leader, Aung San Suu Kyi.' He is able to get away with this as long as no one overhears him. His tour-guide licence gives him the perfect excuse for being with foreigners and, unlike most people, he is, as some Burmese like to joke, 'licensed to talk'.

Most tourists who come to Burma travel along a well-prepared route which takes them through the central areas of the country. They visit the ancient capital of Pagan, with its hundreds of crumbling pagodas set amid the heat-haze of the plains in the very heart of the country. They climb into the hills not far off the road between Rangoon and Mandalay to glide in low wooden boats across the mist-covered waters of Inle Lake. But there are large parts of the country that are off-limits to tourists. The Ministry of Hotels and Tourism publishes a list of forbidden 'brown areas'; these include the horseshoe of mountains which encloses much of Burma and most parts of the geographical tail which borders Thailand. These areas are home to Burma's ethnic minorities. (Though the ethnic Burmese constitute some two-thirds of the population, seven other ethnic groups, within which there are scores of ethnically distinct tribes, make up the rest.) Many of these regions were turned into battlegrounds during the second half of the twentieth century as ethnic groups fought against the central Burmese regime for more autonomy or independence. Though the government has now defeated most of these armies, it still prohibits foreign access. It is in these areas that the full force of military rule is felt. In the southern Mon regions, up to 150,000 villagers have been forced to work on a 100-mile railway line that runs parallel to the Andaman Sea. And a little further north, in the mountains of Karen State along the Thai–Burma border, where the Karen army is still holding out against the Burmese regime, almost half a million people are estimated to have been forced to abandon their homes when villages were razed to the ground by Burmese soldiers.

Because of the travel restrictions, tourists can stay in Burma for weeks and never see any evidence of the regime's more brutal tactics. I have spoken to some tourists who wonder what all the human-rights activists campaigning outside Burma are fussing about. ('Everyone smiles at you—it can't be that bad,' one tourist said with a shrug.) Indeed, everything in Burma does seem normal: people go about their business in the streets, talking, laughing, chewing betel, reading, going to the movies. As one Burmese friend had chided me, 'What did you expect? That we would all be sitting around on the pavements crying?' He gave me an analogy for this disturbing phenomenon of invisible oppression. Burma is like a woman with cancer, he explained. She knows she is sick, but she carries on with her life as if nothing is wrong. She refuses to go to a doctor for treatment. Instead, she swirls *thanaka* (a Burmese cosmetic or sunblock made from tree bark) on her cheeks, puts fresh flowers in her hair, and goes to the bazaar as if everything is normal. She talks to people, they talk to her. They know she has cancer and she knows she has cancer, but nobody says anything.

Around the walls of Mandalay Palace is a moat 75 yards wide and over 10 feet deep. Before the regime launched its international campaign to promote tourism to Burma, this area was subject to a beautification programme. Thousands of local residents were coerced into donating their labour to dredge and refurbish the moat. They had to provide their own tools for the job, and if they didn't have any they used their hands. Almost ten years later, the moat is a popular spot for townsfolk to escape the dry dust of the city. It is a picturesque setting. The palace walls are built of fired bricks that have the colour of pressed roses. Teak canopies with multi-tiered roofs float above the gateways. In the still waters of the moat you can see the reflection of pink bougainvillea and arched palm trees. At the end of each afternoon, young couples creep down to the water's edge to watch the setting sun stir the moat into a dazzling cocktail of orange and red.

NOT FAR FROM MANDALAY, about an hour's winding drive up a steep mountain road, is Maymyo, the former hill station where the British went to escape the heat and dust of the city. George Orwell visited Maymyo at least twice while he was posted in Mandalay. For homesick colonial officials, Maymyo was the closest thing to Britain you could find in the sweltering townships of Burma. Most British memoirs of Burma spare a nostalgic paragraph or two for it, describing a paradise of flower gardens, woodland walks and picnic grounds. Orwell didn't mention Maymyo in his novel *Burmese Days,* but the town makes a surprise cameo appearance in his book on the Spanish Civil War, *Homage to Catalonia,* where he remembers his arrival in Maymyo by train:

> It is a rather queer experience. You start off in the typical atmosphere of an eastern city—the scorching sunlight, the dusty palms, the smells of fish and spices and garlic, the squashy tropical fruits, the swarming dark-faced human beings—and because you are so used to it you carry this at-mosphere intact, so to speak, in your railway carriage. Mentally you are still in Mandalay when the train stops at Maymyo, four thousand feet above sea-level. But in step-ping out of the carriage you step into a different hemi-sphere. Suddenly you are breathing cool sweet air that might be that of England, and all round you are green grass, bracken, fir-trees, and hill-women with pink cheeks selling baskets of strawberries.

I hired a taxi to go to Maymyo, and when I arrived there I booked into the Candacraig Hotel, a former 'chummery', or house for bachelors, which was built by the British to house staff from the colonial Bombay Burmah Trading Company. The Candacraig sits at the top of a long driveway which sweeps past a lawn of manicured flower-beds. It is an impressive mock-Tudor-style mansion, with turret rooms on the first floor and deep-green vines growing up the front wall. The six-bedroom hotel is run by the regime's Ministry of Hotels and Tourism, and the staff, as might be expected, are somewhat strict. The sanitized feeling of a British boarding school lurks in its corridors and swills around in the weak tea served in stainless-steel pots. In the high-ceilinged bedrooms the disused fireplaces are stained with pigeon dropping. I had stayed here a few times on previous visits, and remember the first time, when the front-desk manager asked me what time I would like my supper.

'Seven thirty?' I suggested.

'That, madam, is the correct answer.'

As I turned to walk away, he asked, 'And what would madam like to eat?'

'Um . . . fish?'

'That, madam, is incorrect. There is chicken or there is beef.'

This time I decided to sample the dinner again. The menu was exactly the same. I opted for chicken, and received what looked like the same dry piece of roasted breast meat, accompanied by a pile of green beans and mashed potatoes. All three tables in the dining room were full, and as our knives and forks clattered against our plates there was an awkward hush among the diners. Towards the back of the room a long table had been taken up by an English family of seven. An English couple from Wiltshire were seated in the corner by the French windows, and the man had his hand clasped tightly round a half-empty bottle of beer. He leaned across the large chasm between our chairs.

'How was your soup?' he asked me. After a dramatic, conspiratorial pause he whispered, 'Garlicky?'

The wooden floorboards creaked loudly as a weary-looking Burmese waiter with a limp bow tie trudged between the tables removing unfinished chicken dishes and replacing them with small, ungenerous bowls of strawberries. It was a curiously English, curiously uncomfortable scene.

As Orwell noted, Maymyo doesn't feel at all like Burma. One traveller in the 1920s described it as 'conspicuously un-oriental, more like a corner of Surrey than Burma'. Even today, the remnants of a British hill station are ubiquitous there. The town itself was a British creation, founded in 1887 by its namesake, Colonel May of the 5th Bengal Infantry. ('Maymyo', means literally 'May Town'.) Old colonial houses with sun-faded brick walls sit silent and forgotten behind overgrown hedges and forests of trees. The British army imported Gurkha soldiers from Nepal, and you can still see Nepali sweater-knitters and find Gurkha descendants manning the dairies, balancing tin milk churns on either side of their bicycles. The lanes echo with the clip-clop of horse's feet as pastel-coloured hackney carriages, painted with wreaths of flowers and driven by swarthy Indians in Victorian flat caps, rattle along the winding lanes. Near the old clock tower in the main street is a watch-repair shop which was started by a watchmaker from Madagascar who came here at the start of the twentieth century to cater to the fast-growing British population. The shop is now run by his great-grandson.

Perhaps the most poignant reminder of Britain's colonial days is the old cemetery. Maymyo has one of the last remaining British cemeteries in Burma. Around 1990 the current regime began emptying the country's graveyards, making way for the development of city centres. A Burmese friend told me that many of the old British headstones were bought up by Burmese businessmen in Rangoon as fashionable garden accessories. The Maymyo cemetery is still intact, but only just. It is a desolate place, surrounded by a low brick wall. Many gravestones are broken, and their fragments are scattered around the dry scrub. On part of a shattered white marble cross only the words 'In loving memory of' remain. On another chunk of marble there is only 'thou hast'. On one gravestone an angel's face has been hacked off, and many of the headstones have vanished completely, leaving only a small number carved on a matchbox-sized rock to mark the plot. The grave of one woman caught my eye: that of Dorothea Hopkins Andrews, who died here in 1912. It is overgrown with bramble and surrounded by splinters of smashed marble. The headstone reads, 'Loving thoughts will ever linger round the place where thou art laid.'

Some of the graves had clearly been vandalized. The headstone of a child's grave, that of James Bertrand Petley, who was born in Mandalay in 1901 and buried here in 1903, had been badly whitewashed, as if someone had poured a bucket of paint over it. A mysterious half-burned candle stood on the otherwise neglected headstone of Edith Henrietta Homer, who died here in her mid-forties in 1921. Nearby, one tomb had been completely dug up. As I peered into the macabre hole, I was startled by a young Burmese man walking towards me across the empty cemetery. His hair was neatly parted, and in one hand he held a rolled-up geography textbook, which he beat against his other hand like a truncheon. 'Black magic,' he informed me when I asked if he knew why the grave had been dug up. He showed me other graves that were covered in obscene graffiti, and still others where unknown hands had tried to piece the splintered stones together like jigsaw puzzles. If I wanted to know more I should ask at the church, he said, pointing to a nearby bell tower.

In one of Maymyo's many churches, I later met a Burmese priest who told me that the local authorities had forbidden Christian burials in the graveyard for the past ten years. Christians were now allotted a plot of land far outside the town. The only reason the cemetery still survived, he told me, was because the British lease on the land had not yet run out. He expected the lease to expire any year now. 'They are just waiting to take it back,' he said of the local-government authorities. 'They will dig up the graves and feed the bones to the dogs. They don't care.' He blamed the destruction in the cemetery on the Buddhist belief in reincarnation. 'Buddhists have no respect for our Christian cemetery. We Christians believe the dead will rise again when Jesus comes; the bodies are just resting. If you are a Buddhist, you believe a dead person will turn into an elephant. Or a dog.'

As I left the cemetery I noticed a hunched figure sitting at the entrance: a soldier clad in rumpled olive green with the wooden stock of a rifle nestled between his knees. He hadn't been there when I entered, and when I looked back once more from the top of the road I saw him walking away.

MAYMYO ONCE HAD a reputation as something of a party town. British police officers stationed in Mandalay would drive up on their motorbikes for a game of golf and a late dinner, returning to the city before dawn, the eyes of wild animals glimmering in their headlights as they careered back down the hill. During each hot season the British government administration moved here from Rangoon to escape the heat, bringing in its wake everyone who was anyone in colonial society as Maymyo became the setting for a social whirl of parties and dances.

During one such hot season, in 1923, Orwell came here for a week's holiday with Roger Beadon, a fellow probationary assistant district superintendent undergoing police training in Mandalay. Beadon was later one of the few old Burma hands able to remember much about the writer's time in Burma. It was in Maymyo that Beadon realized that Orwell was not a typical empire builder. He recalled that, though they both enjoyed the trip, Orwell remained aloof the whole time and limited his conversation to what Beadon termed commonplace remarks. 'I realized that he and I had very little in common, I presumably being an extrovert, he an introvert, living in a world of his own: a rather shy, retiring intellectual.'

Everything in Orwell's background, however, indicated that he was, almost literally, bred for the Empire. He came from a long line of colonial families. His father's ancestors had owned Jamaican sugar plantations. His grandfather had been ordained as a deacon in Calcutta, later serving as a priest in Tasmania. And his father spent his entire career in the colonial service in India, overseeing the production of government opium crops. On his mother's side, Orwell's family had lived and worked as shipbuilders and teak-traders for three generations in Lower Burma.

Orwell himself was born in Motihari, a small town in northern India, and first moved to England, with his mother, shortly before his second birthday. Yet, in Mandalay, Orwell acquired a reputation as someone who didn't fit in. According to Beadon, Orwell was thought not to be 'a good mixer'. Beadon described him as a man who was 'sallow-faced, tall, thin, and gangling, whose clothes, no matter how well-cut, seemed to hang on him'. Beadon spent his time living it up at the Upper Burma Club, playing snooker and dancing, but Orwell 'cared little for games, and seemed to be bored with the social and Club life'. He preferred to stay behind in his room at the mess, reading, spending most of his time alone—much like John Flory, who, in *Burmese Days,* 'took to reading voraciously, and learned to live in books when life was tiresome'.

The social life of Mandalay and Maymyo, it seems, was too hedonistic for the young Orwell. One British civil servant recalled in his memoirs how he had driven to Maymyo from Mandalay to meet a friend for drinks at the Candacraig. When his friend didn't show up he went to bed, only to be awoken at two in the morning by a commotion outside. Standing in the middle of the driveway was his friend, wearing a wrinkled linen suit with a fresh flower wilting in the top buttonhole. 'Where have you been?' he yelled over the balcony. 'Out to lunch, old boy,' slurred the friend.

But any gaiety that once existed in Maymyo is now long gone. All guests at the Candacraig were tucked up in bed by nine o'clock and the bar room was always empty. Behind the bar, however, was a small reminder that colonial drinking habits had not been totally forgotten. Stashed in a dusty glass cabinet were five half-bottles of Aster's Strawberry Wine, nine mini bottles of Campari, two bottles of Burmese whisky, one of Gordon's Dry Gin, a bottle of crème de menthe (half-empty), two bottles of Mandalay Beer and one enormous spider (dead).

Though some of the old houses which once played host to all those dances and dinners have been refurbished to attract tourists, many remain unlived-in. One afternoon I cycled past a broken-down wooden gate. Over it I could see a thick tangle of forest that must once have been a grand front lawn. An octagonal tower with broken window panes peered above the greenery. I followed the broken rubble of the driveway to a large red-brick house. The house was derelict. The mandarin-coloured droplets of a vine of golden shower, growing wild, spilled across the cov-ered driveway. The roof shingles were weathered pale as beach wood, and powder-blue paint was flaking off the front door in long strips. Around the back of the house, a door opened when I pushed it and I tiptoed inside. The rooms were empty. The wooden floors were well-worn and termite-riddled, and the fire-places were clogged with dust and cobwebs. But clearly I wasn't the first person to have come here recently: in one corner I saw a few empty bottles of rum, and the sign of Iron Cross—a Burmese rock band—had been scribbled in charcoal on a wall. I went up the creaking staircase, and on the first floor, heavy teak doors opened on to an endless series of bedrooms. The house must have been built for a large British family. It was late after-noon, and the broken windows cast long shadows. The rooms were utterly silent.

Back outside, I sat on the front porch to watch the sun go

down. I had prepared for the occasion with a packet of popcorn (pleasingly known as *pauk-pauk* in Burmese) and a bottle of Maymyo's specialty, damson wine as sweet as cough syrup. As I gazed dreamily at my bucolic surroundings, a *longyi*-clad figure materialized out of the haze and wild rose bushes at the bottom of the driveway. The man said he was the security guard who looked after the house, and he offered to let me go inside. I declined graciously. He pointed to the tower room and told me about a ghost he used to see there, a young blonde woman who paced silently up and down in front of the windows. A Burmese friend of mine who grew up in Maymyo had told me that the town was full of ghosts. She remembered that every night at nine o'clock, when she was sitting in her bed reading, she would hear a heavy splash in the well outside. Her mother would tell her not to worry: it was just the lost spirit of a British woman who had lived there and committed suicide by jumping into the well.

The poor British woman may have been condemned by the laws of karma and imagination to repeat her lonely suicide over and over again, but the ghost in the upstairs window had been released from her nightly pacing. The security man with whom I was talking had been to the pagoda and had offered candles and prayers to her spirit. She never appeared again.

I returned to the hotel after sunset, spooked by the silvery moon shadows that slipped across the lane ahead of me.

A few days later I came face to face with a more tangible British ghost, called Dorothy. She was a child-sized 81-year-old Anglo-Indian. She said that her mother was English and her father was Indian and they had come to Maymyo to work for the

British. Dorothy had sun-roasted and crinkled skin, with mustard-coloured eyes and wavy white hair tied up in a loose bun. She wore a shabby blazer with leather elbow patches and a *tamein,* or sarong. When I met her, I was walking down Maymyo's main street with a Western friend of mine who was visiting Burma. Dorothy grabbed my friend's arm and asked in a perfect English accent, 'Are you Connie? You look exactly like my cousin Connie. Are you her?' My friend, Katherine, was very definitely not Connie and said so. Undeterred, Dorothy went on, 'I thought you were Connie. Connie and the twins, they went back to England, you know. If you come across them, please say you met me here.'

The three of us ended up in a tea shop, where Dorothy reminisced about bygone times. 'It's nothing like before,' she said wistfully. 'Of course, everyone has left now. There was Minnie Rodricks, Barbara Duvall, Christine Hollinghurst . . . all the girls from the convent. They've gone away to England, you know.' In those days things were cheap and life was good, said Dorothy. 'Everything is too expensive now,' she sneered, picking up the greasy samosas that had been placed in the middle of the table and angrily tapping her cup, sloshing tea into the saucer. 'Things are bad now. Nothing like before. Nothing!'

Dorothy looked to the left and to the right, rolling her eyes like a cartoon character. 'But it's not good to say bad things,' she said. 'We mustn't say bad things. Or they will catch us.' She zipped up her mouth with her hand and broke into a ditty in a high-pitched voice: 'Oh, I wish I was a bachelor boy and my money would jingle again.'

As we said our goodbyes, Dorothy tapped Katherine and me for any spare change or pens we might have. Then she took one final look at Katherine and asked, 'Are you sure you're not Connie?'

K HIN NWE was a severe-looking woman in her early sixties with the expressive eyes of an actress from the era of silent movies. She worked in a government ministry in Maymyo, and a tour-guide friend of mine had told me to contact her if I was interested in the history of the town, as she had lived there all her life. When we met, in a shady park, she seemed a little wary of me—hostile even. I asked her some questions about the old houses of Maymyo. Where was the club that the British officials congregated at? (Burned down in the Second World War). Who owned all the British houses now? (The government). And the cemetery: did she know what had happened at the cemetery? She answered my questions without interest, but when I mentioned the cemetery she looked at me keenly for a long time. 'An officer was killed there,' said Khin Nwe finally. She was referring to a murder that had taken place a few days before my arrival. I knew nothing about this and was merely asking about the damaged gravestones, but when I mentioned the cemetery she had perhaps assumed that I was a foreign reporter trying to gather information. 'Of course it was not in the newspapers,' she continued, explaining that there had been a gambling argument: the soldier couldn't pay his debts, and the gambling ring to whom he owed money had killed him. By unwittingly mentioning the cemetery

I had fallen through a reality loophole, and I sensed that Khin Nwe was now going to give me a very different slant on life in the picture-book town of Maymyo.

'I have no hope for the future,' Khin Nwe said blankly. 'How can I? Things are only getting worse.' Economically, she was not able to make ends meet despite holding down a fairly senior job within the government administration. She received a relatively generous monthly salary of 18,000 kyat (less than twenty dollars), but this was still not enough to cover her rent and necessities. She was heavily in debt. She wanted to talk openly to her superiors about her problems, but she was too afraid. Her brother had talked openly in the town, and he was put in jail for six years. Soldiers came to his house and planted a packet of heroin in his bedside drawer. When he came out of prison he was a different man. 'He did not talk openly any more,' said Khin Nwe, wiping away tears. 'He became depressed and died young.' She continued with difficulty, 'We have no voice, no way to complain, no way to change things. If we speak out . . .' She drew her hand slowly across her throat.

Khin Nwe told me that high-ranking generals and drug lords from Burma's Wa State were buying up land and houses in Maymyo, attracted by the cool climate and pleasant lifestyle. 'The streets are paved with white powder,' she said, referring to the heroin that paid for their extravagant retirements. After Afghanistan, Burma is the world's largest producer of heroin. Much of the opium used in heroin production is grown in Wa State, in the rugged north-eastern mountains beyond Maymyo. The business is run by the United Wa State Army (UWSA), a group described by the US State Department as the world's 'most heavily armed narco-traffickers'. The Burmese regime is thought to have been benefiting financially from this illegal trade in drugs since the UWSA signed a ceasefire agreement with the Burmese generals in 1989. But the generals insist they are working to eradicate the drug industry, and from time to time they invite foreign journalists to specially organized ceremonies where enormous mounds of heroin, opium and methamphetamine pills are burned to cinders in front of international television crews.

After an hour, Khin Nwe looked at her watch and told me she had to return to the office. 'It was good to talk to you. Usually I have to keep it all inside. It's good to have this release,' she said. She told me to remember her name. 'Remember it in your head. Do not write it down in any book.'

Fleeting glimpses of a very different world were opening before me and closing up again just as quickly. Hidden behind the dreamy hedgerows of Maymyo there were whispers of murder and drug lords. All you had to do, it seemed, was scratch the surface of one of the town's smiling residents and you would find bitterness or tears.

THE REGIME'S central military academy, where it trains its officers, is located in Maymyo, and soldiers are more visible here than anywhere else I had been in Burma. Cadets march down the streets, dapper in maroon berets, swinging their arms and neatly creased trouser legs in unison. The British had also based their soldiers here, and Orwell spent a month with them doing military exercises as part of his police training. I met an octogenarian Burmese man who could still list the British regiments that he remembered as being stationed in Maymyo—'The Cameron Highlanders, the King's Own Yorkshire Light Infantry and the King's Royal Rifle Corps,' he chanted with pride. He also sported a pencil-thin moustache in imitation of the British officers who had last marched down these streets over fifty years ago. Orwell had an identical moustache—an addition to his appearance which he acquired while he was in Burma and kept for the rest of his life.

I decided to cycle to the British military barracks where Orwell had stayed. Looking on a map, I saw a circular road that ran past the small train station, through the old barracks and back into town. As soon as I passed the station the scenery changed. The British houses were still there—in varying stages of repair and neglect: some were sparklingly renovated; others were semi-derelict, with weed-choked chimneys—but it was clearly a military area. The washing dangling from the lines was all green or khaki. Officers wearing green bomber jackets and shiny black boots cruised past on motorbikes. A barefoot private struggled along with a metal trunk on his back. I could hear the ominous thunder of artillery practice nearby, and I realized, belatedly, that I was somewhere I probably shouldn't be. On either side of the road were grey military barracks, most of which had been built recently and were surrounded by freshly turned earth. I cycled past enormous brand-new meeting halls set in landscaped gardens

among neat circles of daisies and gardenias. All this development—the new barracks and massive auditoriums—gave off an
ominous aura of preparation and power. Few pedestrians caught
my eye, and no one smiled at me.

A soldier stepped into the road in front of me. 'No!' he
shouted. 'No!'

'Am I not allowed to cycle down this road?' I asked in my most
polite Burmese.

'No! You must leave, instantly,' he said, pointing me in the opposite direction. I followed the line of his finger. The road looked
long and empty. The pavement was painted with red-and-white
stripes, and an endless row of pine trees stood to attention on
each side of the road. I headed towards a large gate with iron
bars, and only then did I discover that I had inadvertently been cycling through the regime's Defense Services Academy. Two be-
mused soldiers opened the gate a fraction to let me out and then
closed it again, firmly.

The sun was beginning to set as I pedalled away. I freewheeled
down a hill towards the Candacraig Hotel to pack my bags and
head back to Mandalay. It was a glorious evening. Violet trumpets
of flowering morning glory danced in the hedges, and the air was
smoky with wood fires.

WHEN ORWELL'S YEAR in Mandalay came to end he was
posted to a small town called Myaungmya in the swamp-
lands of the Delta region in Lower Burma, to work as the assistant of a British superintendent of police. Though Orwell would

later dismiss his time in Burma as 'five boring years within the sound of bugles', his stint in the Delta took him straight into the troubled heart of the Burmese countryside, away from the urbane façades of Mandalay and Maymyo, and brought him face to face with the darker side of British rule.

Before I left Mandalay for the Delta I had to return a book to my voracious book-reading acquaintance Aye Myint. It was a collection of writings by Aung San Suu Kyi published abroad under the title *Freedom from Fear*. The book is definitely not part of the government's grand vision of 'A Golden Land', and reading it in Burma felt like an illicit activity. Even though Aye Myint had wrapped this contraband version of the truth in brown paper and had labelled the spine with a Pali word for 'the cycle of life', I carried it nervously in my bag and read it only in the safety of my hotel room. 'Don't show it to anyone or leave it lying around anywhere,' Aye Myint had cautioned me when he gave it me.

Where does the past exist? wonders Winston Smith in *Nineteen Eighty-Four*. If it cannot be read in actual sites or in official records, is it preserved only in people's minds? In Burma, certain narratives may be forbidden and many books may be banned, but this doesn't mean that they don't circulate. They travel between trusted friends, beneath false covers, from hidden libraries all over the country and form a parallel universe of alternative truths and secret histories. I had seen a number of these libraries while I was in Mandalay. One doctor's house I visited was stacked from floor to ceiling with old newspapers and research papers he was working on. Some were taped up inside plastic bags; others sat grandiloquently in piles of Mandalay dust. I met a young writer whose library was organized by subject matter on homemade wooden shelves and covered eclectic topics from female sexuality through Russian literature to postmodernism. And there was Aye Myint's library, neatly packed inside heavy-lidded trunks. All these collections, however, had one thing in common: they were gradually disappearing. Their pages were being glued together by damp and mildew. Pull any book from a shelf in Burma and it will be followed by a sprinkling of powder-like dust, the work of white ants relentlessly munching their way through thousands of texts all around the country.

I walked to Aye Myint's house beneath the shade of an umbrella. On one corner a group of trishaw drivers yelled at me, 'Hey you!' Music blared from a shop selling audio cassettes of Burmese pop songs. There were stores with second-hand televisions stacked in precarious towers, and spare motor parts spilled out on to the street from busy garages. Motorcycles and over-packed buses careered past me. On the other side of the street I saw a stout blind man shuffling slowly along a row of parked cars. He held a pencil-thin bamboo pipe to his lips, and was playing a high-pitched tune. Hanging from his shoulders was a plastic cup to collect donations from passers-by. As I watched, he bumped gently into one of the parked cars, righted himself, and walked on. Long after I lost sight of him I could still hear the plaintive melody of his pipe rising up above the cacophony of central Mandalay.

Aye Myint's house was the only wooden building left on his street. It was almost obscured by a row of white Chinese apartment blocks. I returned his book, and as he poured me a cup of clear tea I asked him a question. A Burmese professor of English literature had told me that Hemingway's *The Old Man and the Sea* was one of the most popular books in Burma. I asked Aye Myint why he thought that was. He answered without hesitation. '*The Old Man and the Sea* is about tenacity,' he said. 'It's about having the strength to hang on.' The book tells the tale of a man and a fish. The man goes fishing and hooks a gigantic marlin. The powerful fish is strong enough to drag his boat out to sea, and for three days man and fish are locked in a battle of strength and willpower. The fish eventually gives in and the man is left triumphant, but with aching arms and a delirious sleep-deprived mind. 'By the time he has sailed home he no longer has the fish because the sharks have eaten it,' said Aye Myint. 'He has only bones to show for his struggle.'

*Two*

# THE DELTA

Nothing was your own except the few cubic

centimetres inside your skull.

*Nineteen Eighty-Four*

MYAUNGMYA IS A TOWN in the middle of nowhere. It is located deep inside the Delta region, where Burma's largest river, the Irrawaddy, spills into hundreds of streams that meander through silt and mangrove forest down to the Bay of Bengal. The Delta is a flat mass of mud and water with rich, fertile soil and the clammy, hothouse heat of a tropical swamp. It is a hauntingly timeless landscape. The rivers are milky brown—the colour of weak cocoa—and water hyacinth grows so thick it sometimes covers the entire surface with softly undulating blankets of vivid green. The banks of the rivers and canals are lined with *dani,* or the nipa plant, which looks like the single leaf of a palm tree planted upright in the water. Beyond these *dani* fences, small paddy fields form a higgledy-piggledy patchwork dotted with an occasional water buffalo or caramel-coloured cow. Small huts of bamboo and thatch sit amid the forests of mangrove and coconut trees, and every so often the golden tip of a pagoda can be seen above the greenery.

An antique steam-powered passenger ferry floats almost silently through this landscape. The upper deck is crammed with passengers who have staked out plots on the hot metal floor by laying out plastic groundsheets and creating small shelters from baskets, buckets and burlap sacks of vegetables. The ticket I bought in Rangoon entitles me to inhabit plot #59 for the day-long journey to Myaungmya. Plot #59 is a piece of the deck about half the size of a suitcase, and when I find it I carefully arrange myself so that both I and my bag fit compactly within its faded white lines. But the hush of the river and the still, pre-monsoon air have a soporific effect on all of us, and any initial attempts at tidiness are soon abandoned. Sleepy legs slide off groundsheets, and drowsy bodies droop themselves languidly across bags and railings.

The cry of a vendor echoes across the boat. '*Sa-ouq-twaaaaaaaaay!*' yells the man as he weaves his way through lazy piles of passengers and produce. 'Boo-ooo-ooks!' Under his arm he carries a stack of books and magazines that can be rented for the duration of the journey. A family near me unpacks an aluminium tiffin box from one of their overstuffed baskets and pours pungent curry-drenched rice on to torn-off sheets of newspaper. Next to me, a woman lies across her husband's legs, smoking a cheroot and reading her horoscope in a two-month-old magazine she has just hired. An elderly woman on a nearby plot, with sprigs of fresh white jasmine pinned in her hair, gazes out at the endless line of *dani* palms, her head resting against the rusting iron rail. Another cry shatters the silence: '*Mohinghaaaa-aaaaaa!*' A vendor emerges from the lower deck and ladles out steaming noodles from an earthenware pot cocooned in rags for warmth. A young girl follows carrying aloft a rattan tray stacked high with chopped watermelon, each red triangle buzzing with flies. Out on the river, hulking dark rice barges and wooden canoes heavy with unripe bananas sail slowly past.

George Orwell arrived in Myaungmya to begin his career as an imperial policeman in January 1924, when the only way to reach the town was by boat. The Delta was then considered one of the worst areas in Burma for a British man to live and work. Maurice Collis, a British magistrate-turned-writer, who spent a brief time in the Delta during the 1920s and enthused wildly about the rest of Burma, described the landscape in this clammy corner of the country as morbid, monotonous and depressing. A travelling British painter wrote that if you wanted a vision of the Delta you had only to paint a stripe of brown for the water, a stripe of green for the paddy fields, and leave the rest blank for the sky.

The Delta did, however, have one particular claim to fame: it was reputed to have the largest, liveliest mosquitoes in the Empire. In a 1920s travel book called *The Silken East,* V. C. Scott O'Connor, a retired British civil servant from Burma, entitled his chapter on the Delta simply 'Mosquitoes'. British residents of the area lived inside fortresses of iron gauze to protect themselves from the region's flying armies. Every window was covered with additional screens, and every door had an automatic closing mechanism so that it would shut as soon as it had been released, giving the insects less time to enter. Some houses, O'Connor noted, even had a special room, 'a kind of inner citadel and last refuge, which is wholly iron gauze, and within it the master of the house sits like a vanquished lion in a cage'. It was said that you could always identify Britons who had been posted to the Delta, as they retained a habitual manner of entering doors with a sudden dart and a slam, to prevent the ghosts of the Delta's mosquitoes from following them.

By most accounts, this was considered an unlucky posting for Orwell. A few weeks before I came to the Delta I met a Burmese author who was convinced it was the reason Orwell had become such a pessimistic writer. He would never have written *Nineteen Eighty-Four* if he had not been posted there, she declared with certainty. 'It was the Delta that ruined him,' she told me. 'If he had not been there he would have stayed in Burma for the rest of his life. He would have learned to love Burma—all foreigners do. But he couldn't learn to love Burma because he was sent to the Delta, where there is nothing but mud, *dani* and poor farmers.' She warned that the Delta had not changed since Orwell's time, and advised me not to stay too long.

The ferry declared its arrival at Myaungmya with an ear-splitting blast of its horn. I hung over the railing and watched as the boat docked against the pier. Along the waterfront was a row of old colonial shop-houses caked in thick peppermint-blue paint and stained with mildew. In the background I could see tall, elegant palm trees, and heavy rain clouds hanging low in the sky. Porters with ragged navy-blue shirts and rough tattoos of dragons and tigers slithering up their arms waited to load and unload sacks of produce. Before the boat was even tied to the pier, a yelling throng of hawkers had surged on board with tin platters of sliced pineapple, lotus pods and steamed sweetcorn for passengers travelling onward to the port town of Pathein. I gathered my bags and climbed down on to the pier, amid the chaos.

T DIDN'T TAKE long for Myaungmya's Military Intelligence to find me. On my first night in the town I was having dinner in a busy little Burmese restaurant—a delicious feast of pennywort salad, spicy fish curry, *daal,* and cardamom-laced vegetable soup. Halfway through my meal the owner of the restaurant, a portly bald man in a grease-stained *longyi,* came up to my table and politely asked me to return to my guest house.

'Why?' I asked.

'Please don't ask questions,' he replied. 'Please go back now, just for a little bit. Later, maybe, you can come out again.' He handed me a jar filled with brown droplets of hardened jaggery—a sweetener made from sugar cane: a traditional way to cleanse the pallet, and a sign that the meal was over.

I walked the five minutes back to the guest house, a cramped four-storey building in the centre of town. There I found the proprietor sitting at his desk surrounded by a pile of papers. He looked up at me and smiled apologetically. 'I have to report you to the authorities,' he said. The arrival of a foreigner in Myaungmya was an uncommon event, and local regulations required that he submit photocopies of my passport to nine different government departments. Each department needed a special form, along with a copy of the page of my passport with my photograph and biographical details, as well as the page on which my Burmese visa had been stamped. I had to sign and date each of the forms and photocopies before they could be submitted to the relevant authorities. The proprietor told me he had to file the forms *before* I spent the night in Myaungmya. I had arrived late in the afternoon, and it was already eight in the evening by the time I registered at the guest house. He had had to bribe the one photocopy shop in town to open up after hours. I asked him how he had found me in the restaurant. He laughed. 'That', he said, 'was the easy part.'

Burma's surveillance machine is frighteningly thorough and efficient. It consists of a number of different departments that come under the control of the Directorate of Defense Services Intelligence (DDSI), known informally in Burmese as MI, for 'Military Intelligence'. MI's mandate is vast: to monitor the entire Burmese population. It concentrates on obvious threats to the regime, which include the armed forces themselves, and targets anyone who has ever criticized the government openly, NLD members, and foreigners both in the country and out. In short, everyone is being watched. A friend in Mandalay had warned me about the omnipresent MI and its informers. He told me that in some towns the surveillance mechanism operates at a neighbourhood level, with local MI minions filing daily reports to their central bureaus. The regime, he said with awe, knows everything. If there has been an anti-government remark made by a drunkard, a basket of mangoes stolen from the local market, or a simple quarrel between husband and wife, the MI will most probably know about it. This method of control is highly effective: Big Brother really is everywhere.

In Orwell's *Nineteen Eighty-Four,* the ever present 'telescreen' monitors the movements of all Party members. When they are at home the two-way screen, which transmits orders as well as gathering information, is positioned so that all activities in the house can be watched. It is through this telescreen that the Party's Thought Police are able to monitor the populace and the minutiae of their day-to-day activities:

A Party member lives from birth to death under the eye of the Thought Police. Even when he is alone he can never be sure that he is alone. Wherever he may be, asleep or awake, working or resting, in his bath or in bed, he can be inspected without warning and without knowing that he is being inspected. Nothing that he does is indifferent. His friendships, his relaxations, his behaviour towards his wife and children, the expression on his face when he is alone, the words he mutters in his sleep, even the characteristic movements of his body, are all jealously scrutinized.

The method may not be so high-tech in Burma, but it is just as efficient. MI is armed with a number of ordinances to monitor the population. A registration system dictates that all members of every household must register with the local authorities. If guests are staying the night, they too must file registration forms. There are also restrictions on travel, overseen by frequent checkpoints on roads throughout the country. All communication equipment such as telephones, fax machines and modems must be registered; anyone using such machines without the correct licence is punishable by imprisonment. 'They are very, very good,' a Burmese journalist in Rangoon told me about the MI. 'They have been trained by the best: the old Russian KGB and China's secret police.' Though it is difficult to investigate their well-hidden inner workings, there is indeed evidence to suggest that the MI have been tutored by these countries, as well as by others with formidable experience in surveillance, including Israel, Singapore and East Germany. So, even without the hidden cameras and recording devices that monitor the lifts and shopping malls of more developed countries, the reach of the MI is all-encompassing. They know where you sleep and with whom; they can intercept your post and read your letters, they can listen in on your telephone conversations. And they have informers in almost every public space, from universities and offices to monasteries and tea shops.

As a British police officer, Orwell was responsible for similar intelligence-gathering. Surveillance was the backbone of British police work in Burma. On the boat sailing out from England, one new officer met a Scottish policeman who gave him some tips on how to control the Burmese people: 'My boy, there are three cardinal rules: the first is supairvision, the second is supairvision, and the third is supairvision.'

British policing methods in Burma placed a heavy emphasis on detection and prevention by carefully monitoring the populace. Known criminals were tagged as 'History Sheeters', and their names and histories were listed on so-called 'Bad Character Rolls', so that the police could keep an especially close eye on them. Policemen would check up on History Sheeters regularly—

often late at night, to ensure they were safely tucked up in bed and not out committing crimes or undermining the authority of the Empire. What the police force lacked in technology, it made up for in bureaucracy—the British administration swamped the Burmese with paperwork. Each provincial headquarters kept a daily crime digest that was fed into a weekly *Criminal Intelligence Gazette* that detailed the latest murders, gang robberies and other serious offences. This document was printed in Burmese and English, sent to the government's Central Intelligence Bureau in Rangoon, and circulated to police stations throughout the country. Some police officers became rabid in their pursuit of Burma's criminal elements. I read one report typed by a subordinate of Orwell's level for his superintendent. Next to the name of a suspected criminal, the superintendent had scrawled in red crayon the words 'I want him! Must have him!'

The proprietor of the guest house where I was staying in Myaungmya handed me the photocopies and forms one by one, and I dutifully signed them all. The nine departments now aware of the arrival of this solitary foreign female were the Township Land Police, the Township Water Police, the District Land Police, the District Water Police, the Immigration Department, the Local Peace and Development Council, the District Peace and Development Council, the Military and, of course, Military Intelligence. A few days later, when I paid my bill as I checked out, I noticed that the proprietor had charged me for all the photocopies, as well as for the 500-kyat bribe (approximately fifty cents) it had cost him to convince the photocopy shop to open after hours.

———

'S O, THE HUNTING DOGS of our military regime have been tracking you down, have they?' laughed Myo Kyi. We were sitting in a tea shop in Myaungmya, and I had just told him about my experiences at the guest house. I had met Myo Kyi's cousin in Bangkok, where he was teaching at a Thai university, and he had asked me to deliver a letter and some money to Myo Kyi since I was planning to go to Myaungmya. His cousin wouldn't write down Myo Kyi's address for me: he had asked me to memorize it. ('What if they confiscate your notebooks and find his name and address in them? It would not be good for him,' the cousin had warned.) I was given vague directions to Myo Kyi's house (third street on your left after you pass the pagoda, fifth house on your right once you cross the canal) and it had taken me the better part of an afternoon to find him.

Myaungmya is built around two main streets that run parallel to the river. Most of the buildings are low-rise colonial shop-houses. On the wall of one building I could just make out the em-blem of the British Crown and the date it was built: 1923. Layers of paint, decades of renovations, were flaking off its columns like the sheaths of skin shed by snakes. The wreckage of the façade was patched together here and there with corrugated iron and tarpaulin, and mildew was creeping up the walls. The town is centred around an old British-built market with elegant pillars and wrought-iron roof fixtures. Inside the market, plump women sit amid baskets of damp greens and fresh flowers. There are stalls selling a rainbow array of plastic buckets and raincoats. Deeper inside, beneath the gloom of the roof, shanks of raw meat hang from metal hooks. And down where the market opens on to the river, where the produce of the Delta is loaded on to boats bound for Rangoon, piles of yellow mangoes glistening wet from the rain are nestled in beds of straw, and bananas dangle like claws from bamboo poles. Myaungmya was once a bustling trading post and attracted merchants from all over Burma. There are mosques and pagodas and Chinese shrines smeared with red paint and golden calligraphy as thick as papier mâché. But as I looked down the side alleys I saw that they drifted off into dirt lanes and jungle.

It was down one of these green lanes that I found Myo Kyi's house. Myo Kyi wasn't at home, but his wife said I could find him at the local tea shop. 'He is there every afternoon from two until five,' she told me.

Myo Kyi was a retired engineer who had spent most of his life designing bridges and dams for government projects. He had a craggy, walnut-brown face, and his lips were stained deep red with betel. 'You must be careful with yourself,' he warned me. 'Our Military Intelligence are everywhere. And where they are not, their informers are.' In Burmese, informers are sometimes called *pasein yo,* literally 'the handle of the axe', signifying that the weapon used to chop down the tree is made from the wood of the tree itself. (Interestingly, the regime also uses this image in dubbing Aung San Suu Kyi an 'axe handle'.) 'They are like the hunter's dogs scavenging for the hunter, searching out prey,' explained Myo Kyi. By using these informal informers, the MI have become incredibly effective, he said. The reason the system works so well is very simple: it is hard to tell who is an informer and who is not.

The tea shop where I sat with Myo Kyi was a small, hole-in-the-wall shop. Its walls had been burnished a molasses colour from the wood fires used for cooking and for boiling tea. At one unoccupied table a tea-shop boy was rolling out pastry to make samosas. He glazed each paper-thin sheet of dough with oil, tossed it on to a blackened wok on top of the fire, flipped it twice, and then returned it to the table, where he carefully smoothed out the creases as if he were laying out freshly ironed handker-chiefs. A monk hunched over a table in one corner of the shop looked blankly out into the bright road as passersby flitted across the entrance like movie extras. A saturnine man entered with a pile of roasted ducks on a large tin plate balanced on top of his head. The tea-shop owner appeared from the back of the shop, picked up each duck, and examined it meticulously, looking beneath its rubbery wings, eventually buying two. A woman walked in off the street, attracted by the ducks that were being sold. When the man had made his final sale, he lifted the plate back on to his head and walked off. '*Beh-tha kin!*' he yelled— 'Roast duck!' I wondered who in this tea shop could be an in-former.

I was always asking my Burmese friends how you spot an in-former or an MI agent. There is obviously no foolproof method, and everyone had a different suggestion, varying from the ludi-crous to the arcane. A retired footballer in southern Burma told me that all MI wear their watch on the right wrist and smoke with their right hand. 'It is their special signal so that they know each other,' he said earnestly. For some time after he told me this I took to looking suspiciously at all right-handed smokers, until I realized that many of my friends and probably more than half the population of Burma smoked with their right hands and wore their watches on their right wrists. The young writer in the Orwell Book Club, Maung Oo, always preferred to sit in the middle of a tea shop, as he was nervous of men who sat around the edges in any seat that afforded a good view of the rest of the shop. Informers, he told me, never choose tables in the centre of the room. An English photographer friend of mine who was trying to record evidence of forced labour in Burma realized he was being followed by an MI agent when he noticed the outline of a pair of handcuffs pressed beneath the man's *longyi*. And one Burmese friend claimed to have a sixth sense: 'You can notice changes in your environment from time to time. I have a sense if there's someone at the gate, or listening on the telephone. All you need is to be clever, to be aware.'

Myo Kyi asked me if I had heard of the panopticon devised by the eighteenth-century British philosopher Jeremy Bentham. The panopticon operates on the same principle as the ever present telescreen in Orwell's *Nineteen Eighty-Four,* which allows people to be seen at all times. It is a prison designed to control a large number of prisoners with only a handful of guards. A central tower has visual access to every cell, and the prisoners can be viewed twenty-four hours a day. It is impossible, however, to see inside the central tower: prisoners can never tell if there is anyone in the tower or not. The system operates on the theory that if you think you are being watched you respond in the same way as if you really are being watched. 'So, you see,' said Myo Kyi, 'it doesn't make any difference whether they have informers or not. It is enough that we believe that their informers are everywhere. After that, we start to do their work for them.'

Myo Kyi sighed heavily, and the piquant scent of betel wafted over me. He stroked the letter I had brought him from Thailand and said, with a triumphant grin, 'But they cannot know everything. What is in my mind? They can not know that!'

I left Myo Kyi at the tea shop and took a circuitous route back to the guest house. When I thought too much about the ever present surveillance I found it incredibly unnerving. I would view everyone I met with paranoia, weighing up the possibilities that he or she might be an informer or a member of the MI. If someone approached me while I was sitting on my own in a tea shop and asked too many questions I would often give him or her the cold shoulder. Afterwards I would feel terrible about it. I had even wondered guiltily about Khin Nwe, whom I met in Maymyo. She had cried while she told me her story, and yet, as I left our meeting, a thought had flitted through my mind that perhaps she was an informer, trying to trick me into telling her what I was doing in Burma.

I tried to develop the mask that I had seen so many of my Burmese friends wear in public. On a previous trip to Burma, one of my friends had introduced me to his card-playing group. I watched him joking and laughing with them over poker, but when we left he told me he trusted only one of the five people he had been playing with. I had read a description of this ability to act so well in public in Czeslaw Milosz's book *The Captive Mind,* in which he describes life in 1950s Poland under the authoritarian influences of Nazism and Stalinism. He writes that in such circumstances people must, of necessity, become actors and actresses. 'One does not perform on a theatre stage,' says Milosz, 'but in the street, office, factory, meeting hall, or even the room one lives in. Such acting is a highly-developed craft that places a premium upon mental alertness. Before it leaves the lips every word must be evaluated as to its consequences. A smile that appears at the wrong moment, a glance that is not all it should be can occasion dangerous suspicions and accusations.' I read Milosz's description to my poker-playing friend and his face lit up. 'Yes, yes!' he said enthusiastically. 'That's just like us. It is as if we are all stuck in some play—in one of Shakespeare's tragi-comedies, perhaps.'

Of course, no matter where we live, we all have to play certain roles dictated by our environment, but for those of us who live in freer societies the game is not such a dangerous one. We will not end up in prison if we say the wrong thing to the wrong person. In Burma, where people can easily be coerced or bullied into informing on those around them, you have to be careful whom you pick arguments with. If you upset a neighbour, he could tell the MI you are a spy, or that you are harbouring anti-government sentiments. And then, late one night, there will be a knock on your door. 'It doesn't matter whether the things they say about you are true or not,' a friend told me. 'You will be taken away to a detention centre and tortured or pressured until you have confessed to something you didn't do. Then you will be sent to prison, and your family might not even be told where you are. They might find out months or years later, when you have been released at some random point in time. Or maybe never.'

WHEN ORWELL LIVED in Myaungmya he spent much of his time on patrol, sailing through the canals, hunting down History Sheeters, visiting crime scenes. I asked at the market if it was possible to rent a boat and explore the canals around the town. I was directed to the police water-transport depot, a small shack on the river's edge. I explained to the officials there what I wanted to do and how much I was willing to pay to do it. 'Come back tomorrow,' I was told. I wasn't very hopeful, but when I returned the next day there was a boat waiting for me. It was a small lime-green vessel with a flimsy wooden roof. A soggy rattan mat had been placed across the planks beneath the shelter, so that I would have somewhere to sit. There were three men on board: a boatman to handle the outboard motor and two other men. I was told that one was a reserve boatman and the other was to be my guide. The latter was a tall man with a military haircut and chiselled features. He wore a sparkling white Lacoste T-shirt tucked into his *longyi,* and had small circular tattoos on his wrists and in the hollows between his thumbs and forefingers— marks believed to make a man bulletproof.

It was an overcast day. As the boat chugged noisily away from the bank, a sticky breeze funnelled its way through my small shelter. I decided to ask my guide some questions about the river, and scrambled out on to the prow, where he was sitting.

'What kind of fish are there in this river?' I asked in Burmese.

'Fish,' he replied.

'Yes, but what kind of fish?'

'*Fish* fish,' he said with a laconic flourish.

I retreated back under the shelter and watched the scenery chug slowly past. The area was lush and extraordinarily fertile. Thick vines and creepers were draped across branches. There were spider lilies with long white tentacles, and scarlet hibiscus whose petals spilled out like party streamers. The floating islands of water hyacinth sprouted a tiny bell-like flower, the colour of pale forget-me-nots. All along the banks were the now familiar dagger-like *dani* with their yellow-tipped leaves. A decade after Orwell had returned to England, he slipped the following paragraph into a book review he wrote:

For an average Englishman in India [Burma was then ruled as part of the Indian Empire] the basic fact, more important even than the loneliness or the heat of the sun, is the strangeness of the scenery. In the beginning the foreign landscape bores him, later he hates it, in the end he comes to love it, but it is never quite out of his consciousness and all his beliefs are in a mysterious way affected by it.

The scenery of the East clearly got under Orwell's skin, and when he wrote about Burma in *Burmese Days* he produced his most elaborate descriptive writing: the novel is given an exotic setting, drenched in mist and tropical flowers. His other books lacked such lyricism—neither Spain nor England produced such vivid 'purple passages', as he called them. And, on his deathbed, it was to the Burmese landscape that Orwell's mind wandered as he searched for inspiration for another novel.

Dugout canoes glided along the edge of the river. Bamboo groves were occasionally revealed, producing patches of luminous green light. A gaggle of people scampered across one opening, bright pink and purple shoulder bags hung like sashes across their torsos. Naked boys wearing cloche hats made of palm leaves slid with whoops and shouts down a muddy embankment into the river. A lone woman wrapped in a lilac *tamein* knelt on a stone in the canal with her back towards us, slowly combing her black, waist-length hair. Mostly, however, all we passed was greenery. In some areas, where the jungle was especially thick, the only hint of habitation was the tail end of a canoe, carved from a single log, poking out from under the foliage.

After a few hours the boatman pulled up to the bank and tied the boat to a tree. 'We'll get off here and walk around,' said my guide. We had arrived at a village of tumbledown houses made from bamboo and palm thatch and surrounded by clay water jars, chickens, pigs and mangy dogs. These motley habitations were stretched out beside a long, narrow track that ran along the river. My guide led me directly to one end of the village, beyond which the police outpost was located. I guessed that we had to report our arrival; my guide said simply that perhaps I would like to see the police station. It took us some twenty minutes to get there. We skidded and slid along a track of butter-soft mud that wound its way through an endless vista of green paddy. Cows picked their way delicately along the dirt embankments between the waterlogged fields. At the outpost, four policemen lived within a bamboo-walled compound. Their shacks were perched precariously on stilts above a bog in which a family of pigs wallowed. 'Very nice,' I said, not knowing what else to say.

A policeman joined my entourage as we headed back to the village. I dropped behind my escorts as we walked along a track lined with rubbish and more mud. In the quiet of the village all I could hear was the sucking of mud at my heels, and then, suddenly, a burst of laughter shattered the silence. I looked up to see an old man laughing at me. 'Aren't the roads in Burma the finest you have ever seen?' he called out to me in Burmese, with a cheeky, toothless grin. He had a kindly weather-worn face and a smart white crew cut. His arms were covered with cabbalistic tattoos, blue-black with age. I stopped to talk to him. He was eighty-six years old, he told me, and had lived here all his life. I asked him if he remembered the British times. 'Yes, they were here once,' he said. 'But they never came out to my village. They were big men; they stayed in their big houses in the big town,' he said, referring to Myaungmya. We hadn't got very far in our conversation when my escorts came schlepping back through the mud to surround us. The old man looked from one to the other and seemed to become confused. Curiously, he no longer understood anything I said, shaking his head dumbly. He's too old for your questions, said the policeman, laughing. We moved on.

I would have liked to talk more to the old man and ask him about the rise and fall of the Delta. He had been born when this muddy swamp was at the booming centre of the world's rice production. He was now living through its hardest times. Before the

British annexed this part of Lower Burma in 1852, the area offered nothing but 'malaria-haunted marshes' and 'amphibious savagery', according to one British civil servant. But the British had seen the potential of the region's rich soil. The colonial administration began settling the area and encouraging rice farmers. It soon became apparent that the land was incredibly fertile, producing 50 per cent more rice than ordinary soil. Adventurous settlers came from all over Burma to carve a living from the marshes. By the time that Orwell arrived here, in the early 1920s, the Delta was leading Burma's exports of over 3 million tons of rice—half the world's supply. But the Delta's heyday is long over, and Burma's reputation as the rice bowl of Asia is in tatters. According to one source, Burma now exports a meagre 20,000 tons of rice. Farmers are forced to sell a quota of their yield to the government at prices as low as one-sixth of the market price. The regime uses the rice to subsidize government employees and military personnel, exporting the rest. Farmers who are unable to meet the quota must barter their valuable livestock, or face imprisonment. Since the Delta's soil is so conducive to rice-growing, farmers here are harder hit than most by this government policy, as the regime relies heavily on the region for its resources. The village already seemed horribly poor. Many people had goitres, swollen eyes or gammy legs. Nobody welcomed us—not even the children who were playing around the ruins of an old pagoda. They stopped their shrieks as our cavalcade approached them, and stood staring at us, still as statues.

The policeman led us inland towards the local school, a one-storey U-shaped building, constructed of cardboard-thin cement. It was after school hours, and we found the headmaster seated behind a desk piled high with tattered exercise books and papers. A short man with a nervous manner, he wore a knitted waistcoat over his grey-white shirt, and had combed his receding hair into a side-lock that sat stickily on his sweating head. We sat around his desk—myself, my guide, the reserve boatman and the policeman—as he spoke to me in broken English. He told me he had been transferred to this village from his home in Myaungmya three years ago. 'I am enjoying myself here very much,' he said, pushing his spectacles up his nose. Hanging on the wall behind his desk was a large framed photograph of General Than Shwe, the top general and military leader of the country. It was an awkward meeting. I got the feeling that the headmaster wanted to tell me something—perhaps about conditions in the village—and I wanted to encourage him to do so. However, though none of my minders claimed to speak any English, they listened intently to our conversation. So, instead of the questions I would have liked to ask, I proffered other ones. 'How many students do you have?' Five hundred. 'What subjects do you teach?' History, geography, mathematics and English.

'OK!' announced my guide. 'Let's go!'

We were all, I think, intensely relieved by this command. As I walked out the door, the headmaster called me back. 'Please,' he said, 'would you write your name down on this piece of paper.' He didn't say why, but it was probably so that he could report our meeting to the authorities. All government civil servants, from

street sweepers to schoolteachers, are required to report any in-
terchange they have with a foreigner. I was sorry to have made
him so anxious.

As we boarded the boat, a group of villagers lined up on the
bank and watched us depart. I waved, but no one waved back.
The skies had turned cloudy and colourless, and the boatman began tying tarpaulin sheets against the sides of the shelter in the
middle of the boat. Halfway back to Myaungmya we sailed into
the storm. Through the flapping sheets I caught glimpses of banana trees on the bank, flailing in the wind like hysterical ban-
shees. A small boy stood at the edge of a paddy field with a plastic
sheet wrapped around his otherwise bare shoulders and a straw
hat, dripping with rain. The water turned slate grey as the downpour continued, and soon all I could see was a heavy fog of rain
and cloud. When the boat finally docked at a pier in Myaungmya,
I said my thanks, climbed inelegantly on to the slippery walkway,
and ran for cover in an abandoned wooden warehouse to wait
out the rest of the storm.


ORWELL SPENT just four months training in Myaungmya,
learning the methods of police work under a British superintendent. He was then posted to the nearby town of Twante,
also within the Delta region. To get to Twante, I had to take a
boat to Ma-U-Bin town, overnight there, and board a bus the following day. Ma-U-Bin is a trading centre for the Delta, a large
market town where rice and vegetables grown in the region are
bought and sold at the local market and shipped on to Rangoon

or down to the Bay of Bengal for export. I could see its dark silhouette as we approached it by boat in the middle of another thundering storm. It was only seven o'clock in the evening, but the entire town was in darkness. Flashes of lightning illuminated the empty skeleton of the large riverside market. I climbed up the pier, past the eerily empty stalls, into the main thoroughfare. The street was deserted in the heavy downpour, and I walked beneath the inadequate protection of an umbrella until I came to a guest house.

A weak light shone from a small booth inside the concrete building. Below the roar of the rain I could hear the steady throb of a generator powering the dim bulbs that lit the long, narrow corridors. I handed over my passport, paid 1,000 kyat (about one dollar) for a night's stay, and was led to a bleak, tiny room that housed a wooden bed with no mattress. Over the bed hung a greying mosquito net stained with betel spit and reeking of beer and sweat. Since I had nowhere else to go, I settled in for the evening. I dried myself off and sat on the bed with a stack of notes I had jotted down from the India Office Records at the British Library in London. They summarized police reports made during Orwell's time here in the Delta. I could remember clearly how unsettled I had been when I wrote them: how the cool hush of the library was utterly at odds with the mayhem they described.

Orwell's first year on the beat was a catastrophic one for the British police force in Burma. Retired civil servant J. K. Stanford wrote in his memoirs of that time, 'Everyone had realized what an astounding assortment of malefactors—murderers, dacoits, thieves, robbers, house-breakers, forgers, coiners, blackmailers, and so on—each district possessed. They seemed to spring up like dragon's teeth, till there were scarcely enough columns in the criminal game-book.' Violent crime in Burma had risen at an alarming rate. Dacoity—defined as crime committed by roving gangs of more than five hooligans—had doubled in the last ten years, as had murder rates, giving Burma the dubious distinction of being the most violent corner of the Indian Empire. As one police report put it: 'Murder stalks through the land with impunity.' The sheer brutality of the crimes astounded British administrators. Dacoits raped women and girls as young as eleven, afterwards covering their victims in kerosene-soaked blankets and setting fire to them. There were descriptions of a dacoit king famous for crucifying his victims. The dead body of an Indian was found in a well with a bamboo stick forced up his anus. A monk was lured out of his dwellings to have his throat slit. A fisherman was hacked to death for his daily catch. 'This year', said the police report for 1924, with considerable understatement, 'has been a very difficult one for the Police.'

Burma's unprecedented crime wave sent the police force into turmoil, and Orwell found himself right in the deep end. 'Crime season', as the police called it, was between January and June, when the demands of agricultural labour were low. And this was exactly when Orwell began his first posting out in the field. The British police authorities set up countless committees to investigate the root causes of what one report called the 'bestial savagery' and to find out how best to deal with it. All police leave during crime season was revoked. Ninety British officers and 13,000 Burmese policemen had to oversee a land of some 13 million people. The Burmese policemen were underpaid and undertrained. Corruption was rampant among magistrates and criminals who were caught were seldom convicted. It was a potentially disastrous situation.

The British authorities desperately searched for solutions. One committee denounced alcohol as the catalyst for murder. The ever present *dani,* which lined the rivers I had sailed through, could be distilled into a lethal brew, and toddy was attainable from any palm tree. The committee recommended total prohibition for Burmans. Another pointed to the demoralizing influence of the imported adventure movies—mostly violent depictions of America's Wild West—that were doing the rounds on travelling cinematographs. One officer blamed the high rates of violence on the Delta's infernal mosquitoes. And there were some, much more disturbing, diagnoses which referred to 'the innate criminality of the Burmese character'. Only one report ventured to look at the impact of British intervention on Burmese culture: the way in which the British government had removed respected headmen and replaced them with its own bureaucratic counterparts. A Burmese police officer added 'a minute of dissent' to one report, pointing out that young Burmese boys now had to attend schools styled on the British educational system and were no longer able to go to the *pongyi kyaung,* or traditional monastic schools. He felt the government should have had the foresight to see that disabling the country's centuries-old religious education system would lead to disaster. There is, he wrote, 'no reason to assume it has come to such a stage that the Burmese people are less moral than any other nation'.

At Hla Htut's bookstall in Mandalay I had found a copy of a book called *The Tiger-Man of Burma and Other Adventure Yarns* by C. F. Argyll Saxby, printed in the early 1920s by the Boy's Own Paper Office, London. The title story—a ripping tale about a young boy called Bob Harwood and his trusty Burmese minder, Pan Yi—seemed to capture something of the spirit of that time. Bob's parents had been killed by a notorious Burmese dacoit known as the Tiger-Man ten years previously, and Bob and Pan Yi have great adventures tracking him down. The Tiger-Man catches Bob, covers him with sugar, and leaves him in the jungle to be eaten alive by ants. But Bob doesn't die: his trusty Burmese servant comes to the rescue. 'You are a brick, Pan Yi! You are a whole cartload of bricks!' says Bob by way of gratitude. The trusty Burmese servant is captured in turn, and is held captive in a pagoda, strung up with a python slithering towards him. Against all the odds, Bob manages to rescue his servant and catch the dacoit. The story ends with words from the Tiger-Man himself: ' "The British always win. I should have remembered that," said the dacoit, thoroughly cowed, and almost pitifully broken in spirit.'

It is hard to imagine the effect of all this violence on the young Orwell, who had spent his childhood in the placid settings of Henley and Eton College. A contemporary of Orwell's at Eton remembered that Orwell spoke about the East, his place of birth, quite often and had a romantic, sentimental idea of the region.

The young Orwell must have gleaned many of his ideas about Burma from his mother's descriptions of her childhood home in the southern port town of Moulmein; one of her sisters liked to boast that their father lived the life of a prince, tended to by thirty barefoot servants. And the India Office examination would hardly have given Orwell any idea of what was to come. He took exams in English language ('write a profile of an old game-keeper'), and history ( . . . 'if Nelson had lost Trafalgar?). A year later, after a regimented but calm existence in the comparative civility of Mandalay, he was launched into the mud and mayhem of the Delta. And there was no way that Orwell could have hidden in his room reading: his superior officers in both Myaungmya and his following posting, Twante, happened to be renowned crime-busters, commended for their work in the annual police gazettes, and in Twante his superintendent was the celebrated winner of the annual revolver-shooting competition. Later in Orwell's life, when discussing the poem 'Spain' by W. H. Auden, he took offence at Auden's description of killing during wartime as 'necessary murder'. Orwell wrote, 'Personally I would not speak so lightly of murder. It so happens that I have seen the bodies of numbers of murdered men—I don't mean killed in battle, I mean murdered . . . Therefore I have some conception of what murder means—the terror, the hatred, the howling relatives, the post-mortems, the blood, the smells.' Again, it seems, the backdrop of Burma was haunting him.

It didn't take long for the voracious mosquitoes of Ma-U-Bin to penetrate the porous net that hung around my bed. In a diary Orwell wrote during the Second World War he recalled, from his days in Burma, the same irritation I was experiencing. It is the Sod's Law of using mosquito nets: as soon as you think you have killed the last mosquito inside your net and have turned off your light to settle down to sleep, another mosquito will, inevitably start whining near your ear.

THE NEXT MORNING I escaped the guest house and walked past featureless grey meeting halls, mouldering colonial shop-houses, and tightly shuttered-up dark wooden homes until I found a tea shop. Just as a steaming shot glass of tea was placed on my table, a man I had not met before came up to me and announced that I had a visitor waiting back at the guest house. I was un-pleasantly surprised. The night before, the man at the front desk had already taken my passport and quizzed me about my move-ments. ('When are you leaving Ma-U-Bin? . . . Where will you be going? . . . And by what method of transport?') Grudgingly, I downed my tea and made my way back. In the dingy corridor a middle-aged man had created a makeshift desk from a flimsy cof-fee table and sat behind it waiting for me. He did not identify himself and wore no uniform, but handed me some official forms to fill in. I told him I had already given the hotel my passport and details. 'Yes,' he said, 'but we cannot read English and we need you to tell us what it says.' He needed to know my country of ori-gin, my name, age, occupation, where I had come from, where I was going to, and the purpose of my visit to Ma-U-Bin. I filled in all the required sections of the form, stating my occupation as something innocuous like 'consultant' and the purpose of my visit as 'tourism'. After I had done that, he told me he was the local immigration officer for Ma-U-Bin and asked if he could be of any help. He had just jotted down the fact that I was getting on a bus to Twante in fifteen minutes.

On my way back to my room to pack my bag, I passed the toilets, an especially grim ensemble of cockroach-ridden squat latrines. A woman was bent down over one of them trying to scrub it clean. She saw me walk past and came to stand by my door and watch me pack. She was a short, dark Indian woman with a boxer's crooked nose and a childlike smile. She wore a threadbare sari top and a torn *tamein* that just covered her calloused knees. I estimated she was in her late sixties, but she told me she was just forty-five. As I asked her more about her life, she started to cry. No one, she said, had ever wanted to know anything about her. She had been married at the age of sixteen in an arranged coupling to a man twenty-five years her senior. He was old now, and sick. She told me he could barely move and she had to do everything for him. They had one son who didn't have a job but spent his time drinking and shooting up heroin. She had been working in the guest house for the past eight years, earning a salary of 4,000 kyat a month with which she supported her son's drug habit and her ailing husband. 'They are bad men,' she said of the men who ran the guest house. 'They make me work all day. I am not even allowed to stop and eat my lunch. I come in every day at five in the morning and leave when the sun goes down. Sometimes, if I do not finish cleaning all the rooms in one day, they hit me.' I gave her 1,000 kyat—barely a dollar. She pushed it back into my hand. 'I did not tell you this story so that you would give me money,' she said. I could hear the proprietor's voice nearby and, worried that he would see me giving her money and perhaps try to take it off her later, pressed an additional 1,000 kyat into her hand, more firmly this time. Again, tears rolled down her cheeks as she folded up the money and tucked it into her bosom. She put her hands together in a prayer position and said, 'Namaste, sister.' Her name, she told me, was 'Sri', after the Hindu goddess of good fortune and abundance.

At the front door of the guest house a man was waiting to take me to the bus station. He wouldn't tell me who he was, but told me he worked for the government and offered me a ride on the back of his motorbike. When we reached the station, he waited until I had found a seat on the bus to Twante, brought me a bottle of water for the journey, and stood and watched until the bus had pulled out.

THE PREVIOUS NIGHT'S RAIN had turned the streets of Twante into quicksand, and as I set out to find the police station where Orwell used to work I had to hop along sandbags and broken sections of pavement. Trishaw drivers wearing wooden helmets splashed through the streets, their vehicles laden with vegetables and baskets of fish. On the corner of one street a woman sold fresh flowers from black plastic buckets. It was a muggy, overcast day, and people sat outside the wooden shop-houses of the main road fanning themselves with sheets of news-paper or palm-leaf fans. Loud, jangling music blared out from loudspeakers attached to a lottery-ticket stall.

Twante's police station is located on a small hill in the centre of town. At the foot of a steep cement staircase leading up to the station is a sign in Burmese saying, '*Kuu-nyi-ba-ya-zay*'—'Allow us to help you.' The main building is a simple one-storey construction, recently whitewashed. As soon as I entered, I was hurriedly ushered into a room where the chief of police was briefing a group of officers from behind a large table. The police chief was an enormous, dark-skinned man with a gravelly voice. 'How can I help you?' he asked, flashing a smile that revealed teeth capped in silver. I told him I was interested in British history and old British buildings, and asked if I could look around the police station. He leaned over and noisily spat a mouthful of betel juice into a spittoon beneath his desk. The officers who were sitting in neat rows in front of him stared silently at me, presumably wondering, as I was, what the answer to this strange request was going to be. The chief looked up from his spittoon and flashed another smile. He declared that he would assign an officer to escort me around the premises, but I would not, under any circumstances, be allowed to take photographs. I agreed.

My impromptu guide was a taciturn young man wearing the regulation police uniform—a dull khaki shirt and matching trousers. He whisked me round the station in lightning time. 'And this is the lock-up,' he said, almost jogging past a dilapidated colonial building behind the main block. Through the iron bars of the building's large windows, I could see the shadowy figures of prisoners kneeling silently in long rows, waiting for their midday meal. Behind the administrative buildings was a wide green glade, in the middle of which grew a large banyan tree. The tree's thick, tangled roots wriggled across the ground like pythons, and miniature white houses were lodged among its branches. Inside one of the shrines was a handsome wooden figurine of Myin Byu Shin, part of a lively pantheon of thirty-seven spirits called *nat* that are worshipped in Burma. His tiny room was filled with freshly plucked yellow flowers, and high above him among the heart-shaped leaves of the tree hung his mount, a marionette puppet of a white horse.

We trotted on past wooden bungalows on stilts that were set in neat rows around the glade. 'This is where the policemen live,' said my guide. Through the open doors of the houses I could see flashes of calendars and posters of Burmese pop stars, small Buddhist shrines, rice bubbling in charcoal-blackened pots. On the verandah of one house a baby slept in a hammock that had been fashioned out of an old *longyi*. A policeman stood washing his mud-caked boots by a well, and nearby a group of women squatted around a vendor, haggling over small packets of herbal medicine containing dried roots, peppercorn-sized pellets, and herbs ground into fine rust-brown powder.

Policemen and their families must survive on ludicrously low salaries. (A high-ranking officer in a similarly sized town once told me he received 8,500 kyat a month, and with this $8.5 he had to support himself, his wife and two young children.) As a result, the police force in Burma is notoriously corrupt. 'That sign outside the station says, "Allow us to help you,"' a Burmese friend told me. 'But they will only help you if you give them money first.' The Burmese police force was founded by the British and was then administered under civilian law. Today all the highest posts in the force are occupied by army officers and it is, in effect, little more than an ill-armed, inefficient branch of the military. The Burmese people I had questioned did not seem to view the police with much respect. 'The police force is like a fruit stuck between two thorns,' my friend had explained. 'One thorn is the military; the other is the people.'

Our brief tour ended back in the main office, where the police chief had rustled up a bottle of fizzy tamarind juice for me. I sat down and made polite chit-chat with the group of officers who were gathered in the room. I asked if they had to deal with much crime in Twante. The chief beamed his silver-toothed smile at me. 'No,' he said, 'there is no crime in Twante.' I had heard from talking to my friends in Mandalay that poverty was forcing people to ever greater levels of desperation: there were rumours that robbery, theft, rape, assault and murder were increasing throughout the country. Yet there is a worrying trend in Burma's police stations. In order to please the central military command, the police leave crimes unreported, so that their division will look good and crime-free, at least on paper. When people go to the station to report crimes, the police often ask them if they are sure they want to file details and try to convince them not to do so. I once had my wallet stolen in Mandalay, and when I suggested to the friends I was with that I should report it to the police they laughed.

When I left the police station, the chief asked me where I was going. I didn't have any exact plans, but said that I might wander over to the old British church. He smiled at me again. 'I hope you have a pleasant visit,' he said. 'Please enjoy our little town, and if you need any help—any help at all—please ask me.'

As it happened, I didn't get to the church until the next day. The church is located in the sleepy outskirts of Twante, about a fifteen-minute walk down winding dirt lanes lined with towering palm trees, past thatched houses with sagging bamboo fences. In a ditch along one of the streets I watched an ominous-looking snake with yellow stripes, a young cobra, swim with its head held gracefully above the water like that of an elderly lady doing breaststroke at the public pool. Children played in the streets— hopscotch and a kind of boule with cheap plastic models of Chinese warriors. Because Twante is just a few hours from Rangoon and tourists make day trips to view the town's age-old pottery industry, people were more friendly here than in parts of the Delta that were less used to foreigners. As I asked directions to the church, I was guided along with delighted giggles and shouts.

The church is a simple building built of dark wood with a slanting tin roof topped by a small cross. The grounds around it are filled with vegetable gardens, and pineapples grow from thorny star-shaped bushes around the edges of the compound. Under colonial rule, Catholic, Baptist and Anglican missionaries were able to proselytize throughout Burma, and the country now has some 2.2 million Christians comprising just under 5 per cent of the population. Today, however, missionaries are forbidden from entering Burma, and the regime is suspicious of Christians and their foreign contacts. As a minority religious group, Christians are openly discriminated against by the government. They often find it difficult to get jobs in the civil service, and if they succeed they are seldom able to get promoted. Though church compounds have been able to retain their land, all the mission school buildings have been taken over by the regime and are used as government schools. The churches are understandably bitter about the way they have been treated, and priests are usually quite outspoken with visitors about their views on the government. Since the Burmese assume that most Westerners are Christians, going to church is a fairly innocent thing to be seen doing, and whenever I arrived in a Burmese town I always visited the local church.

In a dilapidated mission house next to Twante's church building I found a Burmese priest clad in flowing white robes. 'I hope you will stay for tea,' he said simply. We sat around a meeting table on chairs padded with mildewed cushions in the front room of his house. The priest brought out a ceramic teapot and placed a fruit cake on the table. I asked about conditions in the countryside around Twante. He sat quietly for a while before he answered, and then he said very slowly that life was difficult for the villagers. 'The government takes rice from them—as much as it needs to feed the army. The farmers have no choice: they must give it. And if the army wants them to work—to help build a road, or dig a canal—the villagers have to help. The government calls it "donated labour".' He added with a giggle, 'We call it "forced donation".' The priest urged me to take a slice of cake. As soon as I had done so, he quickly wrapped up the rest and took it back into the kitchen.

The use of forced labour has been well documented by groups like Amnesty International and the International Labour Organization (ILO). Their reports are based on interviews with villagers who have fled to refugee camps in neighbouring countries and on information-gathering trips which the Burmese regime occasionally consents to. Forced labour is coerced from villages and towns throughout the country. Construction projects—new roads, bridges, dams, even hotels for tourists—are often built with it. The regime makes no discrimination by age or sex: all over Burma I saw elderly people, women and children working on hard labour. On a road not far from Myaungmya I had watched a group of young children around the ages of nine or ten breaking rocks with pickaxes, loading the rubble into rattan baskets on their heads, and carrying it to the side of a road which was evidently being widened. Their faces, wrapped in rags and hidden beneath straw hats, were smeared with *thanaka* to ward off the harsh glare of the afternoon sun. They peered out from behind these masks, yellow and ghostly. I wanted to ask them if they were getting paid for this back-breaking work, but it was impossible to approach them as a foreman stood nearby watching me warily.

To justify its use of forced labour, the junta uses two pieces of British colonial legislation: the 1907 Town Act and the 1908 Village Act, which entitle the headman or policemen of any town or village to demand that residents provide assistance to government servants. In its 1998 report on Burma, the ILO stated that such practices amount to present-day slavery. The ILO investigators had been appalled by the government's systematic use of unpaid labour and its 'total disregard for the human dignity, safety and health' of its people. The Burmese government dismissed the report as 'one-sided and biased'. The military, it argued, was working with the people to develop Burma. The projects which people worked on, such as irrigation facilities, schools and hospitals, benefited the local population. The second-highest ranking general and head of Burma's Military Intelligence, Lieutenant-General Khin Nyunt, declared that the West was distorting the reality of what was going on inside Burma: 'We feel very strongly that these allegations were largely the result of misperception and misunderstanding of the situation and the mentality of the people.' He insisted that villagers were happy to work for the military, to help speed up development projects. 'In Myanmar thinking, contribution of labour not only brings immediate material benefit in present life, but also merit in future life cycles,' he explained.

As I said my goodbyes to the priest, he told me that two police officers had come to see him the previous day. They had asked him whether a foreign lady had visited the church. I realized that when I had cheerily told the police chief where I was going he had sent his men after me to check if I was telling the truth.

A T MIDDAY the main pagoda in Twante is empty. I took off my shoes at the entrance and walked up the covered stairway to the wide, open platform on which devotees can perambulate clockwise around the golden mass of the bell-shaped spire. The white ceramic floor tiles were scorching hot from the sun, and I had to walk around the platform's edge, in the shadows of the shrines, meditation halls, and banyan trees that lined the perimeter. Dotted along the base of the pagoda are small shrines mark-ing the days of the week, each day evoking the powers of a par-ticular planet in the solar system and represented by a different animal. Monday, for example, is ruled by the moon and repre-sented by a tiger. Tuesday is marked by a lion and comes under the influence of Mars. The Burmese believe that your destiny is determined by the day you were born, and the appropriate shrine has a particular relevance in an individual's cosmological chart. The shrines are colourful, each with a statue depicting one of the animals: a naga (or serpent), an elephant, a mouse. They are draped in garlands, and candles—recently burned—have dripped pools of wax on to the ground beneath them.

Pagoda are the centre of Burmese spiritual life, and every town and village has one. People visit the pagoda daily or weekly to pay respect to the Buddha relics which are often enshrined there, to meditate, to give alms, or to attend the festivals held on religious holidays. The pagoda is considered a place of spiritual-ity and learning. The stairways leading up to the platform are decorated with educational paintings from Buddhist legend, of-ten depicting the moral lessons in the Jataka tales about the Buddha's previous incarnations. The peaceful principles of Bud-dhism, which encourage wisdom and compassion, are instilled through these teachings.

The pagoda in Twante—said to be over a thousand years old—was being renovated and was covered with a web of bam-boo scaffolding. I had read in the government English-language newspaper, *The New Light of Myanmar,* that General Khin Nyunt had been in Twante the previous week to oversee the renovations. It is worth reading the opening paragraph of the article just to get a sense of what makes front-page news in Burma:

State Peace and Development Council Secretary-1 Lt-Gen Khin Nyunt, accompanied by Yangon Division Peace and Development Council Chairman Commander Maj-Gen Myint Swe, the ministers, the deputy ministers, officials from the State Peace and Development Council Office and departmental heads, arrived at Dalla Jetty at 7:30 today. He was welcomed there by No 1 Military Region Commander Col Khin Maung Soe, Yangon South District Peace and Development Council Chairman Lt-Col Sein Hlaing, chairman of Dalla, Twantay and Seikkyi-Khanaungto Township Peace and Development Councils, departmental officials, members of the Union Solidarity and Development Association and members of social organisations.

It was a rare occasion when I picked up *The New Light of Myanmar* and didn't find a photograph of one of the generals overseeing pagoda renovations or the construction of a new pagoda. It was a practice that dated back to the kings of Burma, the royal patrons of the Buddhist religion. Like today's generals, U Po Kyin, the corrupt Burmese magistrate in Orwell's *Burmese Days,* considered himself a good Buddhist. He believed that all the evil he had done in this life—cheating people of their money, jailing innocent men, abusing young girls—would accumulate and result in his reincarnation in the lowly form of, say, a cockroach. He therefore planned to devote the later years of his life to doing good works, to counteract out the bad things he had done and balance the scales of karmic justice. Orwell summed up U Po Kyin's philosophy as follows:

> Probably his good works would take the form of building pagodas. Four pagodas, five, six, seven—the priests would tell him how many—with carved stonework, gilt umbrellas and little bells that tinkled in the wind, every tinkle a prayer. And he would return to the earth in male human shape—for a woman ranks at about the same level as a rat or a frog—or at worst as some dignified beast such as an elephant.

The newspaper report went on to say that Khin Nyunt had offered fruits and flowers to the Buddha image on the upper terrace of Twante's pagoda and had then perambulated the pagoda in a clockwise direction. A ceremony was held later in which local dignitaries made cash donations towards the renovation of the pagoda. The article listed the highest amounts donated. They were astronomical by Burmese standards, and Khin Nyunt himself gave 900,000 kyat (around 900 dollars). The article then described how the general finished his trip to Twante with a visit to a local school, where he handed out 500 pencils to schoolchildren.

In Burma, there is no escape from politics—not even at the pagoda. Many Buddhist monks joined the protests of 1988, and hundreds were shot and killed by soldiers. Two years later, some 7,000 monks walked silently through the streets of Mandalay with their begging bowls, to collect alms in memory of those who had died in 1988. The peaceful remembrance ended in bloodshed as soldiers shot into the crowd, killing and wounding a number of monks. Afterwards, the *sangha,* or holy Buddhist order, launched a nationwide religious boycott of the regime by refusing to accept alms from military families or to oversee their weddings and funerals. The action is known as *pattam nikkujana kamma*—'the overturning of the alms bowl'. This passive protest reportedly upset members of the army, as it robbed them of any control over their spiritual destiny: at Buddhist funerals, monks are necessary to guide a person's vulnerable soul into the next life. The army responded by cracking down on the monkhood. Soldiers raided over 100 monasteries, arresting more than 3,000 monks and novices. The *sangha* now operates under strict government control. All monks must be checked by the government before ordination, even those who take holy orders for only a few weeks or months, as many Buddhist men do. Traditional ceremonies require prior permission from local authorities. And informers, dressed in the brick-red robes of a Burmese monk, are rife within the *sangha* itself. Senior monks are coerced into toeing the party line with threats and bribes. Abbots, who often have influential moral power within the village, are ordered to keep villagers in check.

I walked down the steps of the pagoda and headed back towards the centre of town. In the shadow of the main pagoda there is an old ruined pagoda, a mountain of bricks held up by the vines and bushes that have grown over it. A few small figurines have been placed here and there among the rubble, with cups holding incense and candles—a sign that what powers this pagoda once held may still linger here. Round about, ponies still tied to their covered carts were waiting out the fierce midday sun beneath the shade of surrounding trees. Their owners lay dozing in the carts, or nestled into soft green nooks amid the ruin.

D URING THE UPHEAVALS of 1988, a curious legend circulated in Burma. It told of a small village that was terrorized by an evil dragon. Each year the dragon required the sacrifice of one young virgin from the village. And each year a brave young hero of the village would scale the nearby mountain to fight the dragon. None of the heroes ever returned. When the next man set off on his doomed mission he was secretly followed to see what would become of him. The dragon's lair was lined with gold and gems, and when the man arrived he was able to slay the dragon with his sword. As he sat over the corpse, admiring the sparkling gems, he gradually began to grow scales, a tail and horns, until he himself had become the dragon the villagers feared. The moral of this legend is identical to that of Orwell's book *Animal Farm*.

*Animal Farm* is the only one of Orwell's books to have been translated into the Burmese language—in the 1950s, before the military took control. The translator, the late Thakin Ba Thaung, is a much-loved figure in Burmese history and literature. The Burmese word '*thakin*', or 'master', was used by the Burmese when addressing an English person. Ba Thaung was a founding member of the Thakin Movement, which campaigned for independence against the colonial government and whose members daringly attached the title 'thakin' to their own names. Orwell would no doubt have liked the fact that his book was translated by a key agitator against British rule, who was once jailed by the British for posting a letter with the stamp of King George V provocatively stuck on the envelope upside down.

When Thakin Ba Thaung translated *Animal Farm* he adapted the story to a Burmese setting, giving it the more poetic title *Chi-lay-gyaung Taw-hlan-yay,* or *The Four-legged Revolution*. In *Animal Farm* a group of farm animals decide to overthrow their human owners and run the farm themselves. (In Thakin Ba Thaung's book, Mr and Mrs Jones of Manor Farm have been transformed into U Tha Kaung and Daw O Sa of Yinmabin Field.) The revolution is led by pigs with a vision of an egalitarian utopia free from tyrannical human beings, but their ideals are gradually abandoned as power goes to their heads and they become cruel and greedy. They decree that only pigs are allowed to eat the apples grown in the orchard (nutritionally essential for a pig's brain, they claim), and they breed a terror squad of dogs to police the hens, sheep, cows and horses living on the farm. As the pigs take on the luxuries of the humans they fought to overthrow—sleeping in the farmhouse and swilling whisky—the other animals die of overwork and starvation. Orwell had based *Animal Farm* on the Russian Revolution of 1917 and Stalin's fearsome drive to collectivize the Soviet Union's farmland, resulting in the death of millions of peasants. I preferred to read it as the second part of Orwell's unintentional trilogy on Burmese history.

Burma's miserable experiment with socialism began in 1962,

when the leader of the army, Ne Win, seized power from the elected government that had been set in place after the British left and established what he called a Revolutionary Council. At the time of the military coup, the country was in chaos. Burma had been a key battleground for Japanese and Allied forces during the Second World War, and the country's infrastructure was a shambles. A Communist army was fighting to overthrow the government, and a number of ethnic minorities had begun their armed struggles for independence. Many older people I spoke with remembered a sense of relief as the army brought the country back under control. But, as with the pigs in *Animal Farm,* it gradually became clear that Ne Win was no benevolent leader. He launched what he called 'The Burmese Way to Socialism', a heady and disastrous mix of Marxism and Buddhism. All other political parties were outlawed, and Ne Win's opponents were imprisoned. All private businesses were declared state property. Many foreigners living in Burma, mostly Indian and Chinese merchants, were stripped of their assets and fled or were forced to leave as the country sealed itself off from the outside world. Military men with no business experience were put in charge of Burma's industry and agriculture. Before long they had depleted the country's foreign reserves and were unable to import necessities— spare parts for machinery, or even toothbrushes. The shelves in the shops were soon empty, and people were reduced to queuing for rations of cooking oil and rice. Ne Win and his military had transformed Burma—a country abundant in natural resources— into a wasteland. After twenty-five years of Ne Win's rule, a year before the 1988 uprising, the United Nations declared Burma one of the world's least-developed countries, along with ten other countries mostly located in sub-Saharan Africa.

When I discussed *Animal Farm* with my Orwell Book Club in Mandalay, Tun Lin, the jovial retired teacher, did most of the talking. He had, as he liked to say, lived through a real-life version of *Animal Farm*. Tun Lin refers to the years under Ne Win as 'the time of the green spectacles'. To look at something through green spectacles, he explained, is to look at a thing that is bad and be forced to think of it as good. The phrase has a curious history. The battles and bombs of the Second World War devastated Burma's paddy fields and plantations, and by the time the Japanese army eventually occupied the country farmers found it hard to grow any edible produce. Even the farm animals and pack-horses refused to eat the parched grain, because of its unhealthy-looking white colour. The Japanese, fearful that the donkeys they needed to transport munitions in the mountainous terrain of Upper Burma would starve, came up with an ingenious solution. They fashioned spectacles out of green-tinted glass and wire and hooked them around the donkeys' ears. 'The donkeys saw that the grain was green and happily ate it,' explained Tun Lin. 'That's what we had to do during our years in Burma's *Animal Farm*. The entire nation was forced to wear green spectacles just like those donkeys.'

Knowing that Tun Lin enjoyed jokes, I told him one about Ne Win's misrule that I had learned from my Burmese-language teacher. A soldier is living in a hut on Inya Lake in Rangoon, not far from Ne Win's palatial residence. One lunchtime he goes down to the lake to see if he can catch anything for lunch. He hooks a large, fat fish and excitedly puts it in a bucket of water to carry back to his hut. He decides to chop up some tomatoes and onions and make a fish curry. But, when he looks in his cupboards, he sees that there are no tomatoes and there are no onions: the cupboards are empty. 'Never mind,' he thinks, 'I'll fry the fish in oil—perhaps it will taste better that way.' But, when he reaches for the cooking oil, he sees that the bottle is empty. 'I know,' he reasons, 'I'll grill the fish over the stove; it will taste simple but nice.' But, when he goes to get some charcoal from the charcoal bin, he sees that the bin, too, is empty and there is no charcoal. Finally he realizes he may as well release the fish and go hungry. He walks back to the lake and tosses the still-living fish into the water. The fish jumps in with a happy flick of its tail and yells, 'Long Live Ne Win!'

Tun Lin had heard the joke before but he laughed anyway and reminded me of something Orwell had once written about political humour: 'Every joke is a tiny revolution.'

Za Za Win, the recent graduate in our discussion group, was too young to remember much about Ne Win's time or the 1988 uprising. But one sentence in *Animal Farm* had a particular meaning for her: 'Will there be sugar after the revolution?' She remembered her father murmuring this rhetorical question to himself when she was a child, and it was only when she had read *Animal Farm* the previous week that she had realized it was spoken by Molly, the dandyish white mare in Orwell's book. 'I suppose they were warned,' she said of the animals in *Animal Farm*. 'When Molly the mare asked if there would be sugar after the revolution, the reply was a categorical "No."'

*Animal Farm* was unpopular in Burma when it was first published there in the 1950s. Many of the leading intellectuals at the time had leftist leanings and read it as a criticism of the socialism they admired. When the US Embassy printed excerpts as anti-Communist propaganda, the book's fate was sealed. The society which had sponsored the translation had to give away remaindered copies. But years later, when people began to reread it, they saw the similarities to their own history. I met one university lecturer who told me she had tried to put *Animal Farm* on the syllabus for English-literature students, but the authorities had warned her off: the text was just too similar to what was going on in Burma. A few years ago *Animal Farm* was serialized on the BBC's Burmese radio service. For weeks afterwards, Tun Lin told me, Mandalay tea shops were abuzz with attempts to match the animal characters to Burma's own leaders. Could you compare 'the Lady', as democracy leader Aung San Suu Kyi is known, to the exiled porcine revolutionary Snowball? And which pig was General Ne Win? Was he Major, the imperious old pig with a vision who died so suddenly? (Hopefully.) Or was he Napoleon, the grotesque ruler who grew stronger and more deranged each day? (Probably.)

Ne Win was perhaps a bit of both. He was a famously reclusive leader, known for his foul mouth, many marriages and obsessive superstition. It was his dabblings with numerology that had the most dramatic consequences for Burma. In 1987 Ne Win demonetized certain banknotes, replacing them with new notes with denominations of 45 kyat and 90 kyat—each value neatly divisible by nine (an astrologically auspicious number, and the general's favourite). People's already paltry savings were wiped out overnight and, with little to lose, a year later they took to the streets in the 1988 uprising.

Ne Win died in December 2002 at the age of ninety-one in his lakeside villa in Rangoon. I was in Rangoon at the time of this monumental event in Burmese history. Ne Win had rarely been seen in public since he stepped down from the government, in 1988, and most analysts speculated that he had lost all his political power by the time of his death. This was starkly illustrated by a highly publicized trial which sentenced his son-in-law and grandsons to death for allegedly plotting to overthrow senior general Than Shwe. The only mention of Ne Win's death in the state media was a small and insignificant obituary in the back pages of *The New Light of Myanmar*. The whole event was carefully stage-managed as though nothing had happened. Ne Win's body was cremated in private on the afternoon of his death. I noticed there were perhaps a few more soldiers in Rangoon, and a few tea shops were closed earlier than usual, on the night he died. But other than that there was nothing to mark the passing of Burma's despotic ruler. I asked Za Za Win what she thought was the significance of Ne Win's death. 'Nothing,' she said. 'Nothing will change because he's dead. His death makes no difference. It changes nothing.' She was probably right: I noticed that even after Ne Win's demise people were still uncomfortable about saying his name out loud in tea shops.

Our discussion about *Animal Farm* and Burma's years under Ne Win came to an end when two men sat down at the table next

to ours. One of my companions nudged me almost impercepti-
bly, and Tun Lin leaned in close to the centre of the table. I could
tell from his expression—eyebrows raised into question marks,
the hint of a grin—that it was time for a joke. 'Have you heard
the one about the dentist?' he asked. 'There was once a Burmese
man who travelled many hard miles in order to visit a dentist in a
neighbouring country,' he began. 'When he arrived at the dentist's office, the dentist was surprised to learn how far the man
had travelled. "Are there no dentists in your country?" he asked
the man with concern. "Yes, yes, we have dentists," the man
replied. "The problem is we are not allowed to open our
mouths."'


I SPENT a couple of days wandering around Twante's dirt tracks.
I went to see terracotta pots being moulded by hand out of red
clay. I sat by the riverside watching overladen boats float past and
fishermen returning from months at sea. In Mandalay I had met
a retired Burmese police officer who had been posted to some of
the same towns as Orwell. 'As a British officer in the Delta, Orwell
would have been very lonely,' he told me. 'The British had their
own community, and they didn't mix with the Burmese. As a
young boy in those days I hardly ever saw the British—only sometimes did I see them out riding their horses in the early morning.'
In Myaungmya and Twante there would have been only one
other European living there at the same time as Orwell, or two at
the most, working in the colonial administration. Though Orwell

must have written letters home describing his first impressions of the Delta, none of them survives. His childhood friend Jacintha Buddicom remembered that she received three letters from him detailing how unhappy he was in Burma: 'The first was a long one, in the strain "You could never understand how awful it is if you hadn't been here."' In *Burmese Days*, misery and loneliness plague John Flory, who describes life in Burma as a 'solitary hell'. Each year Flory stays in Burma he becomes lonelier and more bitter amid the 'foreign trees, foreign flowers, foreign landscapes, foreign faces'. He retreats into books and fantasies, dreaming of a female companion, of fleeing for England.

When British candidates applied for a job as an imperial police officer, they had to state which part of the Empire they would prefer to work in. They were allowed to choose five places, and were asked to give reasons for their first choice. Orwell put down Burma first, and next to it, in an inky scrawl, he wrote 'Have had relatives there'. (At that time his mother's family were still living in Moulmein, a town to which he would later be posted.) Were it not for the family connection, Burma would have been an odd choice. Most candidates put it at the bottom of their lists. The country was considered a backwater of the Empire, run as an extra province of India, and government servants were given a special 'Burma Allowance' to compensate for its hardships. An intriguing report in the India Office records noted the 'abnormal number of young police officers who have suffered from mental derangement' in Burma. The report was completed a few years before Orwell's posting, and was concerned with the fact that in recent years six young British officers had suffered mental break-downs and two had committed suicide. It ended with the unsatis-factory conclusion that it was not able to produce any reason why such incidents were so prevalent in Burma.

On my last evening in Twante I went to have dinner at one of the town's street-side eateries. As I was eating my food, a power cut plunged the entire town into darkness. There was the briefest hush as diners adjusted to the dark, and then the clatter of cutlery and the murmur of conversation started up again. Gradually the street began to glow with a warm light as young serving boys ap-peared holding thick candles above each table, like church acolytes. A man at the next table told me that Twante always had electric-ity problems. 'Whenever Rangoon needs the power they cut us off here,' he explained. 'Of course, we had one of the generals down here a week or so ago, and while he was here we had twenty-four-hour electricity.'

The guest house was in darkness when I arrived back after din-ner, and I had to climb blindly up to my room on the first floor. The room had a wide window covered with a clear plastic sheet, and through it I could see a mango tree with long, thin leaves and tear-shaped fruit glowing silvery-green in the moonlight. I turned on my torch, which was powered by cheap batteries I had bought in the market. The light it provided faded in and out, eventually giving out entirely. When I shook it, the torch came back to life just long enough for me to see fat geckos with beady black eyes scuttle across the ceiling, casting shadows five times their size.

I tucked myself under the bright green mosquito net that

hung above my bed. Though a breeze blew in through the gaps around the window, it couldn't penetrate the thick polyester of the net, which only wobbled slightly with each gust of wind, like a giant green jelly. I listened to the noise of the guest house. The acoustics were such that a cough down the hall sounded as though it were coming from right beside my head, from somewhere in the darkness outside my mosquito net. I could make out the garbled strains of a Burmese pop song from a radio being played in a nearby room:

*She doesn't love me any more;*
*Why that's so, I don't know.*

After a while, everything fell silent and the only sounds I could hear were the geckos above me on the ceiling, chuckling delightedly.

*Three*

# RANGOON

Power is in tearing human minds to pieces and
putting them back together again in new
shapes of your own choosing.

*Nineteen Eighty-Four*

**I**N THE HEART of Burma's capital, Rangoon, sits a palatial mansion. Under British rule, this ostentatious Victorian-style structure was known as the Secretariat, and it was built to house the
seat of the colonial government. The building is a sprawling complex, with endless parchment-yellow colonnades, red-brick walls
and high, shuttered windows. Crows flap gracelessly among the
vaulted domes of its vast roof, and the surrounding gardens are
lush with coconut trees and fan-shaped traveller's palms. After independence, the Secretariat was used to house the newly formed
Burmese cabinet, and today it serves as one of the regime's central offices. The entranceway is well-guarded by soldiers in combat helmets. Jeeps and armoured trucks are parked along the
sweeping driveways. At each of the compound's four corners,
soldiers holding machine guns stand in sentry boxes surrounded
by rusting barbed wire.

There are old British buildings like this all over Rangoon. Indeed, parts of the city look as if London had been transplanted into a tropical landscape and left to moulder for a century or two. Down near the docks are the British law courts with their imposing white Doric columns. The courts are still used for legal proceedings, and civil servants wearing sparkling white shirts tucked into thick silk *longyi* hurry between buildings, swinging faux-leather briefcases. Statues of lions, their lips garishly slathered with scarlet paint, gaze down from the roof of the old telegraph building. Above the entrance of the former British department store Rowe & Co. is a blank clock face, intricately bound in iron fretwork. The narrow alleyways that run behind Rangoon's main roads are lined with colonial-era shop-houses. Through the doorways you can glimpse steep wooden staircases twisting upward into dark stairwells. Livid green moss grows along cracks in the plastered walls, and ferns sprout from the disintegrating stone pediments.

After Orwell's year in the Delta he was posted to a police station on the outskirts of Rangoon—first to Syriam, across the river to the south, and later to Insein, a fifteen-minute train ride north of the city centre. Rangoon at the time boasted many grand buildings of Empire, and for colonial officials it was an oasis of Western civilization in the seething tropical swamp of Burma. In Rangoon you could enjoy French cuisine and fine wine at the renowned Strand Hotel on the riverfront, or listen to the latest dance records at the Gymkhana Club. 'Oh, the joy of those Rangoon trips!' reflects John Flory in *Burmese Days*. 'The rush to Smart and Mookerdum's bookshop for the new novels out from

England, the dinner at Anderson's with beefsteaks and butter that had travelled eight thousand miles on ice . . .'

Smart and Mookerdum's bookshop was nationalized after Ne Win's military government came to power, and Anderson's no longer exists, but you can still dine out at the Strand Hotel. When I first came to Burma, in the mid-1990s, the Strand was a dilapidated government-run rest house. The musty rooms were crammed with mismatched furniture, and the beds were made with threadbare linen. A few years ago an international hotel chain renovated the building and turned it into a five-star hotel. Once again French meals are prepared at the Strand—courtesy of a resident chef flown in from France. And an afternoon tea of scones and imported jams is served to guests lounging in rattan chairs beneath whirling black ceiling fans.

Since the regime opened the country up to international investors in 1989, many of Rangoon's older buildings have been demolished to make way for condominiums, office blocks and hotels. There are supermarkets that sell imported snacks (Nutella, Pringles and Pop Tarts), and department stores where you can buy international-brand-name goods (Revlon make-up and Guess jeans). You can have pizzas from wood-fired ovens and Caesar salad at a bar with stylishly scuffed floors, and cappuccinos at a coffee shop that plays MTV on flat-screen monitors. A weekly English-language journal publishes social pages that feature foreign businessmen raising champagne glasses and Burmese belles smiling graciously for the cameras. All these novelties may make parts of Rangoon feel like any other booming Asian capital, but in reality they are little more than window dressing. Most of the amenities are available only to very wealthy businessmen and the families of the generals. Burma has the lowest income of any country in South-East Asia—lower than Laos or Cambodia. While wages remain stagnant, inflation rates in Rangoon are estimated at almost 50 per cent per year. Most people in the city are barely making ends meet, and some are not able to do even that. In the early morning, long queues of people waiting for government rations of food staples such as cooking oil and rice can be seen threaded across the city's streets.

I knew one elderly Burmese woman—a former teacher—whom I visited each time I came to the city. She always insisted we meet at a recently built supermarket near her house. We would spend a few minutes walking up and down the air-conditioned aisles as she admired the goods, carefully examining a bottle of organic shampoo or reading the ingredients on a box of chocolate-covered almonds. She would tell me how wonderfully convenient the supermarket was, how it had everything you could possibly need from all over the world. And she would remind me how there had been nothing like this in Burma during Ne Win's time. She saw the supermarket as a sign of progress for the country. Yet we never had to queue at the checkout counter, because she never bought anything. She couldn't afford to shop in the supermarket and, like most Burmese housewives, purchased all her supplies from the open-air stalls at her local wet market.

Around the side of the Secretariat compound, behind the double layers of barbed-wire fencing, are the outbuildings where the soldiers who work there are housed. They are built in the same style as the Secretariat itself, with red bricks and yellow cornices, but it is possible to see these structures at closer range. Black stains drip like spilled ink from the rain-soaked roofs. Bare light bulbs dangle on wires hung over the decrepit door frames. Most of the window panes are broken and have been replaced by corrugated iron or pieces of cardboard. Dotted between the buildings are small vegetable patches. Chickens peck among the weeds, and a few pigs can be seen half-sunk in mud. At night the Secretariat dissolves into darkness and is visible only as a hulking black silhouette, like the ghostly mansion of a Gothic fairy tale. In the foreground, among the ruins that lie along the edge of the compound, soldiers and their families cook their evening meals over camp fires.

**T**HE FIRST PERSON I went to see when I arrived in Rangoon was my good friend Ko Ye, an expert in the Burmese junta's methods of reality-control. Ko Ye has worked as a publisher in Rangoon for the past thirty years. Every word on every page that runs through his printing press, and through every press in Burma, is checked by government censors before it is distributed to the public. And it is partly due to such rigorous censorship that Rangoon has been able to maintain its veneer of normality.

Ko Ye's printing press is in a busy area of downtown Rangoon where the streets are clogged with buses and cars and vendors have covered almost every inch of pavement with their stalls. There are Buddhist posters, herbal medicines and pirated video CDs for sale. An Indian man clad in a dhoti squats in front of an oil-filled wok stirring bite-sized samosas. A young girl waves a plastic bag over a tray of fresh pomelo to keep the flies off. Noodle soup is served to customers who crouch around low tin tables, and biryani is shovelled out of gigantic vats into styrofoam lunch boxes. Along the roadside, men sit at pavement tea shops, their legs neatly crossed beneath their *longyi,* watching the chaos stream past.

I slipped down a comparatively calm side street and found the ground-floor office where Ko Ye runs his business. As I waited for someone to fetch him from a back room, I watched the well-rehearsed ballet of the printing press—a large black machine as big and noisy as a car. A shirtless man wearing a labourer's knee-length *longyi* worked the levers, and another man crouched beneath the machine to catch the printed pages as they came flying out. A woman sat cross-legged on the floor next to the press. She stacked the freshly printed sheets, folded them inside covers and, with thick thread, sewed the still-warm pages into a book. Next to her, a man with ink-stained hands and a greying white singlet organized a neat pile of finished books. He inked up a rubber stamp bearing the publisher's logo and began punching it firmly on to the front page of each volume.

Before long Ko Ye, a tall man in his early fifties, came striding into the room, a cigarette dangling from his lips.

'Tea?' he asked briskly.

'Of course.'

Ko Ye summoned a young boy who, at the doorway, was tying bundles of magazines on to the back of a bicycle ready for distribution around Rangoon's bookshops. He pressed some banknotes into the boy's hand and sent him out to buy tea. Ko Ye offered me a stool in front of his desk. As he sat down on the other side of the desk, he lit another cigarette from the previous one and launched into his favourite topic: the Press Registration and Scrutiny Department (PRSD). The PRSD is a veritable army of 'scrutinizers' headed by members of Military Intelligence. It has the awesome task of searching through every single printed item—whether school textbook, magazine, calendar or song lyrics—for a word, a sentence, a picture which might be considered anti-government. Ko Ye picked up a copy of a lifestyle magazine that was lying on the desk. Its rough, grey pages were filled with short stories, articles about movies, and profiles of popular singers. He flicked through the magazine and showed me where censors had scrawled with a pink highlighter across certain paragraphs or, as was the case on some pages, whole articles. Scribbled alongside each scrawl was the single word '*hpyoke*', or 'remove'.

'Why these particular pages?' I asked.

'I really don't know,' he replied. 'I don't think even the people at the censorship board know why any more.' The PRSD, he explained, has eleven broad rules outlining what subjects cannot be written about. The rules are impossibly vague. Among other things, they forbid:

- anything 'detrimental to the ideology of the state';
- anything which might be 'harmful to security, the rule of law, peace and public order';
- any 'incorrect ideas' and 'opinions which do not accord with the times';

- any descriptions which, though factually correct, are 'unsuitable because of the time or the circumstances of their writing'.

'They never tell us exactly *why* something is banned,' said Ko Ye. 'We just have to guess.' Some obvious taboos are the NLD leader Aung San Suu Kyi, references to the people's uprising of 1988, and the word 'democracy'. Each month editors are briefed on additional banned topics—the board's decisions are often variable, and depend on what is going on inside Burma—and when I met Ko Ye these included rice (a severe shortage had necessitated the distribution of government rations) and gold (rising bullion prices were a further clue to the country's economic woes). In recent months, political disagreements with neighbouring Thailand had led the PRSD to remove any reference to Thailand from the news. This meant everything to do with Thailand, said Ko Ye—all references to Thai people; all advertisements for Thai products. When one monthly magazine inadvertently ran an advertisement for a Thai company the PRSD banned the entire issue. The PRSD's mandate also covers international news. Reports of events that might mirror Burma's own history too closely, such as the people's uprising which took place in Indonesia in 1998 and precipitated the fall of authoritarian leader General Suharto, are banned from Burma's newspapers and magazines.

The young boy arrived back at the office carrying a plastic bag of steaming-hot tea. Ko Ye placed two mugs on the table and expertly poured it out, holding up one end of the bag and shaking out every last drop.

'It's not just political subjects that are banned,' he continued. Even basic public information, such as a fourfold hike in train fares which took place just after I arrived in Burma, is not allowed to appear in the newspapers. People find out only by word of mouth or when they go to the train station to buy a ticket. 'The generals simply don't want to see anything bad about their country in print,' explained Ko Ye.

In 1914 a film called *Adventures of Kathlyn* was prohibited by the British government of Burma. The film was about a white woman's adventures in a fictional land modelled on India. The British censors didn't even need to see the film. They simply looked at the advertising pamphlet and, in red crayon, circled the phrases they objected to. One referred to the hapless Kathlyn being sold into a slave market, and another boasted, 'You will see her bound by fanatical natives!' The British government felt that images of a white woman in such compromising circumstances were demeaning, and might give Burmese viewers bad ideas. The authorities were very sensitive to the way that Britons were portrayed in the media, and also saw any press criticism as chipping away sentence by sentence at the legitimacy of the Crown. In 1933 the British censors in Burma banned the acclaimed film *The Private Life of Henry VIII*, in which the king is portrayed eating gustily with his hands: they didn't want a British monarch to be seen dining without cutlery, in the same manner as most Burmese still eat today. Using a harsh press-control law dubbed the 'gagging act', they censored newspapers and magazines, and banned books. (The *Kama Sutra* and *Mein Kampf* were both included in their list of prohibited literature.) Any evidence of what the censors labelled 'hatred', 'sedition', 'disloyalty' or 'disaffection' resulted in heavy fines or, in the most extreme cases, prison sentences.

For a brief decade after independence from the British, Burma experienced a free and lively press. But when Ne Win took control he used old British laws to reign in the media and added a few more constraints of his own. In recent years, existing laws have been amended towards even tighter press control. The authorities keep updated biographical-history sheets on all working writers and editors. As in British times, one step out of line can mean heavy fines or imprisonment. One publisher currently faces a three-to-seven-year prison sentence for printing an unauthorized student pamphlet containing poems and campus news. When another publisher overran his registered print run of 200 copies for a book he was heavily fined and his company was closed down for six months, effectively bankrupting him. 'Censorship is getting progressively worse,' said Ko Ye. 'As the number of writers who have been blacklisted gets longer and longer, it becomes increasingly difficult to write about anything, and editors naturally become less and less daring.'

Magazine editors have a particularly difficult time. Magazines can be submitted to the censorship board only after they have been printed, and if the censors demand changes to the content the editor must make them at his own expense. It used to be that offensive pages were simply ripped out, or paragraphs were inked over in heavy black ink, or silver or gold paint (so you couldn't hold the page up to the light and see through to the text). When a magazine editor tried to publish translated excerpts from Or-

well's *Nineteen Eighty-Four* in the year 1984, for instance, the censors had them torn out. Now the PRSD demands a higher level of
sophistication: it doesn't want the public to see that the media are
being censored. But Ko Ye explained how you can still tell if material has been cut. Because editors and their staff need to meet
monthly deadlines and rarely have time to rewrite articles, they
keep pre-prepared blocks of text to fill in the gaps created by the
censors. Ko Ye showed me one magazine in which the editor
filled up the spaces with advertisements for his magazine. You
could see how heavily it had been censored by counting the ads,
he suggested. I flipped through the pages and counted six quarter-
page, seven half-page and three full-page advertisements.

We were interrupted by a loud screeching noise from the
printing press, immediately followed by a chorus of groans from
the workers. The electricity had been cut and the machine had
juddered to a halt. One of the workers went outside to start up
a small generator, and after a few moments the press slowly
coughed its way back to life. Though the power source in Rangoon is more reliable than elsewhere in the country, the electricity still cuts out daily—sometimes for a few minutes, but more
often for a few hours. In some parts of town, such as Golden Val-
ley, a wealthy neighbourhood north of the city centre where
many of the generals live, the electricity supply is fairly constant.
Elsewhere in Rangoon power comes on for only a few hours each
night. For most businesses, private energy supplies are a necessity, and outside the big hotels and condominiums you can see
generators the size of houses growling loudly throughout the
day and night.

Ko Ye tapped the last cigarette out from his packet of London brand. 'The PRSD has been controlling all published material in Burma for over forty years,' he said, 'and now we have a whole generation of young people who have grown up within the curtailed reality it has created.' He told me that his son was reading a political novel from the 1950s, printed during Burma's brief period of press freedom, and was surprised to learn that it had once been possible to criticize the government. He knew, of course, that you could do it behind closed doors (he'd heard Ko Ye enough times), but he never knew you could once do it in print. 'One day they may give us more economic freedom and more freedom of movement,' Ko Ye said of the regime. 'But they will never, never allow us to have freedom of expression. They know that if we published the truth—if people could know the truth— the full truth, they would be forced out within a month.'

ORWELL BELIEVED that it is impossible for literature to survive under totalitarianism. A totalitarian government, he wrote, knows that its hold on power is not legitimate and therefore can never allow the truth to be recorded. To maintain the status quo, it depends on lies. 'Modern literature is essentially an individual thing,' argued Orwell in his essay 'Literature and Totalitarianism'. 'It is either the truthful expression of what one man thinks and feels, or it is nothing.' In short, totalitarianism kills creativity: 'The imagination, like certain wild animals, will not breed in captivity,' he wrote.

'Rubbish!' declared a young Burmese writer, after I had given him Orwell's essay to read. 'Take a walk down Pansodan Street,' he challenged me, 'and you will see that literature is far from dead in Burma.' Pansodan Street is affectionately known as the *lan-bay tekkatho*, or 'street-side university'. It is a busy thorough-fare that runs right through the centre of Rangoon. There are wall-to-wall bookshops, and stalls selling books and magazines cover almost every inch of pavement. There are books everywhere you look, piled on the ground and placed on makeshift wooden shelves: dusty old English classics, scientific textbooks, newly published Burmese novels, books for English-language students, old colonial gazetteers, collections of contemporary Burmese poetry and short stories, and translations of fiction and non-fiction from around the world. Some 100 books are published every month, alongside over 100 monthly magazines, and 80 weekly journals. Clearly, the regime's heavy-handed censorship has not killed the urge to read and write.

Reading between the lines has been developed into a fine art in Burma, and Burmese publishers, editors and writers have found wonderfully creative ways of slipping information past the censors. While I was in Rangoon, a magazine ran a short story about a pack of wolves attacking an elephant. Read between the lines and the story can be interpreted as a fable about Aung San Suu Kyi's tremendous strength against the regime's unrelenting efforts to break down her party. Tun Lin, the retired teacher in my Orwell Book Club in Mandalay, spent an entire afternoon telling me how the cartoon movie *The Lion King* was in fact the story of Burma. Simba, the young lion who is forced to flee his homeland, is Aung San Suu Kyi. His father, like Aung San Suu

Kyi's father, was murdered. Scar, the evil lion who takes over and who turns a once beautiful kingdom into a parched land where animals die of starvation or are forced to flee, is Ne Win. In the end, Tun Lin was pleased to remind me, Simba fights off the evil leader and restores the land to one of rainbows and sunshine where the waters flow crystal clear and all the animals live in harmony.

Allegory is not the only way to evade the censors. Magazine editors publish articles about, say, the health-care system in Sweden and hope that readers will compare it with the virtually non-existent health care available in Burma. Some publishers print translations of introductory-level books on schools of thought like post modernism and deconstructionist theory. 'In this way we try to undermine their system,' one translator told me. 'Through these books we may be able to educate the youth and help them to open their eyes so that they can see the reality around them. It is not a direct method, but we hope very much it is reaching the people.'

On Pansodan Street I noticed an inordinate number of self-help books translated into Burmese. All the best-sellers from the West are available: *Seven Habits of Highly Effective People, Chicken Soup for the Soul, Who Moved My Cheese?* and, its sequel, *I Moved Your Cheese.* I had read somewhere that, because self-help literature teaches people to empower themselves, these seemingly innocent volumes were a cunning way of sending a message to Burmese readers to seize control. 'Could these self-help books indicate a quiet revolution in the making?' I asked a Burmese writer. He dismissed me instantly. 'Name one country where self-help literature is not popular,' he said. Sometimes, I realized, you could read too much between the lines.

While I was in Rangoon I met a well-known writer of short stories who, like many writers and journalists in Burma, had spent a number of years in prison. He was a soft-spoken man in his late forties, and when he talked he illustrated his points with his hands like a mime artist. 'I write stories based on the things I see around me,' he told me. His stories are chronicles of ordinary life, usually highlighting the poverty—both material and spiritual—of people's lives under the regime. Though he still manages to publish some of his writing, most of the stories he wants to write must remain, for now, inside his head. 'I have so many, many stories,' he said. During his time in prison he was not allowed to write, so he became adept at remembering his tales. He described one for me. It is about the power of imagination.

There, he said, was an old man in prison whose job it was to sweep an area of ground around the prison warden's house. It was an area no other prisoners were allowed to go to, and each day the old man spent all day sweeping it clean. The writer felt sorry for this old man, and decided to save his daily rice ration to share with him. It was very poor quality—almost inedible—but he had nothing else to offer. When he gave the old man his leftover rice, the man thanked him and ate it up quickly as if it were the tastiest food he had ever eaten. 'How can you eat such bad rice as if it is fine food?' the writer asked. The old man replied that, each day as he swept the ground clean, delicious cooking smells wafted out from the kitchen where the warden's wife cooked for her family. When he ate the rice, he simply remem-

bered the tantalizing scent of, say, a pork curry stewed with potatoes and kept it inside his head while he ate.

'To my mind, this is such a simple, wonderful story,' finished
the writer, 'and yet I am not allowed to publish it.'

Almost every writer I met in Burma had had at least one book
banned by the censorship board. As a result, there exists in Burma
a secret archive of unpublished books—stories that linger in writers' heads, and finished manuscripts that have been hidden away.
Some writers write stories they know cannot appear under the
current regime. One friend of mine spent hours each day in front
of a run-down computer recording the day's events as he heard
them through the grapevine. 'I have to do this,' he said. 'Nothing
is reported in the official news here, so, if I do not write these
things down, tomorrow they will be forgotten.' I also met a historian who is busy compiling a modern history of Shan State in
eastern Burma. It is a history of the military occupation of the
Shan lands by this government, he explained. 'I know it will not
be published, but I must write it. I must make a record. Then at
least it is there, and maybe one day . . .'

As one Burmese writer joked to me, 'In Burma we are free to
write whatever we want. We're just not free to have it published.'

*Nineteen Eighty-Four* opens with Winston Smith entering his
shabby apartment. There he crouches in a tiny alcove where he is
able to hide a few inches beyond the ever-watchful eye of the telescreen. He sits over a book with blank, cream-coloured pages,
and holds in his hand a smuggled pen. As he writes the date on
the first page of what is to be his diary, he wonders who he is writing it for, since it would never be safe to show it to anyone in the

world of *Nineteen Eighty-Four*. He begins by recording the events of the previous day, and then, after various interruptions, he dips his pen back into the inkwell and dedicates the book: 'To the future or to the past, to a time when thought is free, when men are different from one another and do not live alone—to a time when truth exists and what is done cannot be undone'.

One question I was frequently asked about Orwell while I travelled around Burma was how he had been able to imagine the setting for *Nineteen Eighty-Four*. Orwell was never oppressed himself; how could he write about oppression? It was a good question. *Nineteen Eighty-Four* has been recognized worldwide as a remarkably accurate description of life under a totalitarian regime. The book describes a soulless society ruled by the all-powerful Party, which controls people through ignorance (all history has been erased and current events are rewritten) and fear (through the ever present telescreen and the threat of vaporization).

So, how did Orwell do it? I usually offered the standard, somewhat unsatisfactory explanations. Some academics think that the cold dormitories and frequent canings of a British boarding school may have given the eight-year-old Orwell an early taste of *Nineteen Eighty-Four*. Others believe the time the author spent as a volunteer soldier in the Spanish Civil War in the 1930s and being hunted down by a Russian police force in Barcelona gave him a particular insight. My own theory, which I was becoming more and more convinced of as I learned more about Orwell's time in Burma, was that his work as an imperial policeman had greatly contributed to his ability to write about oppression.

When I shared these ideas with a Burmese poet I knew, he was unimpressed. He told me about an English poet whose name he could not remember. The poet had won an award for a poem written about Russia. After the award was announced it transpired that the poet had never been to Russia and was heavily criticized. 'In my mind this is very wrong-headed,' said my friend. 'The poet wrote from her imagination, and that is the real art: to be able to imagine something you have not experienced.'


I SOON BECAME a regular at a tea shop near my hotel in downtown Rangoon. The shop consisted of a narrow room open to the road. Two rows of waist-high tables surrounded by plastic stools were lined against each wall. In a charcoal-blackened corner at the back of the room a large kettle of tea bubbled over a stove, and round slices of *palata,* or fried Indian bread, sizzled on flat woks ready to be eaten sweet with a small dipping-dish of plain sugar or savoury with a mix of split peas and onions. Customers sat in small groups, chattering over breakfast. A ceiling fan in the centre of the room stirred the warm air into a gentle whirl of cheroot smoke, buttery *palata* smells and murmured conversations.

The shop had about six serving boys who trotted busily among the customers, replenishing the flasks of clear tea on the tables, proffering cigarettes, and scuffling with each other. After a few visits to the shop I befriended one of them, a scrawny boy with velvet-brown eyes and a head that was slightly too large for his body. Each time I came into the shop, he would dash towards my favourite table before I got there, whip out a dirty rag tucked into the back of his *longyi,* and wipe the table with a dramatic flourish. Soon I didn't even have to place an order: I only needed to catch his eye. He would nod at me authoritatively and bellow to the kitchen staff, *'Paw kya t'kwet! Peh palata t'pwe!'* Within minutes, warm *palata* and a cup of strong, not-too-sweet tea would be sitting on the table in front of me.

My perch at the front of the tea shop was an ideal spot for people-watching. The old shop-houses that lined the street must once have offered a stately address. The balconies were decorated with floral stuccowork, and above the doors were antique stained-glass windows, now almost black with decades of accumulated dust. Dingy one-room shops were tucked into nooks and crannies on the ground floor of each building. There was a dressmaker's where seamstresses were bent over foot-operated sewing machines, a snack shop lodged beneath a stairwell, and a tiny photocopy booth with a couple of ageing machines that were often incapacitated by the frequent power cuts. The musical cry of vendors echoed up and down the street. *'Pyaung bu!'* yelled one woman over and over again, stretching out the vowels like an opera singer: 'Sweetcorn!' She carried a round rattan basket on top of her head, and when an old man lounging in a doorway clapped his hands to attract her attention she walked over and set the basket down in front of him. She removed the lid of the basket and a great cloud of steam escaped, fogging up the old man's glasses. After he had chosen two cobs of boiled corn and paid for them, she squatted down to ease the basket back on to her head and strolled on. *'Pyaung bu! Pyaung buu-uu-uu!'* Other vendors included a woman selling yoghurt sweetened with jaggery, a man carrying a fan of brooms on his back, and another with plastic buckets hung on a bamboo pole.

Residents of these tall Rangoon shop-houses had invented an ingenious method for circumventing the staircase. A string tied to each balcony hung down to the ground floor. At the end of each string was a piece of ballast—a bulldog clip, a small bucket, a doorknob—to keep it weighted down, and when I walked down the side streets on a breezy day they clinked together like wind chimes. I watched a deliveryman clip folded newspapers to the end of certain strings. If no one was home, the papers would dangle there waiting to be pulled up later. A vendor tied two plastic bags of noodles to a string for customers waiting above, and a teenage girl sent a lottery ticket flying up to her mother. Once, when I had left a friend's sixth-floor apartment, I realized only after I had climbed down the stairs and stepped into the light drizzle outside that I had left my umbrella behind. As I looked up towards her balcony, I saw that she had already tied the umbrella to her string and was lowering it down to me.

Each time I visited the tea shop I learned a little more about the serving boy. His name was Kyaw Kyaw, and he told me he was thirteen years old, though he looked no more than ten. Young boys from poor families all over Burma serve as a cheap labour source for the capital's tea-shop owners. They are sent by their families and provided with food and board and a monthly salary which, in Rangoon, seemed to average around 4,000 kyat (four dollars). When I questioned Kyaw Kyaw, he would stand next to me grinning from ear to ear and hopping excitedly up and down. He told me he came from a small town in the Delta where his parents worked as fishmongers in the local market. His two older siblings had died—he didn't know how. Two years ago his parents sent him to Rangoon to work in this tea shop so that he could send his earnings back home. 'How often do you go home?' I asked him. 'Two, maybe three times a year,' he said quickly. Then he paused for a bit, twisted his tea-stained rag in his hands, and said, 'No, I haven't been home yet. Maybe I'm not going home any more.'

Our conversation was interrupted, as it often was, by the familiar shushing noise that the Burmese use to attract the attention of a tea-shop boy. Kyaw Kyaw ran his rag quickly over my table, gave me a big white-toothed grin, and dashed off to attend to the waiting customer.

The tea shop was open from six o'clock in the morning until around nine each evening. One night, when I walked back to my hotel, I went over to have a closer look at it. A metal grille had been pulled across the entranceway and secured with chains and a padlock. On a side wall, fairy lights hung around a Buddhist shrine threw a dim orange light around the room. The shop's stools had been neatly stacked against the walls, and the tables had been pushed together into the centre to make a sleeping platform for the boys, who lay curled up against each other in a tangled pile of arms, legs and *longyi*. I recognized Kyaw Kyaw's red-and-green-checked *longyi* and saw him lying with his head on another boy's stomach and one leg dangling over the edge of the tables. The room was still and quiet except for the heavy sound of breathing and the occasional cockroach scuttling across the cement floor.

I N 1925 Orwell spent nine months living across the river from Rangoon, in a district called Syriam. When he visited the capital he had to travel by ferry. Today it is possible to make the short journey by car, and one morning I hired a taxi to take me to Syriam for the day. Just as we set out, a rainstorm came crashing down over the city. People ran for cover, holding up their *longyi*, ducking into doorways and beneath bus shelters. Stray dogs scurried under parked cars. The rain was astoundingly heavy, and as we sped through the deluge I watched the gutters along the side of the roads regurgitate a fetid cocktail of sewage and mud. By the time we reached the bridge to cross over the choppy waters of the Pegu river the storm was over, stopping just as suddenly as it had begun. It felt as if a gigantic bucket of water had just been emptied over the city.

The curving streets and sleepy lanes of Syriam—today called Thanlyin—were gleaming wet. Pools of water sagged in the tarpaulin awnings over shops. The broad branches of the acacia trees that grew on every corner dripped with water, and the red-dirt streets had become flowing rivulets. A bleating goat stood stranded upon a pile of bricks in the middle of a swirling stream. Trishaw drivers removed the plastic sheets from their vehicles and wiped down their handlebars. Tea-shop boys dried off tables and stools that had been placed along the pavements. Beyond the main roads was a watery vista of flooded paddy, shining silver-grey.

When Orwell lived here, Syriam was considered the best-run district in all Burma. It was a prosperous region, home to a large number of oil refineries. Burma has a rich supply of natural oil, and under the colonial government, which constructed oilfields in the flat, dry central plains, it was the second biggest producer of oil in the British Empire. Crude oil was sailed downriver to Syriam for processing into kerosene and engine fuel. The landscape was dotted with towering chimneys emitting black clouds of smoke. The area was also marked by a large population of American oil-drillers. One British policeman who was in Burma at that time recorded with displeasure the presence of these Americans and the filthy language they insisted on using. The Americans were always popping up in his crime files: he found one driller causing a commotion in a car with a prostitute, and had to deal with another who accused a policeman of stealing a watch that had simply been misplaced.

Orwell must also have disliked the American contingent in Syriam, as, over twenty-five years after his time there, he had a dig at them in his unfinished novella, 'A Smoking Room Story'. In Orwell's plan for a scene set in the smoking saloon of a ship sailing back to England from Burma, he sketched a description of the four American oil drillers present: 'Thick fingers of the Americans stuffing sandwiches & pouring whisky between thick lips. Their implied belief that Man is naturally in a state of playing poker & drinking whisky.' (The English characters who are in the smoking room don't fare any better: the notebook continues,

'Competition in offensiveness between the two branches of the Anglo-Saxon race—the English worse.')

Only a handful of refineries are now being run by the Burmese government: the British authorities destroyed most of the oil industry's infrastructure before the Second World War, to prevent Japanese troops from using it. But a few other remnants of the well-run district of Orwell's time still survive. There are a number of churches in various states of decay. On the steps of one locked-up church a half-naked Indian girl sat clutching the yellow-pink peel of a pomegranate, its seeds spilling out around her like confetti. Near another church is an old British cemetery where a farmer squatted on top of a sarcophagus, slowly chewing a mouthful of betel while his cattle grazed among the grass and daisies that grew over the graves. Nationalized mission schools with oversized colonnades and cobblestone archways sit incongruously among wooden houses and bamboo groves. Peeking inside the doorway of one empty classroom I spied an old nursery rhyme written in a neat, methodical hand on the blackboard: 'Hickory dickory dock,/The mouse ran up the clock . . .'

The only recorded Burmese memory of Orwell in Burma dates back to his time around Rangoon. It doesn't show him in his best light. In 1969 the late Dr Htin Aung, a former vice-chancellor at Rangoon University, gave a lecture at the Royal Central Asian Society in London. He described an incident that took place when he was a schoolboy. The young Htin Aung was waiting with some friends at a railway platform in Rangoon when a tall, gaunt Englishman wearing a well-cut grey suit and carrying a cane came down the steps to the platform. Another schoolboy who was messing around with his friends accidentally rolled under the Englishman's feet and caused him to tumble heavily down the stairs. The Englishman jumped up furiously and raised his cane to smack the boy on the head. At the last minute he checked himself and instead the cane came down on the boy's back. The boy and his friends, including Htin Aung, were angry at the unnecessary violence. The stationmaster told them the Englishman's name was Eric Blair, and they followed him on to the train and argued with him until he got off at Mission Road station, where the famous British club, the Gymkhana, was located.

The 1920s, said Htin Aung, were a dark period for Burmese–British relations. Though the simmering energy of nationalism was not to erupt until the following decade, Htin Aung described the British and the Burmese as bitter enemies separated by 'a wall of racial prejudice, harder than granite'. Communications between them, he said, were riddled with 'mutual suspicion, despair and disgust'. The 1920s were indeed a politically tense time. There were nationwide school and university strikes, which began when Rangoon's first university was opened, and students demanded a national education system free from British control. Village political associations were set up to boycott British goods and refuse payment of government taxes. One British historian noted that a favourite hobby of young Burmese was 'police-baiting'.

In *Burmese Days,* Ellis, a violently racist Englishman who manages a timber company in Upper Burma, beats a young boy he thinks is taunting him. When five schoolboys grin at the highly strung Ellis as they walk past him in the street, he demands to know what they are laughing at. One of the boys replies in broken English, 'Not your business.' Enraged, Ellis brings his cane down across the boy's eyes. The other boys pelt him with laterite pebbles. 'You damned dirty little niggers!' Ellis shouts at them. 'You sneaking, mangy little rats!' The boy ends up blinded, and the incident provokes a riot which results in an angry Burmese mob storming the club, demanding that Ellis be handed over for punishment.

Orwell himself would later write about beating servants and coolies in a brief autobiographical sketch in *The Road to Wigan Pier*. As he explained it, 'Nearly everyone does these things in the East, at any rate occasionally: orientals can be very provoking.' I found it almost impossible to imagine Orwell, the champion of the underdog and the chronicler of the down-at-heel, pummelling a coolie. But there are other very un-Orwell-like memories of Orwell from this period in his life. Christopher Hollis, an acquaintance who had been two years above Orwell at his public school, Eton, had dinner with him when he passed through Rangoon. Years after Orwell's death Hollis recalled that Orwell had been every bit the imperial policeman, espousing theories about how banning corporal punishment might be fine for public schools in England but such laxity wouldn't work when trying to control the Burmese. Hollis found no trace of any liberal opinion in the young policeman. An English chemist working at an oil company in Syriam provided Orwell and a fellow officer with lodgings for a few nights. On the first evening at the chemist's house, the guests ended up on the verandah in their pyjamas singing raucous songs. (Included in the repertoire was an old school song, 'Zipping zyder through a straw, haw-haw!'.) The chemist recalled that it was Orwell who led the singing and who complained that there were no longer any good bawdy songs around. In *Burmese Days,* Orwell derides John Flory's younger days in Rangoon, when he emptied bottles of whisky and bawled out songs 'of insane filthiness and silliness'.

Was Orwell just acting a role in Burma, or was there a little bit of the empire-builder in his character after all? Many years later he expressed a hint of nostalgia for his time in the Empire. When Orwell met with the novelist Anthony Powell he reminisced nostalgically about his old police uniform. 'These straps under the foot give you a feeling like nothing else in life,' Orwell told him.

On the way back to Rangoon, the taxi driver and I stopped at the ruins of a Portuguese church that stood on a hill just next to the river. There was not much left of the church—just the roof-less shell of a Romanesque structure that must have been battered into its present state by hundreds of monsoon storms. A thick curtain of vines hung from the cloister walls, and in the centre of the nave was a tomb carved with a crude skull and cross-bones accompanied by two hourglasses. The church dated back to the sixteenth century, when a Portuguese adventurer called Philip De Brito hacked a small kingdom from the wilds of Syriam. He raised his own army and ransacked the nearby Burmese kingdom of Pegu. When the Burmese gathered their forces and retaliated, they besieged Syriam, captured De Brito and condemned him to death by impalement. De Brito died in agony writhing for three days on a stake beneath the blistering sun of his former kingdom.

I sat resting for a while outside the church looking out over the river at Rangoon. The Shwedagon Pagoda, the most revered Buddhist site in Burma, towered like a golden mountain over the urban sprawl of the city. A few grey office buildings jutted up from the landscape, and there were forested patches of green around the inland lakes of the northern part of the city. Down by the mouth of the river I saw a dark mass of clouds gathering ominously, and the taxi driver urged me to return to Rangoon before the rains started again.

I F YOU LOOK at a British map from Orwell's time in Burma you will see a strange star-shaped structure just north of Rangoon. It is large in comparison to anything around it on the map, and is enclosed by a circle. The star indicates a series of halls that fan out from a central tower and are surrounded by a wall some twenty feet high. This is Insein Prison, designed by the British to be the colony's most secure lock-up. Insein—pronounced like 'insane'—was named after the town and district in which it is located, and is now present-day Burma's most notorious jail.

Orwell moved to Insein town in September 1925, and was based there for six months. At the time, the British police force was still struggling with the increase of crime throughout Burma. Insein was among the most volatile districts, with the highest rate of violent crime and the lowest number of convictions. From 1925 to 1926 there was a staggering 68 per cent rise in the number of murders there. The authorities tried a variety of means to quell the seemingly inexplicable bloodlust. More members of the police force were recruited to surveillance work in order to keep a closer eye on History Sheeters, and a special emphasis was placed on the conviction and punishment of violent criminals. One government report suggested establishing a penal colony for habitual offenders. The idea was to put all the 'bad hats of Burma' on to a boat and dump them on a deserted island called Cocos Island, where they could either be re-educated into respectable citizens or live out their days in harmless isolation. Another report touted the 'advantages of a sound flogging' through wider use of the Whipping Act (at least thirty strokes; fifty for particularly brutal crimes). 'In Burma we are dealing with a Mongolian race,' the report stated by way of explanation, 'and Mongolian races appear to have always found an element of cruelty in their punishments necessary.' The easiest method for tackling crime, however, was imprisonment, and the British jails were filled to overflowing. Every year some 20,000 criminals were locked up, and in 1921, a few years before Orwell arrived in the district, Insein Prison was home to 2,335 of 'the worst men in Burma'.

As a policeman, Orwell must have visited Insein Prison a number of times, and he describes the horror of British-run jails in Burma in *The Road to Wigan Pier:* 'The wretched prisoners squatting in the reeking cages of the lock-ups, the grey cowed faces of the long-term convicts, the scarred buttocks of the men who had been flogged with bamboos, the women and children howling when their menfolk were led away—things like these are beyond bearing when you are in any way directly responsible for them.'

Insein Prison was built to hold 2,500 prisoners. Today some

10,000 are crammed within its walls. Among the criminals incarcerated in jails across Burma are an estimated 1,500 political prisoners. These include students, writers, doctors, teachers, members of the NLD, and monks and nuns who have been arrested for voicing their disagreement with the regime. After the people's uprising in 1988, the government began a systematic hunt-and-destroy campaign to purge the 'troublesome' elements from Burmese society. It targeted down student leaders involved in the uprising and, later, outspoken NLD MPs elected in the 1990 election. Hundreds of people were jailed, hundreds more were forced underground, and thousands fled to neighbouring Thailand.

I spent one afternoon driving around Insein in a taxi. Insein is today a pleasant, leafy suburb of Rangoon, with old British-administration buildings still in use and flower-lined pathways leading to small cottages. There is, predictably, nothing to see around the prison itself but external offices and a large gate. The closest I ever got to knowing anything about the interior of Insein Prison was in the small town of Mae Sot on the Thai–Burma border. On a trip back to Thailand to renew my Burmese visa, I travelled up to Mae Sot to meet a group of former prisoners called Assistance Association for Political Prisoners (AAPP), who have set up a tiny one-room museum of Burmese prison life. The museum is looked after by Nay Rein Kyaw (his real name), a 33-year-old former political prisoner. When I went to Mae Sot between my trips to Burma, Nay Rein Kyaw showed me around the simulated prison cell, gallantly opening a cell door for me to climb through.

Nay Rein Kyaw was arrested in 1992. Late one night two Military Intelligence officers, accompanied by soldiers and police, came to his house and searched his bedroom. They found leaflets he had been secretly distributing that called for democratic change. (Among other things, the leaflet demanded the unconditional release of all political prisoners.) He was taken into custody and interrogated. 'They didn't let me eat or drink for three days,' he said. 'I was so thirsty I kept thinking that if I could just get to the toilet I could drink from the water there, but when they let me go to the bathroom the guards stood in front of me and wouldn't allow me to scoop up any water.' Nay Rein Kyaw was beaten repeatedly, and had electrodes applied to his genitals. 'They asked me why I wrote bad things about the government,' he said. 'They wanted me to say I was wrong: that they are not oppressive, that they are being fair. But I could not say those things.'

In *Nineteen Eighty-Four,* Winston Smith's fate is sealed when he opens his diary and writes, against his better judgement, the words 'Down with Big Brother!' Smith attempts to thwart the ruling party by reclaiming his freedom, and sneaks out into the countryside with his girlfriend, Julia, to make love in the bushes. He eventually makes contact with an underground group headed by O'Brien, and swears to die in his struggle against the Party's oppression. But O'Brien turns out to be a double agent working for the Party to rout out dissenters, and Smith ends up in prison at the so-called Ministry of Love, where he is brutally interrogated:

> They slapped his face, wrung his ears, pulled his hair, made him stand on one leg, refused him leave to urinate, shone

glaring lights in his face until his eyes ran with water; but the aim of this was simply to humiliate him and destroy his power of arguing and reasoning. Their real weapon was the merciless questioning that went on and on, hour after hour, tripping him up, laying traps for him, twisting everything that he said, convicting him at every step of lies and self-contradiction, until he began weeping as much from shame as from nervous fatigue.

Though Smith is gradually reduced to an emaciated shell during weeks of torture, he is able to cling to one last shred of dignity. He may have confessed to crimes he never committed—distributing seditious pamphlets, assassinating Party members—but he has not betrayed his girlfriend, Julia. But then he is taken to Room 101, the dreaded room where each prisoner confronts his own worst fear. For Smith it is rats. When a cage filled with large, hungry, squealing rats is moved towards his face, he withstands his fear only until the wire of the cage brushes his cheeks. And then he breaks. 'Do it to Julia!' he shrieks. 'Do it to Julia!'

The Burmese Military Intelligence use similarly brutal torture methods to coerce prisoners into informing on their friends and colleagues. Bo Kyi, a former political prisoner and a founding member of AAPP, told me that many Burmese activists know it is impossible to withstand extreme torture. They can promise their friends only one thing: that they will endure the pain for three days. This, it is hoped, provides others connected to them with enough time to go into hiding. The interrogation process can take weeks or months; then, once it is over, detainees are usually sentenced in a military court and taken from the interrogation centre to the prison.

Nay Rein Kyaw picked up a blue sack that lay on a shelf in the museum and put it over his head. His voice was muffled through the stiff cloth as he said, 'This is how I was transported to Insein Prison.' At Insein he was put into a cell with four other political prisoners. The cell was seven feet by eight feet wide, and had few amenities. Each prisoner had a burlap sack and a blanket to be used as bedding on the concrete floor. A low earthenware tray that was emptied once a day served as a toilet. And just outside the cell was a daily supply of water in a small urn to be shared with the neighbouring cell. Each prisoner was provided with a tin plate to receive rice gruel, bean soup and *ngapi* (a fermented fish paste) twice a day. 'The food was almost inedible,' said Nay Rein Kyaw. 'Sometimes we found grass in the soup, and there were often pebbles or sand in the rice.' Once a week he was provided with his ration of protein: a small piece of boiled meat. Each day he was allowed out of his cell for fifteen minutes to walk around the prison yard and bathe (using a maximum of fifteen scoops of water from the central trough).

Punishments were frequent. You could be punished if you asked for more rice or talked at the wrong time, said Nay Rein Kyaw. He explained how prisoners were immobilized with twelve-pound iron shackles, were made to crawl over sharp stones, or were forced to hold impossible and humiliating positions such as squatting as if they were riding a motorcycle. The worst punishment, he said, was solitary confinement. In Insein Prison, prisoners have been confined in tiny kennels built to hold military dogs.

After six years in Insein, Nay Rein Kyaw was transferred to Mingyan Prison in central Burma, where most political prisoners are kept in solitary confinement. Mingyan is considered among former prisoners to be the most brutal prison in Burma. Nay Rein Kyaw spent two years and two months there. He was not allowed to look at other prisoners as he walked down the corridor to the prison yard, or converse with his neighbours through the walls. Like other prisoners, he was kept busy with futile jobs. 'The prison guards made us shine the iron bars of our cells until they shone like stainless steel,' he said. 'But they did not give us any cleaning equipment, so we had to make it ourselves from the only things we had: rice and sand.'

I met other former political prisoners in Mae Sot. Nyein Aye, for instance, who was first arrested for his participation in the 1988 uprising when he was just fourteen years old. He began his term in Insein, but, like many political prisoners, was later transferred to a jail far away from where his family lived. His mother made the eight-hour bus journey to the prison each month so she could see him for the ten minutes he was allowed with immediate family members. When he was released after three years he tried to complete his high-school education, but no headmaster wanted to enroll a former political prisoner. He was later arrested again and was sentenced to seven years for joining a campaign calling for a student union to be established. While he was in prison the second time, his father passed away. 'Around the time my father died, I had a dream that he had come to visit me in prison,' Nyein Aye told me. 'He said, "My dearest son, what are you doing here? Why don't you come home? Please come home."'

Nay Rein Kyaw and other former prisoners in AAPP are working to document the numbers and conditions of political prisoners in Burma, detailing the reason for each arrest and the length of each sentence. On the walls of their museum are photographs of those currently imprisoned. The pictures are grouped thematically. At the top of one wall are the scores of monks who are in jail, forbidden to wear their robes or to preach. Another collection shows the eighty-five faces of those known to have died in prison since 1988 because of maltreatment or lack of medical attention. The photographs are of varying quality: some are old black-and-white passport shots, others are clipped from snapshots of happier occasions. Many of the men and women they depict are locked away behind the walls of Insein Prison. As I looked at the varied colours and shapes of the photographs, they seemed to resemble a jigsaw puzzle that was gradually being assembled piece by piece, and managed to give the impression that all these broken lives could one day be put back together again.

ASKED a Burmese journalist friend of mine in Rangoon if it was possible to meet former political prisoners who had chosen to stay in Burma. 'It would be too easy,' he replied. 'Just walk into any house in any town in Burma. Everyone has a father or a daughter or a cousin or an in-law who has been or is a political prisoner. And, if they don't, then they have a friend who has been one.'

In Burma, prison exists as an ever present underworld into which anyone can fall at any time. Many of the people I know there have served time in prison for their disagreements with the government point of view. My Burmese-language teacher was incarcerated for four years. The publisher Ko Ye has spent two short periods in prison. And the journalist I questioned endured many years in the solitary confinement of a ten-by-twelve-foot cell. 'You can find many, many sad stories about prison in Burma,' he told me.

One evening a friend took me to have dinner with two former political prisoners. We met in a bustling neighbourhood in Rangoon's Chinatown, down a narrow street of Chinese shophouses. Hole-in-the-wall restaurants served barbecued food cooked in front of their shops, and the entire road was enveloped in the smoke of cooking fires and the tangy smell of garlic. Groups of diners clustered around rickety tin tables, laughing and singing over jugs of beer. Grubby young children wormed their way through the crowds, squeezing hands in search of spare change. Pigeons perched on the telephone wires that were draped above the street, and, in the upper stories of the shophouses, open windows revealed rooms dimly lit with coloured lanterns.

Ohn Mar and Soe Aung were waiting for us at a table tucked between two boisterous groups of revellers and had already ordered a starter of grilled quail eggs and okra roasted in chilli sauce. As we sat down, my friend hailed a passing vendor, who scooped a tin of steamed peanuts out of the large bucket he was carrying, tossed them in oil, garlic and salt, and poured the mixture on to a plate, giving us each a toothpick with which to spear the nuts. Ohn Mar, a woman in her early forties, introduced herself matter-of-factly. 'I have spent almost six years in prison on four different charges of destabilizing the state,' she told me with a girlish giggle.

I wondered what this diminutive woman could possibly have done to threaten the mighty Burmese army (she was discovered lending a copy of a dissident magazine to a friend), but I then realized that the action itself was somewhat irrelevant. The regime could charge people under any number of emergency acts and laws designed to protect the state. '*Thayay-gwin*' they call the law in Burma, or 'rubber band', because it is so flexible. In *Nineteen Eighty-Four*, when Winston Smith unexpectedly meets an acquaintance in the lock-up at the interrogation centre, he asks him what he was arrested for.

'To tell the truth,' replies his friend, 'there is only one offence, is there not?'

'And have you committed it?' asks Winston.

'Apparently I have.'

It is the same in Burma. There is only one real crime, and that is to act against the government.

After we had ordered a dinner of barbecued fish and clear soup, my friend urged me to ask questions about prison. 'You can ask them anything you want,' he said. 'Go on. They are happy to talk with you.' Yet, sitting there, sipping beer and munching peanuts, I found it difficult to talk so directly about what was, for me at least, such an unimaginable experience.

'How did you endure it?' I asked awkwardly.

Ohn Mar smiled gently and told me that she meditated every day and concentrated on small victories. She told me about the time her sister came to visit her bringing a gift of four mangoes, among other things. All packages are taken away and searched by prison staff before they are given to the prisoners and, when the wardens later handed her the package she saw that they had kept the mangoes for themselves. She demanded to know where the mangoes were, telling the guards that they had no right to take something that belonged to her. She told them that if she was not allowed to have the mangoes they must be returned to her sister. In the end the guards capitulated, though they kept the mangoes for two weeks, until her sister was allowed to return for the next visit. 'Of course the fruit was rotten by then and my sister had to throw it away,' said Ohn Mar. 'But at least I had forced them to do the correct thing.'

Ohn Mar's companion, Soe Aung, a journalist, was less forthcoming. He sat silently listening to our conversation, until my friend nudged him into telling me about his attempts to continue writing in prison. Soe Aung had spent over ten years in jail, and had been released only a few months before I met him. He explained in a quiet, slow voice how he had struggled to keep his mind active during his years in prison. Reading and writing are forbidden in most prisons, and he had to bribe the guards with special food parcels delivered by his family so they would smuggle in some paper and a pen for him. When he couldn't get hold of any paper he wrote on plastic bags, using sharpened twigs to scratch out words. He recorded his thoughts about politics, and analysed news he had gleaned from the scraps of newspaper his food parcels were wrapped in. He hid the articles behind bricks inside his cell, and when he was let out for his daily wash in the prison yard he passed them on to other prisoners. 'In this way I was able to continue being a journalist in prison,' he said. My friend commented that Soe Aung was lucky to be able to avoid the censorship board in prison, and we all laughed. When we had stopped laughing, Soe Aung told us that a piece he had written detailing the unjust treatment of political prisoners was discovered and his sentence was increased by seven years.

Despite the dangers, prisons are sometimes considered as alternative centres of learning in Burma. One writer I knew, who spent a number of years in a special annexe of Insein reserved for dissidents, told me he had been the custodian of a secret library. He had books and magazines smuggled into him, and buried them at different places around the prison yard where he was put to work digging vegetable patches. He memorized the locations of some fifty books sunk beneath the soil. When a prisoner asked for a particular title, he would dig it up and sneak it into the prisoner's cell. Another friend of mine who was a publisher once showed me a hand-made book that had been produced in prison—a biography of a modern artist translated from English into Burmese. It was an exquisite volume, with text inscribed in a tortuously miniature script on pages the size of a cassette tape.

Even without access to books and pens, Soe Aung said, prisoners are able to find ways of learning. There are usually four or five prisoners in each cell, and they take turns to tell stories and share what knowledge they have. A monk may whisper Buddhist sermons. A university professor can teach English grammar. Poets compose poems in their heads and pass them on from cell to cell. When the guards are not around, cellmates debate the necessity of a national constitution for Burma or discuss the literary style of Mandalay writers. Everyone has some knowledge to share, he said.

A haunting wail came from somewhere deep in the crowd, and I turned around to see a beautiful woman with chestnut-coloured skin. One of her legs was badly withered, perhaps from polio, and she hobbled along on crutches. After a couple of steps she stopped to sing a few lines from some indecipherable song, holding out a cup to collect donations. A man at the next table gave a waiter some money to pass to her, and she moved on slowly through the crowded street.

Readjusting to life outside prison is very tough, said Ohn Mar. In the early days after political prisoners are released, Military Intelligence agents follow them constantly and their friends and colleagues are often warned by the authorities not to associate with them. Many former political prisoners end up suffering from severe depression or turn to alcoholism. Ohn Mar told me she was lucky to have the support of her family. She took a long, thoughtful sip of her soft drink and said, 'Perhaps, though, being on this side of the prison wall is not so different. Even after we are released we still find ourselves living in a prison. It's just a much larger one, that's all.'

Around nine o'clock we said our goodbyes and I took a trishaw back to my hotel. We rattled along a lively main street where the low tables of busy pavement tea shops were tucked around cars and trucks that had parked for the night. Shops selling music tapes played bouncy Burmese pop songs and vendors sold roasted palm shoots and vegetables deep-fried in batter to passers-by. In the quieter neighbourhood near my hotel, two men played chess on a board marked out in blue chalk on the pavement. Around them stood a small and silent crowd of onlookers. As the trishaw swung into the street where my hotel was, a pack of stray dogs trotted busily past us howling at invisible intruders.

Not long after our dinner I met the prison librarian again. He was still an enthusiastic procurer of books and I told him I needed something to read. 'What would you like?' he asked. I wondered if he could find me a novel by Charles Dickens, and a few days later he delivered a copy of *Little Dorrit* to my hotel. The book was borrowed from a friend's private library, and had been well read. The spine was falling off, and some of the pages were torn. One reader had left a few pencilled notes in the margins, and I read them with interest. He or she had clearly interpreted *Little Dorrit* not only as the story of a young woman whose father is stuck in a debtor's prison, but as a comment on the confines of society as a whole. The book contains a description of faded gentry living in cramped apartments who stubbornly deny their own poverty and insist on maintaining the illusion of a grander life. Next to these paragraphs was a note written in neat cursive script: 'Prison! Pretences, isolation, enclosure.'

———

THE LARGEST OFFICIAL ceremony in Burma, Armed Forces Day, is celebrated annually on 27 March. The date is, in effect, the army's birthday, as it commemorates the recently formed Burmese army's first time in combat against the occupying Japanese during the Second World War, in 1945. I was in Rangoon, where the main celebrations take place, and watched preparations begin weeks before the actual date. Battalions are trucked into the city to rehearse for elaborate military parades. Security is heightened, government buildings are spruced up and repainted, and billboards promoting the army are hoisted above major intersections and roundabouts. The oversized boards look more like movie advertisements than army propaganda. Painted in soothing pastel colours, they depict handsome soldiers in pistachio-green uniforms marching down pale yellow roads and cheered by crowds of onlookers. Above the parade, a fleet of pink fighter planes glides placidly through a postcard-perfect blue sky.

In reality the generals' big day dawned on a sunless and humid morning, and I learned that the soldiers would be marching not through the streets of the capital, but inside the confines of Resistance Park, just north of the city centre. All roads leading to the park were closed by barbed-wire barricades and trucks, and as I walked towards the park I found the area almost deserted. Across the road from one of the park gates, a small huddle of onlookers stood on tiptoe, craning their necks for a glimpse of the parade. I nudged my way to the front of the crowd, but there was nothing to see. Tall trees around the edge of the park obstructed any view of the events going on inside, and soldiers patrolled the park's perimeter to make sure that passing pedestrians kept their distance. The only hint of any activity inside were the thunderous sound of thousands of boots stomping up and down and the occasional glint of a bayonet, glimpsed through the trees.

I walked along the empty roads to the other side of the park. Every so often something shifted in the foliage and I caught sight of an armed soldier dressed in camouflage crouching uncomfortably in the bushes. The shrill scream of a distant siren rose to a climax as a cavalcade of military motorcycles and shiny black limousines with darkened windows zoomed past me. After twenty minutes or so I arrived at the wide promenade which serves as the park's main entrance. Still there was nothing to see. I stuck my head through the bars of the closed gate and called to a soldier who stood on the other side. He wore brand-new olive-green fatigues and gripped a rifle across his chest.

'Where can I go to watch the military parade?' I asked him.

'Nowhere,' he replied.

'You mean the army isn't marching?'

'No, the army is marching.'

'Then you mean I can't go to see the parade?'

'Yes, you can't go to see the parade.'

Before I could ask anything else the soldier smartly turned his back on me and refused to respond to further queries. It was already late in the morning, and the celebrations were scheduled to finish before the blistering midday heat set in. I realized, with some disappointment, that I wasn't going to be able to see the army on parade. I consoled myself with a special edition of

*The New Light of Myanmar.* The cover showed a photograph of the Commander-in-Chief, General Than Shwe, his shoulders and chest heavily draped in military epaulettes and medals, as he addressed his army. It is difficult to come up with a generous description of Than Shwe's appearance: he is a stocky, dark-skinned man with large spectacles that squat above a flattened nose. Now over seventy years old, Than Shwe never finished secondary school and has spent almost his entire life in the army. Like all the senior generals, he hides behind a fortress of secrecy from which only a few titbits have escaped: he likes chewing betel, and is said to enjoy watching international football matches and reading Chinese martial-arts sagas.

*The New Light of Myanmar* printed Than Shwe's Armed Forces Day address in full. The speech ran through a brief history of the *Tatmadaw,* or Burmese army, and emphasized how the soldiers have always worked 'hand in hand with the people'. 'The *Tatmadaw* is born of the people and is one with the people,' said Than Shwe. The Burmese army was formed to battle for independence from British rule. The army's founding father was Aung San, a student nationalist who in 1941 led a small group of fellow freedom fighters to Japan for training. The so-called 'thirty comrades' (one of whom was Burma's recently deceased leader, Ne Win) marched back into Burma with the conquering Japanese forces during the Second World War. After witnessing the brutality with which the Japanese occupied their country, the comrades soon switched sides and ended up fighting alongside the British to evict the Japanese. After the war the hugely popular General Aung San negotiated with the British for Burma's independence and was set to become the leader of the newly independent country. But in July 1947, just months before independence came into effect, he and most of his newly formed cabinet were assassinated by a rival politician while in a meeting at the Secretariat. It was Ne Win who ended up in the position of Commander-in-Chief of the army and, later, ruler of the country.

The big problem the regime has with producing a potted history of these events is Aung San himself. Throughout the Ne Win years the army claimed Aung San as the great martyred hero of the military, its source of inspiration and guidance. Then, in 1988, the legendary general's daughter returned to Burma and formed a political party which became the army's biggest rival. As if to add insult to injury, Aung San Suu Kyi bears a striking resemblance to her father: she has the same high cheekbones and captivating almond-shaped eyes. It seemed inconceivable that the man considered to be the father of the army could also be the father of the army's greatest enemy.

The regime's response was gradually to extract Aung San from his historical role. This was no easy task. Aung San is a revered Burmese hero, and his portrait hangs in homes and offices across the country. His name graces the national sports stadium and Rangoon's central market, among other buildings, and his face was printed on Burmese banknotes. New banknotes began to appear bearing less complicated figures, like the mythical Burmese lion, the *chinthe*. Martyr's Day, once a solemn army commemoration of Aung San's death, was downscaled, and Aung San's name is no longer mentioned in army speeches.

In a similar manner, the generals have also been trying to edit

Aung San Suu Kyi out of present-day politics. She has spent most of the fifteen years since her return to Burma under house arrest in her run-down family home. When she was released for the first time, in 1995, it soon became apparent that her popularity remained undiminished. Euphoric crowds gathered in front of her gate to hear her speak, and foreign journalists flooded into Burma to interview her. The authorities placed barbed-wire barricades at each end of the street on which she lives and resorted to publicly ridiculing her, publishing demeaning caricatures of her and running a television programme in which she was featured as a toothless hag.

But, despite the regime's efforts, father and daughter remain, in *Nineteen Eighty-Four* speak, stubbornly unvaporized. Aung San is still a symbol of wise and just leadership, and Aung San Suu Kyi remains an adored figure of hope for many Burmese people. Photographs of Aung San Suu Kyi are forbidden from circulating in Burma. But in some markets around the country you can still buy a family portrait of Aung San bouncing his toddler daughter on his knee.

On the afternoon of Armed Forces Day I met an American friend of mine who was living in Rangoon. He showed me a warning that had been issued by the US Embassy to American citizens living or staying in the city. It stated that a bomb had exploded near the Sule Pagoda, a well-attended pagoda located next to Rangoon's City Hall. Two bystanders had been killed, and others had been injured. Another bomb had been discovered elsewhere in the city. The warning suggested that the bombs were intended to disrupt Armed Forces Day, and advised American citizens to avoid major tourist sites and central Rangoon for the rest of the day.

That evening I watched the news on television. There was no mention of the bombs, but there was a lot of coverage of the Armed Forces Day parade. Even on the small television in my hotel room, it was an awesome and formidable sight. The parade took place within the shadow of the golden bell-shaped spire of the Shwedagon Pagoda. Hundreds of soldiers in dress uniform marched in perfect unison across the wide parade ground of Resistance Park. After the parade, soldiers knelt down as the generals' wives hung thick garlands of white jasmine flowers around their necks.

The only time I have ever talked to an army man at any length was when I happened to hire a trishaw that was driven by an ex-soldier. He told me he had been dismissed from the army because he had killed a man in a drunken brawl. 'Weren't you put in jail?' I asked. He replied vaguely that the army looks after its own. Before he joined the army, he said, he had worked on his father's farm in a small village in central Burma. Like many young men from poor rural families, he was lured to a military career by promises of a sustainable and prosperous future. His children would be able to benefit from the superior education at an army school, and if he or his family became sick they could be treated at army hospitals. He told me he missed his life in the army. 'The *Tatmadaw* was my family. It was my mother, and it was my father,' he said, echoing a well-known military slogan.

One friend of mine has a younger brother who is a major in the army. 'I can't talk to him any more,' my friend told me. 'He has been totally brainwashed by them, and is no longer able to think for himself.' When his brother came to visit him at his office once, his wife was furious that he had let an army man into their building. As soon as the soldier left she scrubbed the seat he had sat on with milk to symbolically erase the taint of the *Tatmadaw*.

T**HE NEXT TIME** I met the publisher Ko Ye was in a posh Rangoon hotel called Traders. The hotel's high-ceilinged, air-conditioned lobby is an oasis of calm after the noisy, steaming-hot streets of central Rangoon. Pages in silk *longyi* pad softly around the marble floors, and Western businessmen in smart suits stride purposefully about with copies of the *International Herald Tribune* tucked under their arms. Ko Ye had called me a few days earlier to tell me that the Foreign Exchange Certificate (FEC) was about to be removed from circulation. The FEC was used by the government as a method of shoring up reserves of US dollars. One FEC was equivalent to one dollar, and tourists had to exchange 300 dollars for FECs on arrival at Rangoon's airport. Though both FEC, and dollars could be used at hotels and for large purchases, the kyat was still the most common currency in use in Burma. When Ko Ye called, I counted up my remaining FECs. I had twenty left—enough for afternoon tea at Traders, we reasoned.

The Traders tea lounge is lit by twinkling chandeliers. The silk-lined chairs and glass-topped tables are set among a forest of indoor plants. Ko Ye and I chose a quiet corner and ordered a cappuccino each. Nearby, two expatriate housewives sat over slices of Black Forest gateau and a pot of Earl Grey tea. A group of foreign and Burmese businessmen were drinking early cocktails at another table. As piano music tinkled across the room, Ko Ye leaned back in his chair, lit a cigarette, and gave me the gossip on the mysterious events that had precipitated the FEC's removal.

A few months earlier, when rumours rippled through Rangoon that one of the country's private banks was about to go bankrupt, it was thought the other nineteen private banks might also be on the verge of collapse, and depositors flocked to the counters to withdraw their savings. Banks were forced to put a weekly withdrawal limit on each customer's account, and people had to queue for hours and weeks to take their money out bit by bit. Soon the banks ran out of cash and had to cease transactions. There were reports of a major kyat shortage—which meant that businesses, and perhaps even the government, might not be able to pay their staff at the end of the month. Economists speculated that the banks had been dispensing loans well beyond their capital reserves and the government's central bank was unable to bail them out as would be the case in other countries. Others thought the generals had simply run out of ink and paper to print money. Whatever the truth, it was impossible to know for sure, said Ko Ye, because the government had ordered a ban on all news connected with banks.

A waitress lifted two extraordinarily frothy cappuccinos from a silver tray and placed them in front of us. I took the opportunity to interrupt Ko Ye. The news blackout was an aspect of Burmese life that particularly intrigued me. If you can't read the news in newspapers and magazines or watch it on television, how do you find out what's going on around you?

Ko Ye grinned as he poured sugar into his coffee. 'We Burmese', he began, 'are experts at looking for what's not there. It's something you should learn to do too. You must look for what's missing, and learn how to find the truth in these absences.' He gave me an example. Before the country's banks started to collapse, you could read about the banking system in magazines. At the peak of the crisis, however, the country's leading economics magazine carried a cover story about traditional dyes for silk *longyi*. Sophisticated news-watchers, knew that something must be afoot. 'When a subject drops from the news you can be pretty sure there's something going on in that field,' said Ko Ye.

'The other thing you can do is look carefully at the environment around you,' suggested Ko Ye. 'And you don't need a newspaper to do that.' The exchange rates on the black market were one informal indicator. The black-market rate had risen from 1,000 kyat to 1,300 kyat to the US dollar, but since the recent shortage the kyat had gained strength and a dollar was now worth only 900 kyat. (Incidentally, the official rate remained the same: an unrealistic 6.3 kyat to the dollar.) 'As I go around town each day, I look for clues,' said Ko Ye. 'I see ration queues getting longer, and notice that cigarettes have gone up by five kyat per cigarette.'

I thought back to my own experiences in Rangoon, and realized that I had also been stumbling upon discreet hints about what was going behind the scenes: I just hadn't known how to read them. I recalled the energetic newspaper boys who plied the busy intersection near Rangoon's central market, beneath the towering spire of an old church. Whenever I was in a taxi stuck in the congested traffic amid the diesel fumes and the impatient blare of car horns, one of the boys would come and tap on the car window. The boys sold used copies of the *Bangkok Post* and other English-language newspapers from around the region. The papers had been discarded by foreign guests at the big hotels and were sometimes weeks old, but the boys always did a good sales job and I often bought one. If there was a photograph of Aung San Suu Kyi, they would have the paper folded open at that page, careful to keep it covered by a football magazine or some other innocent rag. As soon as they had my attention they would wink and reveal the Lady's photograph. Now, thinking about it, I realized I hadn't seen the boys for days. The only hawkers at the intersection were selling cigarettes, ready-wrapped betel quids or strings of flowers for drivers to hang over their rear-view mirrors. At the time, Aung San Suu Kyi had been released from house arrest and was allowed to travel to certain parts of Burma with other NLD party leaders. The newspaper boys had been tolerated while Aung San Suu Kyi was safely under lock and key, but, now that her enduring popularity was being demonstrated by enthusiastic crowds which welcomed her wherever she went, the government wanted to keep any possible reminders of her out of sight.

Ko Ye summoned one of the elegant waitresses moving around the room, carrying slices of cherry-topped cakes and multi-layered sandwiches. As she leaned down to talk to us, I caught a whiff of jasmine from the fresh blossoms pinned in her hair. Ko Ye asked her if we could pay for our coffee with FECs. 'Of course,' she said, 'but today is the last day. Tomorrow we will no longer be able to accept them.' I still had ten FECs to spend, so we ordered another cappuccino each and as the waitress went to see to our order Ko Ye turned to me and said, 'You see? That's how you can pick up little snips of information. You ask an innocent question and you get a little bit of knowledge here and a little bit there, and then you add it all up and work out what the situation is.'

A few days earlier a friend of mine had explained how he used this pick-and-mix method to sort through the many rumours that flitted around Burma. 'We must carefully analyse everything we hear,' he said. 'We are told rumours by our friends, our family, at work, in the bazaar. And then we have to analyse the sources. It's like a game. The truth is hiding from us, and we must try and find it.' As an example, he mentioned three rumours that were doing the rounds in Rangoon: a skirmish between monks and police had taken place in a suburb of Rangoon, a navy ship had been sunk in the harbour, and thirty schoolchildren had died after their teachers had slipped sleeping pills into their jaggery drink. It's important to be able to tell which of these is false, said my friend. (It was the third one.) In the newsless society of Burma, events can easily be exaggerated or distorted. 'It's like Chinese whispers,' I suggested. 'No,' he corrected me: '*Burmese* whispers.'

By far the most trusted source of news are the daily radio programmes broadcast to Burma by the British Broadcasting Corporation (BBC), the Voice of America (VOA) and the Democratic Voice of Burma (DVB). To try to prevent people from listening to these, the government occasionally jams the signals. A few years ago a 70-year-old man was sentenced to two years in prison for listening to a VOA broadcast in a tea shop. The radio stations use secret correspondents in Burma who take great risks to get stories out of the country, using borrowed phone lines or hidden satellite phones which are difficult to track. But, for most Burmese, communicating with the rest of the world is next to impossible. While I had been in Mandalay, a Muslim friend of mine had asked me to help him pass on some news about a riot that had taken place in a small town in northern Burma. A local mob had set fire to Muslim houses and shops, including a *madrasah,* or Muslim school. My friend gave me a note which reported that 250 of the 300 boys who had been in the *madrasah* were still missing. The note was hurriedly written on a scrap of paper, and many of the words had been crossed out and corrected. Coming, as it did, so far from any of the resources of Rangoon, where there are foreign embassies and non-governmental organizations (NGOs), it had the desperate air of a message stuffed into a bottle and tossed out to sea.

The anti-Muslim riot also had a greater significance. The regime uses communal violence as a technique to deflect attention from other big news events in the country, and riots are usually instigated by fake monks—soldiers who shave their heads and don robes.

As Ko Ye and I finished our final cappuccinos, I gazed at the potted plant behind him. Ko Ye leaned back comfortably into the cushions of his chair, and lit a cigarette. There was nobody sitting in the seats next to us. A waitress glided past in her velveteen slippers and smiled sweetly. I looked at the plant again, and began to worry that it might be bugged. It seemed placed so strategically close to the table. As I wondered whether to tell Ko Ye what I was thinking, he grinned at me through a cloud of cigarette smoke. I decided that I was becoming excessively paranoid. A few days earlier I had lost one of the notebooks in which I had recorded my interviews with people I had met in Burma. Though I had taken care never to mention people's real names, and had invented such an elaborate code for places and events that I sometimes had difficulty deciphering them later, its loss was deeply unsettling. I turned my hotel room inside out to search for it, and eventually found it exactly where I had hidden it: behind the toilet cistern.

Instead of telling Ko Ye about the possible bug in the potted plant, I asked him how he stayed sane. 'I operate with the understanding that they always know what I am doing, that they are always watching me,' he said. 'Every move I make is a calculated risk. And I make it knowing that I can answer for everything I do. Doing anything in Burma—anything at all—is risky. But that's the only way to live. You can't exist within this system without taking risks.'

I handed the last of my FECs to the waitress and we walked out of the cool interior into the sauna-like heat of a Rangoon afternoon.

ONE OF MY favourite streets in Rangoon was not far from the regime's ministerial offices at the Secretariat. It was a quiet road, just east of the hectic downtown area. The buildings on either side were built by the British to house government staff who worked at the Secretariat. There were small houses and two-storey apartment blocks constructed of brick, with wrought-iron balconies that had been painted a cheerful Granny Smith green. Palm trees arched high above the houses. Children played in the scrappy gardens, and grandmothers sat gossiping on their porches over glasses of lemonade. At one end of the street was a pavement tea shop open only in the early mornings. Plastic stools were spread out beneath the shade of a rain tree. When the sun moved higher in the sky and the shade disappeared, the tea-shop owner packed his stools and kettle on to a trolley and wheeled his business elsewhere.

Whenever I was in Rangoon I always found an excuse to wander along there. One morning, as I turned into the street on my way to visit a friend, I noticed a large truck parked in front of one of the houses. Piled on to the back of the truck was a small mountain of furniture tied down with jute rope. There were wooden beds, rolled-up bamboo sleeping mats, an antique vanity table with a cracked mirror, and boxes of kitchen utensils and children's toys. A few days later I saw more trucks and smaller vans being loaded up with household goods; everyone on the street seemed to be moving. Within weeks the buildings had been emptied. I walked up to one of the houses. Sheets of newspaper fluttered about in the desolate hallway, and the shards of a broken vase littered the doorstep.

In the local newspaper I read a report about the multi-million-dollar development project that had been planned for the area. The complex would include luxury housing, shopping malls and state-of-the-art office space catering to Rangoon's resident and foreign business community. The demolition work began almost as soon as the last resident had been evicted. Men with heavy pickaxes smashed out the windows and broke down the brick walls. The street took on the feeling of an archaeological site as women in tatty straw hats picked among the rubble and sorted it into piles of reusable material. They prised rusty nails out of wooden window frames, and scraped the plasterwork off bricks and beams. The roof shingles were stacked into neat rows along the road for waiting trucks to take away. Almost every scrap of these old British buildings was destined for reuse.

Before I left Rangoon to travel to Orwell's next posting, in Moulmein, I went back to the street to have one final look. There was nothing left except a shack on the side of the road that was patched together from faded blankets, splintered wooden shutters and doors too riddled with termites to reuse. The empty foundations where the houses and apartments had stood were now ponds filled up with rainwater, and the palm trees towered jarringly above the empty swamp. Three naked boys played in one of the ponds, splashing the sluggish grey-green water high into the air.

*Four*

# MOULMEIN

In the end the Party would announce that two and two

made five, and you would have to believe it.

*Nineteen Eighty-Four*

ISN'T IT TOO beautiful?' asked the grey-haired woman sitting next to me at the dinner table as she handed me a porcelain plate.

The plate, slightly yellowed with age, was decorated with a quintessentially English scene: a thatched cottage surrounded by bushes of pink and lavender flowers. A gravel path wound through the garden towards the front door, which had been left ajar. On the upper floor of the cottage, a smiling girl with blonde plaits waved her hand from a window the size of a postage stamp. The scene was surrounded by minuscule forget-me-nots that formed an intricate wreath around the edge of the plate.

I admired the plate for a respectable few moments, and then passed it to another elderly woman sitting on my left. She took it reverently with both hands. 'This plate is probably older than all of us,' she said. 'You simply don't see such beautiful things in Burma any more.'

I was sitting in the house of Beatrice Thompson, an Anglo-

Burmese woman who lives in the southern town of Moulmein. I had met Beatrice's sister a few years ago while studying the Burmese language at London University. She gave me Beatrice's telephone number, and told me to call her before I went to Moulmein. When I rang Beatrice from Rangoon, she insisted on coming to pick me up from the train station. How will I recognize you? I asked. 'You will know me from my blue eyes,' she replied.

The day-train from Rangoon travelled north around the Gulf of Martaban and then south towards Moulmein. At the station in Rangoon I had been told that foreigners were only allowed to purchase upper-class tickets, and so I spent the ten-hour journey on a tatty reclining seat in an almost empty carriage as the train rattled noisily past endless paddy fields, tiny villages and the towering limestone outcrops that characterize the scenery of southern Burma.

It was dark by the time I arrived in Martaban, the nearest stop to Moulmein, and an evening drizzle had sent the station into chaos. Vendors spread tarpaulin sheets across their stalls, and passengers huddled beneath the leaking roof of the station platform. The electricity was not working, and the only light came from the dozens of candles which vendors had lit above their stalls. Crowds of people were moving in all directions, and the muggy air was thick with the smell of betel and engine oil. Candle wax dripped like cake icing on to a small mound of papayas. A basket full of plucked chicken carcasses glistened ghostly pink. A group of laughing monks, swathed in blood-red robes, loomed out of the darkness, their shaved heads luminous in the candlelight. I wandered blindly around the station, trying to find the exit. Suddenly, above the babble of the crowd, I heard a crisp English accent close to my ear: 'Hello, dear.' I turned round to find Beatrice standing calmly amid the mayhem. She wore a pearly-blue top and a matching *tamein* tucked tight around her bulging hips. Her silvery hair was tied on top of her head in a perfectly round bun. She smiled at me warmly and, in the gloomy light, I could just make out the pale blue of her eyes.

Moulmein lay across a river from the train station, and Beatrice hustled me along to the docks where we would catch a boat to cross the waters. She was a model of efficiency, poking people with her black umbrella, nudging vendors out of the way, and bad-mouthing a boatman who tried to overcharge me for the crossing. On the boat, she pulled two empty plastic bags out of her voluminous handbag and laid them across the damp wooden plank that served as a seat: one for her and one for me. As the boat set off across the pitch-black waters, she opened her umbrella and held it over us to fend off the night rain.

Moulmein loomed ahead of us, a dark mass of low buildings, lit here and there by the occasional lamp. Above them, I could just make out the outline of a high ridge on which a number of pagodas stood decked in sparkling fairy lights. Beatrice and I huddled beneath her umbrella and watched as the town came into focus. Dark box-like shapes gradually turned into closed-up shop-houses with barred windows and padlocked doors. The fringed silhouettes of flame trees appeared along the waterfront. Before long, the boat was tied up at an empty pier and passengers scrambled hurriedly up the slippery incline of the gangplank. Beatrice, commanding the steady hand of one of the boatmen, alighted with regal aplomb, while I shuffled inelegantly behind her. She quickly summoned a waiting trishaw driver from the shadows and took me to my guest house. There she gave me fifteen minutes to drop off my luggage, freshen up, and join her and her friends for a late supper.

Beatrice's friends consisted of three other Anglo-Burmese women. They were retired schoolteachers, none of them had married, and they referred to themselves as 'our merry band of spinsters'. We sat in Beatrice's front room—a simple space lit by a large church candle that stood in a surprisingly grand pewter candle-holder (from her English father's family, Beatrice explained). Tea consisted of Burmese cold noodle salad with chicken curry. The women ate with their hands, apologizing graciously for doing so. 'It just tastes so much better this way,' said one. After supper Beatrice laid out a plate of peanut brittle and began pouring tea from a large teapot. The teacups were decorated with a fleur-de-lis pattern, but they were cheap reproductions from China and everyone commented on the difference. Beatrice explained how hard it was to preserve the old English porcelain. All her pieces had cracked during the past decades. All she had left from her childhood, she said, was the pewter candlestick and the plate with the waving girl.

'Moulmein used to be such a prosperous town,' sighed the thin, pinched-faced woman who was sitting next to me. 'The town was famous for its food, you know. I remember when we fed on lobster every night. Now a lobster costs more than all our monthly incomes put together.'

The women reminisced for a while about the golden days of

Moulmein, and then Beatrice interrupted them with a heavy sigh. 'You know, dear,' she said to me, 'our government is bad— very bad. It took our wonderful, precious country and broke it into pieces. Now we are all condemned to living in a kind of purgatory from which there is no release.'

'Careful what you say, Beatrice,' chided one of the women in a sing-song voice. 'Careful what you say!'

I wanted to hear more about what Beatrice had to say, so I tried to keep her on the topic by commenting on how huge crowds of people were showing up to see Aung San Suu Kyi and hear her speak as she travelled across Burma. Perhaps, I suggested, this was a sign that the generals might be easing up and that change would come soon. Nobody said anything. The pinch-faced woman's eyes followed the lilies around the rim of her teacup. Beatrice busied herself with folding up a napkin. After a painfully long silence I reached for a piece of peanut brittle and commented on how delicious it was.

The conversation immediately resumed in a safer vein. We talked about my train journey. 'The railway system is an absolute disgrace these days,' said one woman, shaking her head in disgust. 'I have never been on a train in recent years that arrived on time!' Another woman asked in quaint English where I was 'putting up'. 'What a shame that you can't stay with one of us,' she said. Beatrice explained that she had asked the local authorities if they would allow her to have a foreign guest at her house, but they had refused. 'And of course there's nowhere really respectable to stay in Moulmein any more,' muttered the thin woman next to me.

The women wouldn't talk directly about politics, but they were, I realized, happy to criticize the government indirectly by blaming the generals for the rising cost of lobsters and the late trains. An hour later, when they still hadn't worn themselves out, Beatrice suggested I might want to retire after my long journey. I excused myself gratefully and returned to the guest house, promising to drop in for afternoon tea the following day.

ORWELL'S MOTHER, Ida Mabel Limouzin, grew up here in Moulmein. I had asked Beatrice and her friends about the Limouzin family, but none of them had recognized the name. One of the women thought there was a street named Limouzin somewhere east of the town centre, down by the old timber yards. I had seen the street mentioned in an old English guide-book, and the following day I set off to find it.

It is easy to see how Moulmein was once considered the most beautiful town in Burma. The main road is lined with graceful old buildings that once belonged to colonial merchants. But the pink and cream façades are now faded, the stuccowork entablatures and rosettes that decorated them are cracked, and patches of damp have spread across the walls like a watercolourist's impression of a moody monsoon sky. There are aged mosques with curvaceous ogee arches and sky-blue domes. Though more recently built shop-houses are dotted between the older buildings, with stores selling electrical goods, stationery or groceries, the road has an abandoned feeling to it, as if everyone has shut up shop and gone away for the summer. The windows are covered with wooden shutters, and behind gates locked with rusting pad-locks the gardens are choked with weeds.

The first Limouzin recorded in Moulmein was a Frenchman, from Bordeaux, called G. E. Limouzin, who moved here just after the British annexation of Lower Burma in 1826. At that time Moulmein was little more than a fishing village. It was, however, strategically located at the confluence of three rivers that pour down from the surrounding mountain ranges. It has a naturally sheltered harbour which connects it to the Andaman Sea, and it once provided a useful link to caravan routes that led over the mountains into Siam (present-day Thailand). The British con-quered the area and laid the foundations for Moulmein with a sin-gle street that ran along the river, a military garrison and a bazaar. The forests around the settlement, populated by tigers and ele-phants, proved to be a valuable source of teak, and the area soon attracted timber merchants and shipbuilders from around the world. One of these was Orwell's great-grandfather—G. E. Limouzin. In the one-street British outpost of Moulmein, he founded Limouzin & Co., a company that specialized in building wooden ships. By the time he died, in 1863, Moulmein had become a cosmopolitan trading centre for Indian, British, Ger-man, French, American, Armenian and Chinese merchants, and Limouzin & Co. was one of the most prosperous companies in town.

Limouzin was survived by at least two sons, one of whom was Orwell's grandfather, Frank Limouzin. Little is known about Frank except that he was reputed to have been an expert painter, a fine singer, and a lively fixture on the Moulmein social circuit.

After Frank's first wife died, he married again and had nine children, among whom was Ida, Orwell's mother.

A year before Orwell arrived in Moulmein to head the police headquarters in 1926, his grandmother—well known in the town for her popular dinner parties and tennis gatherings—died. By that time Moulmein was already enshrouded in what one British travel writer described as 'an air of gentle decay'. In the mid-nineteenth century, as the British took over parts of Upper Burma, they set up their capital in the more developed city of Rangoon. Moulmein's boom time was over, and the once busy timber mills and shipbuilding yards were closed down. The town evolved into a favourite retirement spot where British colonial servants came to unwind and live out their days. In the 1960s, after Ne Win nationalized all private businesses in Burma and drove foreign merchants out of the country, Moulmein witnessed a mass exodus of English, Anglo-Burmese and Indian families. The town's renowned mission schools, once staffed by British and American priests and nuns, were taken over by the government. And Moulmein was left to slide still further into decay. As a friend in Rangoon said to me, 'There is no longer anything left in Moulmein. There is no business, no life, no nothing. Moulmein is nothing more than a village with big buildings.'

I walked down the street away from the town centre, and the old merchants' houses began to give way to small wooden shacks interspersed with white-cement shop-houses. I passed an old teak mill, overgrown with vines and wild banana trees. A tall brick chimney stood in the middle of the yard, festooned like a maypole in long, green tendrils. Not far from there I found the street sign I was looking for. It was a bright blue sign imprinted with Burmese script which read '*Leimmaw-zin*', the nearest Burmese pronunciation for 'Limouzin'.

I walked up Limouzin Street. It was a tidy little street with a smooth tarmac surface and tin-roofed houses tucked away behind low white walls. Here and there unruly fronds of orange bougainvillea spilled over the fences and on to the pavement. A row of manicured bushes ran along the base of a pagoda wall. As I strolled up the slight incline I heard the faint sounds of radio music seeping out from some of the houses, but I didn't meet a single person. At the top of the street, where it connected to a busier main road, I asked a passer-by if he knew what the street name, '*Leimmaw-zin*', meant. Yes, he said confidently: '"*Leimmaw*" means "orange" and "*zin*" is a kind of shelf. In Burmese, we call this Orange-Shelf Street.'

I RETURNED to Beatrice's home later that afternoon. I noticed it looked much more shabby by daylight. Beatrice lives alone in two rooms on the ground floor of a concrete house. She has one room for a bedroom, and uses her front room as her kitchen and dining area. In her small back garden grows a guava tree bearing fruit the size and colour of tennis balls. Beatrice apologized to me for the condition of her house. She used to live in a beautiful place down on old Dalhousie Road in the centre of town, she told me, but it had been torn down and now this was all she could afford.

Beatrice had already prepared the tea, and her matching

teapot and fleur-de-lis cups sat waiting on a plastic tray. On a plate next to them was a selection of biscuits arranged in neat circular whorls. 'Shall we take tea in the garden?' she asked. 'It's such a beautiful afternoon.' It was indeed a glorious day, with brilliant blue skies and cotton-wool clouds that might have been lifted straight out of a child's storybook. I carried the tea tray out to a small fold-away table in the garden, and we lounged back into two deckchairs which Beatrice told me she had borrowed from a neighbour for the occasion. As she poured the tea, Beatrice described how she used to teach piano and sewing to girls at the local convent. 'That was the way I was brought up, you know. I could dance and draw passable portraits of my sisters. And . . .' She stopped herself. 'But these are not things which are important any more.' Beatrice now works from her front room as a seamstress, mending clothes.

Beatrice's father was English, born into an army family in the Maymyo hill station. He grew up in Burma and worked in the telegraph service for many years, marrying a Burmese woman and staying on even after independence. But he left Burma shortly after Ne Win came to power, when Beatrice was just eighteen years old. 'Sometimes I think of him more as a Burmese man than an English one,' she said. At home in Burma with his wife and six children he spoke Burmese and ate Burmese food. 'When he returned to England he sent me a long letter complaining about the weather,' said Beatrice with a laugh.

Though there are few Anglo-Burmese left in Burma, the country reportedly had more Eurasians than all of India. The ofspring of liaisons between British men and Burmese women formed a close-knit group who hovered above the Burmese yet beneath the British in the colonial social spectrum. Anglo-Burmans were generally not welcomed into British society and were forbidden from joining the European-only clubs. Orwell paints a frightful picture of two Anglo-Burmese in *Burmese Days*.

In Katha, the town where John Flory lives, there are two Eurasians, named Mr Francis and Mr Samuel. Francis is 'as brown as a cigar-leaf, being the son of a South Indian woman' and Samuel, whose mother was from the Karen ethnic minority, is 'pale yellow with dull red hair'. The woman Flory is courting, the pink-skinned Elizabeth Lackersteen, is horrified that Flory deigns to talk to them. She finds him one day standing at the club gates listening to Francis describe his father, an American Baptist missionary with two wives and who wrote a booklet called *The Scourge of Alcohol* (sales of which were dampened by the missionary's well known passion for rice wine). Francis explains that when the bishop used to visit his father the young Francis was dressed in a *longyi* and was sent to stand with the neighbouring Burmese children so as to remain incognito. The two Eurasians greet Elizabeth enthusiastically: 'Good evening to you, madam, good evening, good evening! Most honoured to make your acquaintance madam! Very sweltering is the weather these days, is not?' Elizabeth, however, ignores them, considering it an impertinence that they should even address her. Later, Flory tries to explain to her how wretched their lives are: how they live around the bazaar doing odd jobs for an Indian moneylender, and how they would probably starve if the Burmese didn't provide them with charity. 'Their drop of white blood is the sole asset they've got,' he says.

'Another biscuit?' offered Beatrice graciously. Each time I took one, she carefully rearranged the plate so that the empty space I had created was filled. I asked her why her father hadn't taken her back to England with him. 'I was in school at the time,' she explained. 'It just seemed best to remain behind with my aunts and finish my studies. And soon it was too late.' As Ne Win's rule progressed and the country gradually closed itself off to the rest of the world she lost her opportunity to travel abroad. Her father never came back to Burma, and ten years after he left the country he died in England. Most of her cousins and some of her siblings had seized the opportunity to leave before it became too difficult, and Beatrice's family is now scattered across the world from San Francisco to Sydney. 'Moulmein feels like a ghost town to me now,' she lamented. 'This whole street used to be all Anglo-Burmans,' she said, vaguely waving her hand toward the houses beyond her tiny lawn. 'Now it is filled with new people. There are only a few of us left—not very many at all. And most of us are rather old.'

Many of the remaining Anglo-Burmans who didn't leave Burma have been totally assimilated into Burmese society. They have married Burmese partners, and the handful of their children that I met don't look as if they have any European blood. This living legacy of Burma's colonial era has effectively vanished itself. However, when Beatrice spoke about the Burmese she didn't say 'we', she said 'they' , so I asked her whether she felt Burmese or English. 'I am not accepted as Burmese and I cannot be English, so I prefer to just be,' she replied. 'I am simply living my life as best I can. I don't feel any need to label myself as one thing or the other.'

Beatrice changed the subject abruptly, picking up the topic she had begun the previous night before her friends had hushed her. 'Burma is a bad place now,' she said again. 'You just have to stand up in this country and you will get shot down before you know what has happened.' She spoke without self-pity, and had a melodious way of enunciating each word like a patient English teacher. 'You see, we are intelligent people. We know right from wrong, and yet we are not allowed to make any decisions for ourselves. Our lives are totally controlled. If there is anything we want to do we must first apply for permission from the authorities. And they always say no. We are treated just like children. But, when we have problems, there is no one for us to turn to. There is no one we can ask for help. We must solve our problems by ourselves.' She briskly wiped some biscuit crumbs off her jade-green *tamein* and then continued, 'Suppose the electricity is not working. What can we do? We can go to the municipality and complain, but they will tell us they cannot do anything about it. And if we complain one too many times they will start to make trouble for us.'

This fear of the authorities was a constant refrain from the people I spoke to in Burma, and I had asked a retired Burmese psychiatrist living in Rangoon about how the regime has so effectively cowed people into submission. 'It is generally accepted that humans should live by a set of unspoken rules,' he explained. 'If you are unhappy with something in your environment, you can speak out. In your country, you might write a complaint letter to a newspaper, or join an organized protest. Here, in Burma, people cannot do that. Here we have no such rules. The only rules we have are those of the generals.' Since the generals can use the rules in any way they want to, with their 'rubber-band' laws, people are too scared to speak out—even to complain about a power shortage or a broken telephone line. 'The randomness inherent in this system means you can never be sure what the consequences of your actions may be,' said the psychiatrist. 'The people here live in terror. It's better for us just to keep our mouths shut.' When the European Parliament awarded Aung San Suu Kyi the 1990 Sakharov Prize for Freedom of Thought, she emphasized this point in her acceptance speech, which was read *in absentia* and was later published in her book *Freedom from Fear*. She listed the different kinds of fear that paralyse people in Burma: 'Fear of imprisonment, fear of torture, fear of death, fear of losing friends, family, property or means of livelihood, fear of poverty, fear of isolation, fear of failure.' And she concluded, 'It is not easy for a people conditioned by the iron rule of the principle that might is right to free themselves from the enervating miasma of fear. Yet even under the most crushing state machinery courage rises up again and again, for fear is not the natural state of civilized man.'

The sun had set while Beatrice and I were talking, and mosquitoes were dancing around my ankles. The sky was a lapis-lazuli blue, and bats as small as hummingbirds flitted around the branches of the guava tree.

'Do you regret not leaving when you had the chance?' I asked Beatrice. 'Yes, to tell you the truth, I do,' she said. 'But that was my life at the time. I cannot take it back. And, at the time, who could know the future? This country used to be a fabulous place, you know. It was rich in nature and people, and so very beautiful. They have managed to turn a paradise into something not much better than a living hell.' In the 1950s, when Beatrice was a teenager, all her family lived together in Moulmein. 'They were good times for us,' she said. 'We used to have dances every Saturday. Oh, they were such fun! If you had only been around then I could have taken you to one of the dances and you would have been able to see what fun we had.'

Before I left, Beatrice wrapped up the last three biscuits in a piece of paper and pressed them into my hand. 'In case you get a little peckish in the night,' she said.

The streets were empty as I walked along the river back to my guest house. In a dark mosque, an inner chamber glowed brightly revealing a small gathering of Muslims sitting cross-legged in a circle murmuring over prayer books. Further down the street I heard an insistent metallic beeping and the sound of laughter: in the ground-floor living room of a shop-house, a group of children clad in pyjamas were crowded around a video game. On the pavement nearby, a kerosene lamp lit up a string of snacks in plastic bags hung along a bamboo pole. Out across the river there was nothing to see but darkness. I could just make out the tangled shapes of water hyacinth flowing past, and the air had the slight, salty tang of the sea.

A N ADDRESS I had been given led me to one of the merchants' houses on the main street in the centre of Moulmein. A metal grille, caked with rust, was drawn across the front of a colonnade of creamy pillars. I forced a partial opening, which I was able to squeeze through only by turning sideways, and found myself in a spacious, high-ceilinged room. The floor was made of teak planks worn shiny and smooth from over a century of use. Black splotches of mould spread across the pale-green walls like bruises. There were a few chairs and a desk piled high with papers and half-empty teacups. A mangy pigeon hopped through the opening I had made and flapped skittishly around the room.

I called out a tentative hello. The sound of footsteps reverberated on the planks above my head and someone hollered down from a ladder tucked against the back wall. 'We're up here. Come up!'

The room upstairs was equally spacious, but, though it had the same worn teak floors and mildewed walls, the atmosphere was completely different. World maps and posters of English fruits were hung on the walls. Books and magazines were stacked in precarious towers, and in one corner an elderly man sat among a group of young students playing Scrabble. When he saw me he leaped up with surprising agility and shook my hand. Tha Win

Kyi used to be an English teacher at a government school, and now makes his living by conducting private English-language tutorials. I had been given his address by someone in Rangoon who learned English from him many years ago.

Tha Win Kyi instructed his students to continue with their game of Scrabble and led me to some seats in another corner of the room. He told me that he currently had more students than he could handle, and taught seven or eight hour-long classes a day. 'Our education system is absolutely going to the dogs,' he said. 'It's just getting worse and worse.' He moved some crossword puzzles aside and dusted down a chair for me to sit on. 'They no longer teach anything in the schools,' he continued. 'The pupils simply learn their lessons by heart. Everything is memorized, even subjects like mathematics. Students do not understand *why* seven multiplied by three is twenty-one: they just remember it. If you ask them to do a sum that is not in the multiplication tables they have learned they will not be able to answer you.' He leaned over and glared at me over his thick glasses. 'This is not what you or I would call an education,' he said.

Burma was once renowned for its high literacy rates and educational standards, and the wilful destruction of the education system is perhaps one of the most tragic things about the country. Many of those I spoke with referred to 'a lost generation' of young people who were not able to get a decent education, and I had met countless parents who were concerned about their children's prospects. I knew a young mother who had three daughters ranging in age from nine to sixteen. She herself had never completed secondary school, but she knew enough to be appalled by the way her daughters were being educated. She had pushed her eldest daughter in front of me and told me to ask her what she wanted to do when she finished school. The girl giggled shyly and replied that she didn't know. 'What *can* she do without knowledge?' demanded the mother. 'Without learning there is nowhere to go. You ask kids these days what they want to do and they haven't got a clue. If there is no future for them in this country, how can they have any dreams about what to do with their lives?'

Tha Win Kyi had taught for seventeen years in a government high school. In 1991 he was forced to resign. That year, after the government refused to acknowledge the result of the general elections which the NLD had won in 1990, it began weeding out disloyal civil servants. Everyone listed on government staff rosters had to sit an exam which posed thirty-three questions about the current state of affairs in Burma. Anyone who answered the questions incorrectly was sacked, forced to resign, or transferred to some distant inactive posting in the countryside.

With some questions it was obvious which answer was required:

- 'Do you support those governing the country?' (Yes)
- 'Do you support what is said on foreign radio stations?' (No)
- 'Do you want the situation to return to what it was in 1988?' (No)

But there were trickier questions:

- 'For whose benefit is the military working and what is it doing?'
- 'What would be the most suitable political system for the country?'

'I answered the questions honestly; I could not lie,' said Tha Win Kyi. A few weeks after he had completed the questionnaire the headmaster summoned him and asked him to resign. 'The reason they did this is because they don't want anyone who thinks differently from them,' said Tha Win Kyi, 'Now they have removed all the good teachers and filled our schools with yes-men.'

The grand plan, if there is a plan at all, is to abolish the power of thinking, believes Tha Win Kyi. 'Children are not encouraged to question their teachers, and when the teacher asks them a question they dare not answer. It has come to the stage where they see a thing which is not true and they dare not say that it is not true.' Tha Win Kyi told me that, in the old monastic schools, pupils were encouraged to question everything they were taught. 'The Buddha himself encouraged questioning and thinking,' he said. 'He taught us that we shouldn't blindly believe what we are told by our parents or our teachers. We must think for ourselves.'

In a corner of the room I noticed one of Tha Win Kyi's students sitting alone at a desk reading an English-language encyclopedia. The book's binding had split into three or four chunks which were held together with thick masking tape, and the tissue-thin pages had crumpled like crêpe paper. Tha Win Kyi followed my gaze and laughed. 'That encyclopedia is almost an antique,' he said. 'It was printed in 1976.' He called to the student, a skinny young man called Tin Aye, who obediently came over and sat down at Tha Win Kyi's feet, tucking his *longyi* around his knees. 'This boy is twenty-six years old and he still hasn't finished his university degree,' said Tha Win Kyi.

Universities in Burma have been closed on and off ever since the student-led uprising of 1988. When I asked a university lecturer what the schedule was for university term times in Burma, he answered, 'We don't know. They decide. This week the universities will be open; next week they will be closed.'

In hesitant English, Tin Aye told me how he had begun his five-year-long bachelor's degree in geology eight years ago. He had studied for one year and then the universities were closed down when student demonstrations broke out in Rangoon in 1996. He took a three-year enforced sabbatical, working as an assistant in a bicycle shop. When his university reopened, it was only for a few months. He is now finishing the penultimate year of his degree.

As a result of this sporadic university opening, many courses have been shortened to clear the backlog of students, and the quality of education has plummeted. Tha Win Kyi told me he had tutored a final-year geography major who didn't even know where Canada was, and he knew students studying for a degree in chemistry who had never performed a chemical experiment ('The teacher just draws the test tube on a blackboard,' he said.) I told him about a graduation ceremony I had attended at a university near Rangoon. I had been invited by a friend whose daughter had just been awarded a master's degree in English literature. Her daughter spent the sweltering morning cloaked in a nylon black gown, posing with friends and family for countless photographs. As I wandered among the crowd I tried to chat to some of the students, and was surprised to discover that few of the English-literature graduates actually spoke any English. Tha Win Kyi clapped his hands together triumphantly, 'You see?' he said.

'Now it is almost impossible to fail a university exam in Burma,' said Tha Win Kyi. 'Teachers are afraid of getting into trouble with the authorities if their students are unsuccessful, so they often give them the exam questions in advance.' Students can also bribe poorly paid teachers for higher marks. Tha Win Kyi told me he had recently been called into the school where he used to work to help mark the English exam papers when two of the other teachers had fallen ill. Attached to one exam paper, he found an envelope containing 300 kyat and a note which read, 'I did not learn the essay for "My School" or "My Town". I have only learned the one for "My Father", so that is what I have written about. Is that OK?'

'I think,' said Tin Aye clearing his throat nervously, 'that you can fail an exam in Burma only if you are completely absent from the examination hall, or if you hand in a blank sheet of paper.' He recalled waking up early to go and check the first-year-geology exam results, which were displayed on boards outside his faculty. When he got there he was disappointed to find only a sign which read, 'All students who attended the exam have passed.'

After 1988 the regime began to split the larger universities into smaller colleges. A friend of mine in Rangoon pointed out how all the new campuses were located outside the city, often across a bridge which could easily be closed down if the students began to protest again. The government also instigated a programme known as distance education. With distance education, taught by correspondence and on television, students are kept safely in their home towns and need attend the central campuses for only ten days in each academic year, in order to sit their exams. A staggering 75 per cent of Burmese students are now estimated to be studying for their university degrees through distance education.

'Few people have any faith left in our education system,' said Tha Win Kyi. There is a popular joke in Burma in which a village elder asks a young boy which standard he is studying in school. The pupil replies that he has just completed the tenth standard, the final year before university. 'Ah,' says the elder, 'so you've finished your education then.'

The ladder on the other side of the room began to shake as another group of students climbed up to attend Tha Win Kyi's afternoon English class. They were wearing the national school uniform, a green *longyi* and a white shirt, and had come straight from school for extra tutorials. Tha Win Kyi excused himself and asked Tin Aye to escort me back to my guest house.

Tin Aye dutifully gave me a ride on the back of his bicycle. It was a hair-raising journey as we swerved violently to avoid stray dogs snoozing in the road or mopeds that pulled suddenly out of gateways. Only when we got to the guest house did he tell me his bicycle had no brakes. 'It's OK,' he assured me, 'I've found an alternative method for stopping it.' He cycled forward for a short stretch and then began pedalling backwards with a fearsome momentum, his knees almost knocking against his chin and his *longyi* billowing around him like a parachute.

PERHAPS ONE of the most evocative phrases ever written by an Englishman about Burma belongs to Kipling's poem 'Mandalay':

> For the wind is in the palm trees, an' the temple-bells they say:
> 'Come you back, you British soldier, come you back to
>     Mandalay!'

The poem has undoubtedly been responsible for luring a number of travellers to the country. I once met a young British backpacker in Burma who told me he was disappointed with his Burmese tour guide for offering to sell him some opium. The guide in turn had been surprised when the tourist declined his offer. 'Isn't that what you came here for?' he asked. 'No,' declared the indignant young man, 'I came here for Kipling!'

Orwell also heard Kipling's call. As a child, he read Kipling's stories and poems which evoked all the exotic romance of the Raj in their depictions of brave British soldiers adventuring across India. And later in life Orwell admitted that the poem 'Mandalay' conjures up a compelling nostalgia that few can resist. You would have to be a snob or a liar, he wrote, if you couldn't derive at least some pleasure from such classic Kipling lines.

It is curious to learn, then, that Kipling never went to Mandalay. He visited Burma in 1889 on a ship en route from Calcutta to Japan, and stayed only three days. He spent one of those days in Moulmein, and 'Mandalay' is based on a pagoda he visited there, the Kyaik-thanlan Pagoda. One morning I went to see the site that had inspired him to send out his siren call to generations of British travellers, and perhaps to Orwell.

Moulmein is bordered to the east by a high green ridge dotted with pagodas, and Kyaik-thanlan is the tallest among them. I walked along the meandering and sometimes steep path to the top of the ridge. The brick walkway was shaded with tamarind and banyan trees, and scorpions waited under the fallen leaves, their tails arched upwards, like miniature dragons. On the top of the ridge the path wound past sleepy monasteries hidden behind moss-covered walls. The old buildings were topped with layers of rusting corrugated-iron roofs, and the walls were painted a deep orange, the colour of bruised peaches. I had removed my shoes to enter the pagoda grounds, and my feet crunched over a coarse sand of crumbled plaster that had slid from the walls. Scruffy stray dogs were curled up in damp, shady corners, and I saw groups of monks kneeling at their morning meal inside unlit teak structures.

Four covered walkways, each aligned with one of the cardinal points, lead up to the golden pagoda, which sits in the centre of a tiled platform. The compound was constructed in the ninth century, and was augmented over the centuries by successive Burmese kings. There are pavilions with ornate green-and-gold-tiered roofs that look like doll's houses piled one on top of another. A fine, golden latticework carved out of painted tin hangs like lace from the eaves. Shrines housing statues of the Buddha are covered in a dazzling mosaic of splintered mirrors and silver shards. The temple bells of Kipling's poem are hung at the highest tip of the pagoda on the *hti,* a small crown of bells and jewels that tinkles gently in the breeze. And, enshrined inside the glittering golden mass of the spire, is a single hair from the Buddha's head.

When Kipling visited this pagoda, however, he had other things on his mind: 'I should better remember what that pagoda was like had I not fallen deeply and irrevocably in love with a Burmese girl at the foot of the first flight of steps,' he wrote in his travel journal. 'Only the fact of the steamer starting next noon prevented me from staying at Moulmein forever . . .'

Kipling's other poems about Burma are less well known and much more gruesome. In one, called 'The Grave of the Hundred Head', Kipling championed the brutal reprisals wreaked by the British army on Burmese villagers who refused to succumb to foreign rule. In the poem, an Indian regiment revenge the death of their English lieutenant who was killed by Burmese rebels. They massacre an entire village and pile the severed heads of the dead above the lieutenant's grave, placing the village leader's head on top of the mound. Kipling's message to the Burmese was clear:

*That a white man's head*
*Must be paid for with heads five-score.*

Orwell maintained a love-hate relationship with Kipling all his life. 'I worshipped Kipling at thirteen,' he stated in an essay about the author, 'loathed him at seventeen, enjoyed him at twenty, despised him at twenty-five, and now again rather admire him.' This means that when Orwell first arrived in Burma he appreciated Kipling's somewhat rabid take on colonialism, but after years working within the Empire he found Kipling's politics repulsive and labelled him 'a jingo imperialist'. In his late thirties Orwell returned to a grudging respect for the poet, calling him a 'good bad poet' whose poems were a sort of guilty pleasure to be indulged.

Kipling even makes a cameo appearance in *Nineteen Eighty-Four*, when Winston Smith recognizes one of his fellow inmates in prison, a poet from the Records Department where he used to work. The poet's job had been to rewrite the classics of English literature so that they adhere to Party ideology. He was arrested after making a mistake when translating one of Kipling's poems into 'Newspeak', the soulless party dialect which eliminates all possibility of thought that is antithetical to Big Brother's rule. The poet had allowed the word 'god' to remain in the poem. ('I could not help it!' he told Smith. 'It was impossible to change the line. The rhyme was "rod". Do you realize that there are only twelve rhymes to "rod" in the entire language?') The poem in question is another bloodthirsty chant called 'Loot', in which British soldiers are egged on to plunder the pagodas of Burma:

*Now remember when you're 'acking round a gilded Burma god*
*That 'is eyes is very often precious stones;*

*An' if you treat a nigger to a dose o' cleanin'-rod*
*'E's like to show you everything 'e owns.*

From the pagoda platform I could see all of Moulmein and the surrounding countryside. The town spread out beneath me in a jungle of palm trees, and the tin roofs of houses were marked by rust-brown patches amid the blanket of thick greenery. I saw a few sturdy church towers and the tapering golden tips of other pagodas. And beyond the town, where the river spills into the sea, green islands shimmered in the haze of the horizon.

The voice of the good bad poet can still be heard in Burma. Aung San Suu Kyi, an avid reader, is said to be an admirer of Kipling's writing. She and her British husband, Michael Aris, named their son after the plucky hero of Kipling's novel *Kim*. And Aung San Suu Kyi used a Burmese translation of Kipling's poem 'If' at one of her rallies during 1988. The poem begins:

*If you can keep your head when all about you*
*Are losing theirs and blaming it on you . . .*

**M**OULMEIN IS FULL of old English churches built during colonial times. One day my search for remnants of Orwell's family led me through the open gates of an old Anglican church. It was a large building with narrow lancet windows and flying buttresses along its sides. The red bricks of its walls were tinged black from the humidity, and large patches of grey cement had been plastered here and there in places where the bricks had begun to rot away. The wooden door beneath the square clock tower was padlocked shut. Next to it was a greying marble plaque attributing the design of the church in the late nineteenth century to the architects St Aubyn & Wadling of London.

I walked along an overgrown pathway in search of someone who might be able to help me. Around the back of the church I came across a man asleep in a hammock on the verandah of a small hut. He seemed a little startled to see me, but eagerly offered to help me look through the church's old gravestones for members of the Limouzin family. Informing me that he was the caretaker, he disappeared into his hut and emerged a few moments later with his grotty singlet covered by a collared white shirt. As we walked back to the front of the church he picked up a large stick and began poking in the foliage of weeds and thorny vines alongside the path. I heard his stick tap something hard and watched him uncover a headstone that lay flat on the ground. Together, we unearthed a few more discarded headstones, but they were impossible to read—the metal inscriptions had fallen off, and the stones were caked in the mud and grime of some 150 years.

These stones were remnants from Moulmein's main cemetery, which used to be in the centre of town, explained the caretaker. Around ten years ago, the local authorities demolished the cemetery to make way for a central police station. A memo had been handed to the church informing relatives that bodies could be exhumed and moved to a new site that had been allocated for Christian burials on the other side of the ridge. The graveyard was very old, and only a few people still living in Moulmein had relatives there, so the churches gathered together members of their parishes to help salvage some of the headstones. The caretaker suggested we look inside the church, where more of the stones had been stored. We stood in front of the padlocked door for a good ten minutes while he rattled through a large collection of keys hung around a metal band that was tied to his waist. Finally one of the keys clicked in the lock and he was able to wrench open the rusting padlock. With a reluctant groan, the doors creaked ajar, emitting an acrid stench of mildew and neglect.

Inside the church were rows of worn pews, and high above them a wooden ceiling seemed to sag dangerously. The brick pillars along the nave were stained with white waves of what looked like icing sugar—damage caused by Japanese soldiers, who had used the church as a warehouse for storing salt during the Second World War, explained the caretaker. I found only a few hints of the church's former grandeur. The choir stalls were made of oak which must have been shipped from England, and were beautifully carved with vines bearing plump grapes. And, on the floor around the altar, cream, black and red tiles shone through the dust.

The caretaker led me round behind the vestry, where a narrow corridor was filled with old furniture, brooms and the remaining rescued gravestones. He dragged out the stones one by one. With a corner of his *longyi,* he wiped off the fine red dust that covered them and laid them out on the cold stone floor beneath the choir stalls. I noticed a white wooden cross, as tall as a man, leaning against a far wall. It was inscribed with a Burmese name and a recent date. 'What is that doing here?' I asked the caretaker. He told me that a few years ago the graveyard had been moved yet again—this time to make way for a new train station, which has yet to be built. The deceased man's family had emigrated, and the caretaker wanted to save the cross for them in case they ever came back. Hanging from one arm was a forlorn plastic bag filled with a few handfuls of dirt. 'Some soil from around the grave,' said the caretaker. 'We didn't have the time or resources to dig up all the bodies, and what is in this bag is all we could retrieve of this man for his family.' The new cemetery is located outside Moulmein, near a Muslim settlement. 'But there are still problems with it,' said the caretaker. 'The Muslims living there are not happy about having Christians buried on their ground. I attended a funeral there a few months ago, and we were accompanied by armed soldiers in case there was any protest from the Muslims. Imagine—soldiers at a civilian funeral! On our gravestones it says "RIP", but here in Burma even our dead cannot rest in peace.'

The caretaker pulled a small slab of black marble from the stack of headstones. He wiped the dust off the surface, and I watched with growing excitement as the words 'Eliza Emma Limouzin' appeared beneath his hands. Eliza was Frank Limouzin's first wife, who had died at the age of twenty-three in 1865. The headstone provided no details about how she died, but noted that her children Arthur (two years and eleven months) and Emily (one year and four months) were buried with her. All three of them must still lie beneath the central Moulmein police station.

We didn't find any other remnants of the Limouzin clan, and I disappointedly helped the caretaker slide the headstones back behind the vestry. Our footsteps echoed through the silent church as we walked back to the door. I looked again at the cement that held parts of the church walls together, like patches on a leaking ship, and asked the caretaker how he managed to keep the building from collapsing. He told me that the church had a very small parish as only a handful of Anglicans remained in Moulmein. 'There is much work to do here, but we cannot afford it,' he said wearily. 'All we can do is pray that the church won't fall down.' Before I left the church, I pushed some banknotes through the cobwebs strung around the donation box.

I visited a few more churches around Moulmein, hoping to find parish records that might tell me more about the Limouzin family. In one church I met a priest who couldn't help me with my search for records but was particularly outspoken against the regime. We sat in one of the empty pews as he told me how the numbers in his congregation dwindled each year. 'In the last ten years they have turned Buddhism into a fanatical religion,' he said. 'The government are building Buddhism up to be a state religion, and soon they will wipe out all other religions. They say they hated the colonialists for how they ruled Burma, but they themselves are doing the same thing. They are enforcing one language, one religion, one way of life.' The priest felt that the Burmese people are gradually being intimidated into believing that Christianity is a dangerous religion. He often found discarded crosses or statues of the Virgin Mary tossed over the wall into his church garden. 'They are told by their soothsayers that things are going wrong in their life because they have a cross or a Bible in their house,' he said.

As we talked, a sparrow flitted through a broken stained-glass window and landed on one of the pews in front of us. The priest clapped his hands to scare it away. 'How can one small handful of people rule over so many? Terror! That is the only answer,' he said. 'People are too scared to stand up to them. And they, too, they are afraid. They cannot give up power now. They know only the gun, and they are scared because they have so much blood on their hands.' I asked him if he thought the generals believed in any kind of religion. 'They have no gods,' he said with disgust. 'They are always building new pagodas and renovating old ones. They think they are making merit, but God is no fool.'

I did eventually find an old church that still retained some records, and asked one of the priests to check for any trace of the Limouzin family. When I returned a few days later he presented me with a birth certificate for one George Limouzin born on 30 September 1860 and baptized seven weeks later. The parents' names were recorded as 'Eugene Limouzin' (possibly a brother of Orwell's grandfather, Frank) and 'Ma Soe'.

'Ma Soe?' I asked, my mind racing with the implications of hearing a Burmese name linked with Orwell's family.

'Yes, Ma Soe,' said the priest, looking a little embarrassed. 'From her name, I guess that she must be a Burmese Buddhist, but I couldn't find a marriage certificate for the couple.' If one of Orwell's great-uncles had had a child with a Burmese woman, I reasoned, Orwell must have had some Anglo-Burmese cousins here in Moulmein. I thanked the priest for his help and hurried to Beatrice's house to ask her advice.

Beatrice, meanwhile, had been doing some sleuthing of her own. She had asked around the remnants of Moulmein's Anglo-Burmese society, and had found a man who remembered the Limouzin family. 'I'll introduce you to him tomorrow,' she promised me.


**W**HAT EXACTLY are you doing here in Burma?' asked Khin Maung U. I dreaded this question, and always found it difficult to answer. Unfortunately, it was usually one of the first questions that people in Burma asked me. Khin Maung U was the Anglo-Burmese man that Beatrice had tracked down, and he had come to her house to meet me. He was a rotund man with peach-coloured skin and a shock of wavy white hair. When we met he took my hand and held it for a long time in both of his. In answer to his question, I told him I was doing some research into the life of George Orwell.

'George Orwell?' He asked.

'Yes, the English writer . . .'

'Oh, you mean Uncle Eric!' he exclaimed, referring to Orwell's real name, 'Eric Blair'.

While Beatrice sat inside working at her sewing machine, Khin Maung U and I sat on a palm-leaf mat which she had spread out for us in the garden. (The deckchairs had been returned to her neighbour.) Khin Maung U told me he had never met Orwell himself, but his father had been a good friend of Orwell's, and his aunts and uncles had all known Orwell while he was in Moul-mein. Khin Maung U's English father had worked as a civil ser-vant in the British administration, and he and Orwell had played football together. 'Of course they were prevented from becoming truly close friends by Orwell's nasty addiction to the tobacco,' said Khin Maung U with a mock frown. 'Father couldn't stand the smell of smoke, and when Orwell came visiting he had to leave his rolled-up cigarettes outside on the gatepost.'

'What about the Limouzin family?' I asked. 'Do you remem-ber them?'

Khin Maung U did remember the Limouzin family. He told me they were an Anglo-Burmese family who had left Burma for England, or perhaps Australia, in the early years of Ne Win's rule. 'They lived in a part of town we called "Little England" because it was packed full of Anglo-Burmese families,' he said. If the Limouzin family were indeed Anglo-Burmese, as Khin Maung U remembers them, then Orwell had cousins who were partly Burmese. I wondered whether he had known of them or spent time with them while he was in Moulmein.

In nothing I had read about Orwell had I ever found any hint that there might have been Burmese blood in his family. Could he have been ashamed of his part-Burmese relations? The racism in-herent in colonial society was a key element of *Burmese Days*. Or-well's anti-hero, John Flory, has sallow skin, black hair and a large dark-blue birthmark which runs from his left eye to the corner of his mouth. The other members of the club like to joke that Flory may have a 'lick of the tar-brush'.

Racism, Orwell believed, was a necessary element of British

rule. Years after he left Burma, he wrote a wonderful piece on the topi, the tan-coloured pith helmet which all colonial officials wore to protect themselves from the harsh rays of an eastern sun. Orwell wrote that the British had an almost superstitious attitude to the effects of the sun and rarely dared to go outdoors without a topi. ('Take your topi off in the open for one moment, even for one moment, and you may be a dead man.') The Burmese, who were believed to have thicker skulls, did not require such protection. The topi, Orwell concluded, was a way of emphasizing the difference between the British and the Burmese—a simple but effective tool of imperialism: 'You can only rule over a subject race, especially when you are in a small minority, if you honestly believe yourself to be racially superior, and it helps towards this if you can believe that the subject race is *biologically* different.'

Yet, observed Orwell elsewhere, no matter how racist the British were, they were still able to enjoy relations with Burmese women. While the Burmese could not walk through the door of the European-only clubs, Burmese women were warmly welcomed into British bedrooms. In the early days of the British colony, many British civil servants enjoyed Burmese 'keeps', or girlfriends they kept in their houses. The practice was so common that illegitimate children of British subjects were provided for under the education code, with government grants given to any 'European child under 18 years of age whose father is dead or has left the country or cannot be found'. By the time Orwell arrived in Burma, however, the British government was actively discouraging such liaisons, and distributed circulars warning civil servants against the 'practice of co-habiting with native girls, or accepting them as presents'. The names of two horses raced at the Rangoon Turf Club around that time give some idea of how the circulars were received: 'Government Circular' versus 'Physiological Necessity'.

Khin Maung U and I chatted a bit more over the dregs of his childhood memories, but he couldn't remember much else about Uncle Eric or the Limouzin family. As we said our goodbyes, he told me that after Orwell left Burma he continued to keep in touch with his father, sending him copies of every book he wrote. After reading the novels, Khin Maung U became curious about Orwell's time there. 'They made me wonder if there was something terribly pessimistic in Eric's personality—something like you find in Charles Dickens, a streak of gloom which runs through all his work,' he said. 'I often think something really unpleasant must have happened to him when he was here in Burma.' Khin Maung U beamed widely at me. 'It would be wonderful if you could find out what that something was,' he suggested.

It would be wonderful, I thought, but at this distance in time it would be impossible to know what, if any, life-changing event could have happened to Orwell in Burma. Yet there was one aspect of his life in there that I was sometimes guiltily curious about, and that was whether he, like many of his colleagues, had taken a Burmese mistress. If Orwell did have a mistress in Burma, he never spoke openly about it, and there was only one person who remembered him ever talking about Burmese women. The English writer Harold Acton, who met Orwell later in his life, noted how Orwell reminisced nostalgically about their sweetness. He speculated that, if Orwell hadn't been hampered by such a strong social conscience, he might have given in to their charms and ended his days as a Kiplingesque hero in Burma.

The surviving scraps of Orwell's earliest experiments with writing revolve around Burmese women. The handful of poems are written on Government of Burma notepaper, indicating where they were probably composed. They are not particularly happy poems. One poem, called 'The Lesser Evil', is written in the first person and describes regular visits to a Burmese 'house of sin' where the bamboo floors are stained with betel spit and the prostitutes beg their customers to return more frequently. The poem ends when the narrator has a change of heart and, instead of going back to the brothel, chooses the 'lesser evil' and walks into a church.

Another poem, called 'Romance', begins more hopefully with the lines

*When I was young and had no sense,*
*In far off Mandalay*
*I lost my heart to a Burmese girl*
*As lovely as the day . . .*

But the three short verses turn out to be a rhythmic description of bargaining for the services of yet another Burmese prostitute.

It had always interested me how Orwell's fictional characters never fare very well with women. One recurring feature of his novels is the pre-kiss apology. In *Nineteen Eighty-Four,* as Winston Smith and Julia tumble into a grotto thick with bluebells, Winston ruins the moment by asking if Julia can even bear to look at him with his false teeth, his varicose veins, and the wear and tear of his thirty-nine years. In *Burmese Days,* John Flory and Elizabeth stand in the moonlight outside the club, surrounded by the sickly-sweet scent of the frangipani tree. As Flory pulls Elizabeth to his breast, he asks if she minds the disfiguring birthmark that covers half his face.

There is always a great sense of shame attached to male–female relations in Orwell's novels. One of the key characters in *Burmese Days* is Flory's Burmese mistress, Ma Hla May. Orwell describes her vividly as a doll-like character who smells of jasmine flowers, sandalwood and coconut oil, and has skin the colour of copper and hair coiled into an shining ebony cylinder. But Ma Hla May becomes Flory's undoing. Flory dismisses her when he begins to court the Englishwoman, Elizabeth. One fateful Sunday morning, Ma Hla May storms into the church where Flory and the rest of the British community are sitting in the pews and screams at him to give her more money. Elizabeth is horrified by the scene, but it is only when she looks at Flory and sees his dark birthmark, which seems to symbolize the taint of the colonized race, that she realizes that their relationship is over: 'She had never known till this moment how dishonouring, how unforgivable a thing it was.'

IN A BURMESE SCHOOL textbook for ten-year-old pupils there is a lesson about the eight major ethnic groups that live in Burma. Dotted around a line map of Burma are pictures of

chubby-cheeked cartoon couples wearing the traditional cos-
tume of each race. There is a Shan farmer with his flamboyantly
large rattan hat and flared trousers, and a Kachin woman with
striking geometrical designs embroidered across her *tamein*. The
text beside the map tells schoolchildren how Burma's ethnic minorities live together in blissful harmony—or, as the Burmese
phrase puts it, 'without breaking an egg or damaging the nest'.

Orwell would have scoffed at this classroom propaganda. The
sheer numbers of the many ethnic groups living inside Burma's
borders were, he believed, a time bomb waiting to explode.

Burma is one of the most ethnically diverse countries in the
world. Within the eight main ethnic groups, anthropologists
have counted over 130 distinctive sub-groups, ranging from the
former headhunting clans of Naga warriors, crowned in feathers
and the tusks of wild boars, to the Taron, a disappearing race of
Asian pygmies living in the foothills of the Himalayas. The kings
of Burma ruled over these numerous ethnic groups with varying
degrees of control. Some groups in outlying areas acknowledged
the Burmese kingdom by paying occasional tithes. Others were
only nominally linked to Burma, if at all.

When the British arrived they put Burma on the world map:
British cartographers marked out the Empire's new territory and
drew the boundaries of the country as we see it on the globe today. These lines, often heavily debated with Siam, China and the
French colonizers in neighbouring Laos, imposed upon the variety of peoples a single Burmese homeland. Like the Burmese
kings before them, the British allowed different areas varying degrees of autonomy, and they left Burma with a chaotic map of dis-

parate political needs. Some of the larger groupings, such as Shan State, an area the size of England and Wales put together, and the tiny Karenni State to the south of it, signed a tentative agreement to acquiesce to Burmese rule for a trial period of ten years, after which they would be given the right to secede. The Karen, one of Burma's largest ethnic groups, who are concentrated along the border with Thailand, refused to sign any such agreement and prepared to fight for the independent state they had hoped the British would grant them. (It was not until 2004, after over fifty years of fighting against the Burmese army, that Karen rebel forces began negotiating a ceasefire deal with the regime.)

Orwell predicted that these age-old ethnic fault lines would be the downfall of Burma. He once met a Karen in Burma who said to him, 'I hope the British will stay in Burma for two hundred years.'

'Why?' asked Orwell.

'Because we do not wish to be ruled by the Burmese,' the Karen replied.

With so many different ethnic groups hoping for at least some form of autonomy, Orwell reasoned, it would be impossible to maintain the sovereignty of the Burmese state. In a newspaper column written a year before independence, Orwell described what he thought was the essence of the problem: 'Whenever A is oppressing B, it is clear to people of good will that B ought to be independent, but then it always turns out that there is another group C, which is anxious to be independent of B. The question is *how large* must a minority be before it deserves autonomy.'

Over the course of the second half of the twentieth century,

ethnic nationalist armies in Burma multiplied and divided like living cells. They formed alliances, splintered into smaller armies,
disbanded, and started up again in what has now become a dizzy-
ing spin of abbreviations. In Shan State alone, groups that have
battled against the regime include the Shan State Army (SSA)
South, the Shan State Army (SSA) North, the Shan State National
Army (SSNA), the Shan Nationalities People's Liberation Organization (SNPLO), the United Wa State Army (UWSA), the Pao
National Organization (PNO) and the Palaung State Liberation
Party (PSLP).

For half a century, the embattled Burmese military has been
surrounded on all sides by this chaotic dissent. It used also to have
to fend off the well-armed Communist Party of Burma, which
wanted to instigate a revolution and overthrow the state. Gradually the Burmese army was able to regain control of ethnic areas:
as the state propaganda used to put it, the insurgents *ahman-taya
pyan-deh*—'came back to the truth'. In the mid-1970s Ne Win
launched the notorious *hpyat lay byat* or 'four cuts' policy, which
was designed to cut insurgents off from their key means of survival: food, funds, recruits and information. The theory was that
insurgents derived their strength from villagers who supported
the ethnic armies fighting on their behalf. Burmese soldiers razed
whole villages to the ground, forcing their inhabitants into mass
relocation camps. Villagers were, and still are, used as living shields
between the Burmese army and nationalist forces. They are
coerced into walking in front of the army's troops to act as human
minesweepers for landmines laid by the insurgents. I once met a
Padaung woman, with brass rings wound around her neck, who

was living in a refugee camp in Thailand. When the insurgent army in her area began blowing up electricity poles erected by the regime, she and her friends were forced by Burmese soldiers to stand beneath the poles to protect them from the rebels. The women had to stand alone throughout the night, one woman to a pole, and hope that the forces on their side would see them before they attacked. Hundreds of thousands of villagers caught in the crossfire of these conflicts have fled to neighbouring countries and are now stranded in and around refugee camps along Burma's borders with Thailand and Bangladesh. The sheer brutality of the *hpyat lay byat* campaign is astounding. One Karenni freedom-fighter I talked to on the Thai-Burma border joked that the four cuts included a fifth command issued to Burmese soldiers who fought against ethnic insurgents: cut off their heads.

The world of *Nineteen Eighty-Four* is divided into three power-ful superstates, one of which is Oceania, where Winston Smith lives. These three states are permanently at war with each other, fighting in the murky frontier areas between their territories. But, because the states are evenly matched, the war serves no purpose other than to boost nationalism and support for each ruling party. The details of who is fighting whom are irrelevant. The im-portant thing is the state of war itself, which means that power must be held by rulers who are able to ensure the survival of the state. 'The object of war is not to make or prevent conquests of territory, but to keep the structure of society intact,' wrote Or-well. As the Party slogan puts it, 'War is peace.'

Similarly, the main *raison d'être* of the ruling generals of Burma is to hold the country together at all costs. The regime's

'Three National Causes', listed on giant public billboards across the country, emphasize the need to maintain the unity of Burma and to prevent any external or internal forces from threatening Burmese sovereignty. Though the wars against ethnic nationalist armies are almost over—by the end of the 1990s most groups, wearied after decades of fighting, had brokered ceasefire deals with the regime—the Burmese army continues to grow. Over half of the government budget is spent on building the army's strength (education reportedly receives a paltry 4 per cent of the budget). Burma has no enemies outside its borders and now very few actively fighting within them, yet the generals have built up a troop force that is almost equal to that of the US army.

Without any real military adversaries, the generals have had to manufacture some mythical ones. One method they have used is to evoke threats from anything or anyone considered to be non-Burmese—that is, from 'the other'. For example, a government billboard orders Burmese nationals to 'Oppose those relying on external elements, acting as stooges, holding negative views.' One of the regime's main targets is Aung San Suu Kyi, whose 'otherness' they derive from her marriage to a British man. She is often referred to in the local media after her late husband's name, Mrs Michael Aris, and is labelled as an 'evil tool of foreign interests'. She has also been accused of being manipulated by the long-defunct Communist Party of Burma and of being in league with right-wing groups preparing to attack the government, with foreign embassies, and with Burmese exiles living abroad.

When the junta isn't attacking Aung San Suu Kyi it aims its xenophobia at international NGOs (which it accuses of spreading make-believe stories about atrocities committed by the Burmese army in ethnic areas) and the CIA (which it claims runs drug-smuggling cartels in the Wa hills). Bombs are periodically found in strategic locations around Rangoon, as when I was there on Armed Forces Day. The devices rarely explode, and many believe the regime plants the bombs itself, in order to create a threat to the state, or the impression of perpetual war which it needs to justify its rule.

The best-known of the seven commandments in *Animal Farm* is the final one, which states that all animals are equal. Later, as the ruling pigs grow in greed and power, they add an addendum: all animals may be equal, but some animals are more equal than others. In Burma it is the ethnic Burmese who are more equal than others, and the Burmese government practises a policy of 'Burmanization' in ethnic areas. The Shans are the largest ethnic group in Burma after the Burmese themselves, but in Shan State the Shan language is no longer taught in schools and fewer and fewer Shan-language books are allowed to be published. Shan place names have been Burmanized, and a few years ago all Shan street signs were pulled down. In 1991 the regime destroyed a key symbol of Shan heritage, an old palace in a town called Keng-tung, to make way for a government-run hotel. The palace was once the administrative home of the most powerful of the thirty-three *sawbwa,* or chieftains, who ruled Shan State until they were arrested or disappeared under Ne Win's regime.

On the other side of Burma a similar cultural genocide is taking place in Arakan State, which runs for hundreds of miles along the wild coastlands around the Bay of Bengal. A minority

Islamic group called the Rohingya, who live in the area, bear the brunt of the regime's racial hegemony. The Rohingya, descendants of Bengali, Arab and Moorish traders who first settled there centuries ago, are treated as foreign nationals and are not allowed to apply for the identity cards which Burmese citizens must carry with them at all times. Their mosques and *madrasahs* are routinely burned down, and in the early nineties some 250,000 Rohingya fled into neighbouring Bangladesh. In both Shan and Arakan states, as well as in other states in Burma, there are reports that Burmese soldiers have been issued with orders to rape ethnic women in a literal spreading of Burmese seed.

Meanwhile, in the school books, the cartoon couple that represent the Burmese stand to one side of the map, an arrow reaching from them to central Burma. The woman, her long *tamein* draped behind her like a wedding dress, stands demurely with her hands held in front of her. Next to her the Burmese man wears the traditional *kaung baung,* a silk turban still worn on special occasions, and black cropped jacket. He smiles and holds his arm out towards the map of Burma in a welcoming gesture.

ONE DAY, Tin Aye, the young student I had met at Tha Win Kyi's house, invited me to tea. He came to pick me up at my guest house, and I perched side-saddle on the back of his bicycle as we careered through the streets of Moulmein towards his favourite tea shop. This was a featureless concrete block in a glorious setting. A narrow balcony ran around the outside of the building, overhanging the river, which gently slapped water hy-

acinth against the foundations. From our table we had an unob-
structed view of the green-blue whale-like humps of islands that
seemed to float between us and the sea.

Tin Aye had brought along his best friend, Ye Min Kyaw, another geology student who had yet to finish his degree. The two
of them were keen to practise their English, and we had arranged
that they would read 'Shooting an Elephant', an essay of Orwell's
based on events which took place in Moulmein, and we would
discuss it together. Tin Aye rustled around in his shoulder bag
and pulled out the photocopy of 'Shooting an Elephant' I had
made for him when we last met. It had been well read: the edges
were already frayed, and large question marks were dotted in the
margins. Ye Min Kyaw ordered three cups of tea and placed on
the table a Tupperware box of *lapet thoke,* or tea-leaf salad, which
his mother had made. Slowly and methodically he stirred up the
pungent mixture of fermented tea leaves, sesame seeds, nuts, gin-
ger and garlic. We were now ready to begin.

'Shooting an Elephant' is a short, compact piece of writing
which has become one of Orwell's most celebrated essays. Written in the first person, it describes a British policeman who is
called out early one morning to see to an elephant in must that is
rampaging through the streets of Moulmein. As the policeman
follows the elephant's path of destruction (an overturned garbage
truck, a dead Indian coolie), a growing crowd of Burmese begin
to follow him. By the time he finds the elephant it has calmed
down and is placidly chewing grass in a paddy field. But the policeman, compelled by the expectancy of the crowd around him,

decides he must shoot the beast anyway, and the essay ends with the elephant's slow and agonizing death.

Moulmein used to be full of elephants, said Ye Min Kyaw. He told us that his grandfather had once owned a stable of twelve elephants that he rented out to haul logs in the timber firms still operating in Moulmein when he was a young man. Ye Min Kyaw had read bits of Orwell's essay to his 90-year-old grandfather ('I had to shout it at him, because his hearing is not so good any more,' he said laughing). His grandfather told him that during Ne Win's time many Burmese people also had to kill elephants. When the timber firms were nationalized and many of them became defunct, Ye Min Kyaw's grandfather could no longer afford to feed his unemployed beasts. 'He had to set them free in the jungle, where they died of starvation or snake-bites because they did not know how to find their own food,' said Ye Min Kyaw. 'Lots of people had to release their elephants in this way, and my grandfather told me that the jungle is full of elephant bones.'

Ordinary domesticated elephants have been part of Burmese life for centuries, but there is one particular type of elephant that has played a key role in Burmese history: the rare and revered white elephant, which is believed in Buddhist legend to be a symbol of purity and power. The kingdoms of Burma, Siam and Cambodia collected these pinkish, pearly-eyed elephants from the wild, housing them in palatial stables and honouring them with elaborate rituals. The prestige of the white elephant was so great that in the sixteenth century a war was waged between the kings of Burma and Siam over the disputed title of 'Lord of the

White Elephant'. In Burma, the white elephant's significance faded after the British exiled the final Burmese monarch in 1885 and housed his last remaining white elephant in Rangoon Zoo, where it later died. Over a century later, towards the end of 2001, a white elephant was discovered and captured in the jungles of western Burma. The Burmese regime created a media fanfare. White elephants, claimed the state newspapers, appear only during the reign of righteous rulers. The eight-year-old bull elephant was conveyed to Rangoon with much pomp and finery, shaded by traditional white umbrellas and accompanied by a military battalion. One of the most powerful three generals, Khin Nyunt, himself performed the religious rite of pouring holy water over the elephant, which was given the Pali name 'Yaza Gaha Thiri Pissaya Gaza Yaza', or 'Royal Elephant that Bestows Grace upon the Nation'. Since then, two more white elephants have been discovered, and each has been welcomed with equal ceremony into a specially built shed outside Rangoon, where the public can admire the auspicious beasts.

I asked Tin Aye and Ye Min Kyaw what they thought about these white elephants. Tin Aye turned away towards the river and feigned interest in a wooden fishing boat which drifted lazily past the tea shop, a cloud of white nets drawn up on its deck. 'We all think it is a little silly,' said Ye Min Kyaw, seeming to choose his words carefully, 'but we know that it is not a good idea to say that it is silly.' Tin Aye, who still had his back towards me, nodded energetically. I dipped my spoon into the *lapet thoke* and waited for one of them to say something else. 'Perhaps', suggested Tin Aye, 'we should discuss Orwell's essay.'

I told them about a professor I had met in Mandalay who had what I believed to be a unique interpretation of the essay. He suggested that the essay was an exploration of the Burmese phenomenon of *oan*. The Burmese word *'oan'* means literally 'to swarm', and it was the power of *oan,* or collective curiosity, theorized the professor, that made the British policeman shoot the elephant.

Ye Min Kyaw frowned slightly; he clearly had his own ideas about the essay. 'I have decided that the elephant in Orwell's essay represents colonialism,' he said. He explained that the way the elephant destroyed huts and created havoc in Moulmein was similar to the way in which colonial forces had taken over Burma. The policeman bravely tries to kill this raging spectre of colonialism, but it is too big and too powerful and will die only at its own pace. 'I also think', he added, 'that the writer is a bit confused. He is part of the colonial government, but in his heart he is on the side of the Burmese people. He wants to be on the same side as the Burmese people, but he cannot. He is a white man, so he must act like a white man.'

By the time Orwell moved to Moulmein he was most probably ambivalent about the colonial state of which he was a part. The Kipling-inspired romance of the Raj had been worn thin by the daily realities of his job in which, as he wrote in 'Shooting an Elephant', he witnessed 'the dirty work of Empire at close quarters'. The essay begins with the line: 'In Moulmein, in Lower Burma, I was hated by large numbers of people—the only time in my life that I have been important enough for this to happen to me.' Orwell writes how he was trapped between his own resentment towards the Empire and the Burmese people's resentment towards him. In his isolation, he imagines that Burmese monks are jeering at him, and when he is tripped up on the football field by a Burmese player the referee deliberately looks the other way while the crowd roars with laughter. As a member of the ruling power, Orwell is cornered into doing what the 'natives' expect of him: 'He wears a mask, and his face grows to fit it.'

Tin Aye poured some tea into his saucer to cool it down, and sipped from it noisily. 'So did he really shoot the elephant?' he asked. This was a question that has obsessed Orwell's biographers. Just as Orwell often used scenes from real-life in his fiction, so, it has been suggested, he may also have included fictional elements in some writing presented as autobiographical. Throughout his life Orwell was known as an animal-lover, and he was remembered by his colleagues in Burma for his motley collection of strays. His various lodgings were overrun by goats, geese and other farmyard creatures. Nevertheless George Stuart, an old Burma hand who was interviewed in the late 1980s, said that he clearly remembered having drinks one Sunday morning at the Moulmein club when Orwell received news that an elephant had escaped and went off to hunt the beast down. 'He was very nonchalant over the whole affair,' said Stuart, recalling that Orwell showed little emotion other than stroking his toothbrush moustache. Stuart speculated that the incident probably ruined Orwell's colonial career. An elephant was considered a valuable asset to any timber firm—more valuable even than the Indian coolie it trampled to death—and Orwell would have been severely reprimanded for such unnecessary slaughter. It was not long after the incident that he was transferred from Moulmein to a quiet post in Upper Burma called Katha. For most of Orwell's friends who were interviewed there was no question that the deed had been committed. When one biographer questioned Orwell's second wife, Sonia, over a bottle of wine or two in a London restaurant she replied, 'Of course he shot a fucking a elephant. He said he did. Why do you always doubt his fucking word!'

I once met a former Burmese game-hunter, a frail, white-haired old man, who complained that Orwell's elephant took so long to die. He told me with some irritability that it was easy to shoot an elephant and there was no reason for Orwell to have messed up the shot. 'The trick is to aim for the eye–ear line. It is a line that runs from the right eye to the left ear and the left eye to the right ear. You aim for the point where they cross, and that is where the elephant's brain is,' he explained. 'If you hit the brain, the elephant will die instantly. If not—if you aim for the heart or the lungs—it will take hours to die.' Orwell aimed his rifle several inches in front of the ear, where he thought the elephant's brain was located. And when he fired his rifle the crowd behind him erupted in a 'devilish roar of glee'. The elephant stayed still for a long moment, and then sagged to its knees. It was not until Orwell had fired a third shot that the elephant's trunk-like hind legs collapsed beneath him. The elephant lay on the ground, still breathing, and Orwell emptied shots down its throat, but the laboured breathing continued. It took the elephant another half-hour to die, but by then the horrified police-man had fled the scene.

As Tin Aye, Ye Min Kyaw and I finished off the *lapet thoke,* the conversation turned to more personal topics. Both of them were in their final year at university, and I asked what they hoped to do when they eventually graduated. Ye Min Kyaw was uncertain whether the university would stay open long enough for him to finish his degree, and he was already looking for a job. 'I have been searching for a year already and I still cannot find anything,' he said. 'Everywhere I apply they ask for my USDA number, and when I tell them I do not have one they tell me they cannot hire me.'

The Union Solidarity and Development Association (USDA) is a government-run social organization that has some 18 million members—just over a third of the entire population of Burma. USDA membership is compulsory for all civil servants, including teachers who work in government schools. Members are offered a number of perks, such as free or low-priced training in English or in computer studies, and are more at liberty to travel around the country or apply for job opportunities. I asked a number of people what they thought of those who joined the USDA voluntarily, and one friend gave me a vehement reply: 'They're all spies!' she said with conviction. 'They have no self-respect. They just want benefits from the government.'

The USDA was founded to mobilize support for the regime, and Aung San Suu Kyi has likened its members to the Brownshirts of Nazi Germany. USDA members are used as rent-a-crowds for mass rallies—called 'Expressions of the People's Desires'—staged by the regime. Some of these rallies have been organized specifically to denounce Aung San Suu Kyi, with crowds

15,000-strong calling for her to stop opposing the generals—just as each day at his office in *Nineteen Eighty-Four* Winston Smith has to attend the compulsory 'Two Minutes Hate' session in which workers are encouraged to vent their anger at a screen that shows footage of Emmanuel Goldstein. A former Party leader, but now the enemy of the people, Goldstein has written an anti-government book that circulates clandestinely and is rumoured to command a shadowy army called the Brotherhood. 'The horrible thing about the Two Minutes Hate,' reflects Smith,

> was not that one was obliged to act a part, but, on the contrary, that it was impossible to avoid joining in. Within thirty seconds any pretence was always unnecessary. A hideous ecstasy of fear and vindictiveness, a desire to kill, to torture, to smash faces in with a sledge hammer, seemed to flow through the whole group of people like an electric current, turning one even against one's will into a grimacing, screaming lunatic.

Young members of the USDA have been used in an even more thuggish capacity by the regime. In 1996 an USDA mob attacked Aung San Suu Kyi's car as she was driving through Rangoon—government security personal assigned to the NLD cavalcade simply stood aside and watched. More recently, local USDA members have harassed Aung San Suu Kyi as she has been travelling around the country. In the ancient Arakan capital of Myauk-U, the local fire bigrade threatened to hose down a crowd of some 20,000 people who had gathered to hear her speak. In Kale town in northern Burma, where 35,000 people had travelled from towns along the Chindwin river to witness the opening of an NLD office, local USDA members played music through loud-speakers to drown out the sound of her speeches. Crude pamphlets were also circulated in the towns she visited, showing pictures of her house in England 'to where she will soon flee' and her two half-English sons, stating that, though she was born of Burmese parents, she was not able to be the mother of Burmese sons.

Both Tin Aye and Ye Min Kyaw told me they would never join the USDA. I wondered what prospects they would then have in Burma if most job opportunities were closed to them. All over Burma you can meet people grossly overqualified for their menial jobs—doctors moonlighting as taxi-drivers, or law graduates working as tour guides. I knew a young woman in Mandalay who had graduated from Rangoon University with a master's degree in psychology. Unable to find work, she had set up shop as a seamstress. Her tiny stall, tucked into the corner of a building, behind a noodle stall, was strewn with texts by Sigmund Freud and Abraham Maslow.

As the heat of midday gave way to a breezy afternoon, from somewhere outside the tea shop I heard the noise of *chinlon,* a game played with a small rattan ball. There was the soft tap of the *chinlon* as it was passed on from player to player, and the occasional yell when the ball was dropped. Tin Aye folded up his copy of 'Shooting an Elephant' and Ye Min Kyaw shook the last few strands of the *lapet thoke* into the river before putting the empty Tupperware box back into his bag.

———————

A **FEW DAYS LATER** Beatrice insisted on taking me to the station to help me catch the train back to Rangoon. I felt sorry to be leaving someone who had been so kind and helpful to me, and on our way to the station I asked if there was anything I could bring her when next I came to Moulmein. 'Do you know something?' she said. 'I have rather a taste for tinned corned beef. It's not available at all in Burma, and if you could bring just a few tins with you next time you come it would make me very happy.' I made a mental note.

Beatrice saw me on to the train, making sure I had a seat next to a fellow female passenger and giving me a packet of jam biscuits and a bottle of water, which she tucked into the pocket in front of my seat. As I arranged my bags and snacks around me, Beatrice stood on the platform with her hand resting on the frame of the open window. A whistle blew and the train lurched into motion. I leaned out the window to wave goodbye. The red-brick walls of the station grew smaller and smaller as the train moved away through the palm trees on either side of the tracks. A gradually diminishing Beatrice stood alone on the platform in her shimmering pink *tamein* and waved until I was out of sight.

*Five*

# KATHA

From now onwards he must not only think right;

he must feel right, dream right.

*Nineteen Eighty-Four*

AS THE DRIVER TWISTED his key in the ignition, a wave of excitement passed over the passengers on the bus. The woman sitting next to me smoothed down her *tamein* and swiftly twisted her hair into a shining black knot on top of her head. An elderly man in the next row scooted to the edge of his seat and, holding on to the seat in front of him with both hands, leaned into the aisle to look through the front window. A mother lifted up her toddler so he could wave from the window as we pulled away. At the front of the bus, the conductor rifled through a pile of cassettes and slid one into the tape-player. It was a Burmese version of the thigh-slapping country-and-western hit 'Jambalaya'. The toddler giggled with delight. The old man tapped his fingers to the music, and I found myself humming along merrily. We were on our way.

I had travelled back up to Mandalay to get the bus to Katha, a small town tucked into the foothills of the mountains of northern Burma. We were due to arrive there at dawn, after an overnight journey along a narrow road between Burma's great river, the Irrawaddy, and the mountains of Shan State to the east. As the sun began to set, I settled happily back into my seat. The bus hurtled past valleys carpeted with lush paddy fields. White pagodas rose out of the hills, and small villages were tucked behind clumps of palm trees. It was a spectacular sunset, with mauve-coloured clouds and pink-red streaks that unfurled like ribbons across the sky. As oxen pulled carts with giant wooden wheels across the fields, they left rosy clouds of dust in their wake.

After a few hours we made a pit stop at a large open hall built of palm thatch and lit with fluorescent lights. The passengers piled enthusiastically off the bus. Most of the women, including myself, hurried around to the back of the hall to queue for the toilets, a row of unlit shacks, built on stilts, which shook precariously as we took turns to step into them. Back in the hall, the evening meal had already been cooked and laid out on the tables. Dozens of dishes were placed beneath plastic screens to keep off the flies. I lifted one screen to find a cold chicken curry swimming in oil, a watery *daal* and some sad-looking fried eggs. Deciding to forego these offerings, I ordered a cup of hot water and Coffee Mix, a handy sachet containing a mixture of instant coffee, powdered milk and lots of sugar. I sat at a table by myself and listened to the slurps and clatter of dozens of people wolfing down the food. Just when a serving boy placed the hot drink on my table, a series of impatient blasts on the horn signalled that the bus was ready to depart. The serving boy was well-prepared: he poured my Coffee Mix into a plastic bag which he tied with a tight knot and handed to me along with a straw.

By this stage in our journey the bus already had a lived-in feeling, and the satiated passengers eased themselves back into their now-familiar places. People had spread blankets over the worn faux-velvet seats, bags of snacks hung from the window catches, and bottles of water were tucked in between the luggage that was crammed into overhead shelves. The bus roared off into the darkness, and the conductor switched on a television which hung in a steel box at the front. Static crackled out through the loudspeakers as he adjusted the controls and found the video channel. A movie flickered on to the small screen, and people readjusted themselves in their seats to get a better view. A spicy-sweet scent spread around the bus as someone crushed a betel quid in their mouth, and I could hear the festive, firecracker popping of sunflower seeds. The video soundtrack was so choked with static that I could only guess that the story was a comedy revolving around a mismatched Burmese couple living in a neoclassical mansion. Everyone else was mesmerized by the screen, and as I gazed out the window I saw scores of smiling faces reflected against the dark shapes of the palms along the side of the road. Halfway through the story the video came to a crackling halt. The conductor replaced it with a Chinese movie set in an ancient era of flowing scarlet robes and flashing swords, but the video automatically fast-forwarded itself every ten minutes or so, making the narrative impossible to follow. Again the machine clicked off before the end of the movie. Nobody seemed to mind and, en masse it seemed, the passengers settled down to sleep. The woman next to me rolled up a towel, tucked it around her neck and leaned back comfortably, and soon I too dozed off.

Around one in the morning I was awoken by a stomach-churning lurch as the bus came to a standstill. There was a long, ominous silence. Looking out at the pitch-black scene around us, I could tell that we must be far from any town or village. Eventually I heard the muffled voices of the driver and conductor as they walked around the vehicle. There were some desultory clanking noises and then more silence. I realized with some frustration that the bus was going to have to spend the night here, and wondered if it was worth getting off to hitch a ride onward. I couldn't hear any passing traffic, and few of the other passengers had even woken up. The old man near me was snoring softly. There were a few soft murmurs and the rustling of blankets as bodies settled into more comfortable positions. Somewhere in the silent darkness of the bus someone lit a cheroot, and its smoke wafted over the sleeping bodies.

Only when the misty dawn crept across the paddy fields did the passengers begin to stir. A few people climbed groggily off the bus to have a look around. A gruff voice from the back row asked where the nearest tea shop was. Some of the women combed their hair and retied their *tamein*. Gradually, word spread that the axle had broken and that the conductor was just setting off to the nearest town to find a mechanic. I got out and watched as the conductor hailed a passing ox-cart. To the north I could see the blueish haze of mountains, and I wondered dismally if we would reach them before nightfall. The sun rose higher in the sky and the passengers congregated on the road in the shadow of the bus. A crowded van drove by, and a few people grabbed their bags and squeezed on to it, disappearing in a cloud of dust.

Long after midday had passed and we had shifted for shade to the other side of the bus, the conductor returned in a truck with a replacement axle. His arrival was greeted with weary indifference. A wizened old woman squatting next to me stared resolutely out towards the mountains, fanning herself with a sports journal. A small crowd of men gathered around the conductor and driver as they worked on the repair. Eventually we filed back on board, shuffling over the debris that had spilled into the aisle—pips, orange peels, soggy plastic bags. By the time the driver turned his key in the ignition the windows had taken on the soft golden hue of late afternoon. The conductor played 'Jambalaya' again—'Son of a gun, we'll have good fun on the Bayou . . .' But all the excitement had been squeezed out of us. The old man looked blankly ahead at the seat in front of him. I leaned against the sun-warmed window and watched as the bus wound its way slowly onward.

KATHA WAS George Orwell's last posting in Burma, and he used the town as the setting for his novel *Burmese Days*. I had brought along a copy of a sketch map he had drawn. On it you can see asymmetrical roughly drawn boxes marking the location of John Flory's house, the church, the bazaar, the jail and the British club. Orwell's publisher was at first reluctant to publish *Burmese Days*. He was concerned that Orwell had described Katha too realistically, and that some of his characters might be based on real-life people. The novel was thought to be potentially libellous. As a result, *Burmese Days* was first published further afield, in the United States, in 1934. A British edition appeared a year later, but only after Orwell had altered the characters' names and tried to disguise the setting. The town's name was changed to 'Kyauktada', and all references to its location in Upper Burma were removed. If a character walking down a street had turned left in the original manuscript, he now turned right. The sketch map I had was drawn by Orwell to facilitate some of these geographical disguises. (Apart from a few later editorial changes, the edition of *Burmese Days* available today has been restored to the original form.)

Katha is today, as it must have been in Orwell's time, a fairy-tale setting. The town sits on a bank of the wide Irrawaddy river, and is surrounded on all sides by the jagged outline of distant mountain ranges. The air is laced with the crisp, fresh smell of fir trees. Decaying colonial mansions and teak houses the colour of cooking-chocolate are hidden amid a forest of mahogany trees and rose bushes. If you've read *Burmese Days,* it is hard not to think of Katha as a fictional town. Though the colonial society which peopled its pages has long since moved away, all the novel's key buildings still remain. Walking through the streets of Katha is therefore an eerie experience—a bit like walking on to an abandoned stage set.

When the bus I was on finally arrived in Katha, in the early evening, I settled into one of a row of guest houses along the river. Its sparse cubicle-size rooms were separated by fresh-cut wood panels, thin as wafers, and the mattresses were piled high with synthetic Chinese blankets.

Before I came to Katha I had shown Orwell's sketch map to a former resident who now lived in Rangoon, and she had added her own knowledge to the diagram, indicating where various colonial buildings had been located, including the old police officer's residence in which Orwell would have lived. The next morning I decided to rent a bicycle and put the map to use.

The proprietor of the guest house was lounging behind an empty desk in the entranceway, snuggled up in a shining green bomber jacket. I asked him if he knew where I might be able to rent a bicycle. He frowned at me silently, then picked up the telephone and called the police. I heard him ask a police officer if a foreigner was allowed to travel around Katha on a bike. There was a rapid burble of Burmese at the other end of the phone. Every few moments the proprietor interjected a sharp '*Hoke-la?*'— 'Is that so?' Then he put down the phone and frowned at me again.

'Why do you need to rent a bicycle? What's wrong with walking around town?' he asked. I guessed that the answer had been no, and I asked him why foreigners were not allowed to rent bikes. He thought for a while, frowning all the time, and then said, 'It is because of safety. The roads are not so good in Katha, and nobody wants anything to happen to you.' I looked at him dubiously, but he didn't continue. 'You can rent a trishaw and driver,' he suggested, trying to be helpful. 'Then the driver can look after you.'

I set off on foot.

Tumbledown wooden shop-houses lined the road that ran along the river. I passed a few dry-goods stores and a one-room lending library where schoolchildren sat cross-legged on the floor engrossed in well-thumbed cartoon booklets. A stall selling freshly made betel quids was set up beneath a large banyan tree by the river, and a small cluster of people were gathered round it, wrapped in scarves and shawls against the morning chill. Stray dogs jogged up and down the street, and a black-and-white sow rolled contentedly in the mud along the steep riverbank, sliding slowly down towards the water with each roll.

When Orwell was in Katha the town had a tiny population of some 3,000 Burmese, plus a small group of Europeans who worked as British government officials or the managers of timber firms operating in the surrounding jungle. The old European quarter was located slightly inland from a curve in the river, and it was here that most of the scenes in *Burmese Days* take place. The well-appointed neighbourhood was equipped with the club, a golf course, a battalion of the Indian Army, and the large colonial homes in which Orwell and his characters lived. I came across a group of houses that had once belonged to the Steel Brothers company, a big colonial trading firm. Now the old houses are home to high-ranking government officials based in Katha. Corrugated-iron sheets have replaced the tiled roofs, and the cream-coloured plaster on the walls has flaked off, revealing red blotches of naked brickwork. Cabbages, vine tomatoes and yellow-green gourds grow in small allotments across the sprawling lawns.

Not far from these dilapidated buildings I found the former district commissioner's home, an immense mansion built of wood and brick. It was set back in a wide field of lilac thistles, and an empty flagpole stood in the curve of the sweeping driveway. The house itself, reminiscent of the colonial mansions I had seen in Maymyo, looked derelict. The wooden planks of the balconies had been chewed into a spongy pulp by termites, and spiders had knitted thick cobwebs across the missing panels of the front door. Scrawled in white paint on the brick wall next to the entrance were Burmese words reading, 'If no one is home, do not enter.' I peeked inside and saw two mud-splattered tractors parked on the stone tiles in front of a disused fireplace. The room was dominated by an imposing wooden staircase with banisters lovingly carved into voluptuous curves. At the back of the house, the scent of honeysuckle hung around the flowering vines that had grown over the locked-up outdoor kitchen.

In small colonial outposts such as Katha, the police officer's house was often near that of the district commissioner and, according to my map, the solitary British policeman in Katha would have been housed next door to this old mansion. I walked on down a small lane and found another, much smaller, colonial house set in a well-tended garden of banana trees and bougainvillea. It was mock-Tudor in style, with cream-coloured walls and timber beams stained sticky black. An army jeep was parked in the covered driveway. As I stood at the gate, a sturdy middle-aged Burmese man sauntered out to the patio, his hands tucked nonchalantly into his slacks. 'May I help you?' he asked in English. I apologized for intruding and mumbled something about being interested in old British architecture. The man came out into the garden to ask me more questions. 'Where are you from? . . . Why are you interested in architecture? . . . What are you doing here in Katha?'

When I had answered to his satisfaction, he invited me into his house for tea. Though I was thrilled to be allowed a chance to see inside a house that Orwell might once have lived in, I was also apprehensive at being entertained by a military man—and a fairly high-ranking one at that, judging by the size of his house and the shiny, air-conditioned vehicle parked outside. I followed him into a dark wooden foyer off which were four gloomy rooms. He led me into a sitting room and offered me a reclining chair in which I had to lie uncomfortably half-prone. 'Please,' he said as he went off to rustle up some tea, 'make yourself at home.'

I looked around the room. The fireplace was filled with half-burned logs, and sepia-toned family photographs in polished wooden frames hung on the walls. Some of the photographs were from an earlier era of Burmese history, showing women with their hair curled into towering cylinders and men wearing *kaung baung,* traditional Burmese headdresses, tied like giant bows around their heads. Among the pictures was a portrait of the man who was making my tea. He was dressed in an army officer's uniform, with a smart cap and striped epaulettes on his shoulders.

'So what is it that you do?' I asked when he returned bearing a single cup of tea in the centre of a lacquerware tray. 'I am a merchant,' he said, and before I could ask anything else a plump, pale-faced woman came into the room. 'Please allow me to introduce my wife,' said my host. We sat and talked about the house for a while. They told me it was almost uninhabitable, because the floors were rotting away and the roof was leaking badly.

It was an awkward conversation; we all seemed a bit nervous. Relief came in the form of a green-eyed tabby cat that slunk into the room and began weaving its way around my shins. We talked happily about cats for a good ten minutes, and then the conversation stopped again. I realized there was nothing else to say. I'd had these kind of meetings before, where everyone sits round and makes polite chit-chat and we all stubbornly avoid any mention of the current political situation in Burma. We discuss the weather, and I am asked if I have visited the ancient capital of Pagan, and then the conversation generally peters out. When the same thing happened in this case, the man's wife gave a little bow and left the room. I told my host that I had to be going as well, and he walked me to the door. 'You're lucky we're having such splendid weather at the moment,' he said as we shook hands and said goodbye.

SHELTERED BENEATH a banyan tree at one end of the town I found a quiet open-air tea shop. Statuettes of Burmese spirits stood in shoebox-sized shrines among the branches of the tree, surrounded by offerings of candles, fresh jasmine and slices of cake. The tea shop's stools and tables—painted strawberry red—were tucked around the tree's roots. On a wooden plank hung above the bubbling kettles, a Burmese sign read, 'The Golden Banyan Tree Tea Shop'. Sitting on one of the stools, I had a panoramic view of the murky, fast-flowing waters of the Irrawaddy. The water was relatively low, and on either side of the river there were wide sandbanks like beaches. The several brightly coloured *longyi* that had been laid out to dry on the sands looked like an enormous patchwork quilt lining the river.

One afternoon while I sat at the tea shop I watched a man playing chess at the next table. He was a round, energetic man who moved his chess pieces with hurried impatience. Though he played a number of games, he never won any and always ended up sweeping his hand across the board and toppling his king. When I asked if he would let me play against him, he told me with a winning smile that he wouldn't like to embarrass a lady by beating her at chess. 'I will not compete with you on the board,' he declared. 'But I will buy you a cup of tea.'

We talked, over our cups of sticky-sweet tea, of many things: the weather, what American fast food tasted like, and traditional Burmese puppetry. After a while, I asked him how he found living in a country like Burma. 'We Burmese people are totally content,' he replied, gazing calmly into my eyes. 'Do you know why? Because we have nothing left. We have been squeezed and squeezed and squeezed until there is nothing left.' He swept his hand across the table in the same frustrated gesture he used over the chessboard. 'Nothing!' he said. 'I have lived in Burma my whole life—over a half a century now—and each year I watch things get worse.'

Then he slapped his thigh and said, 'Ha! That's enough!' He pushed his stool back abruptly and walked off, forgetting that he had offered to pay for tea.

ONE ENDURING BRITISH legacy remains in Katha, tucked behind a neat, white picket fence. It is the Katha Tennis Club, its single court a remnant of the former colonial club. The court and the tiny changing room are perfectly maintained, complete with umpire chairs and night-time floodlights. Though the court is freshly marked with white lines, long cracks have riven the asphalt surface. In the cool, lime-washed changing room a poster of the 1970s tennis star Jimmy Connors hangs on the wall, and on one of the benches is a yellowed copy of a book called *How to Succeed in Tennis*—published, I noted, in 1979.

Down a tree-lined lane behind the tennis court is the club, the most important building on Orwell's sketch map and the physical and spiritual centrepiece of *Burmese Days*. Orwell described it as a dumpy one-storey building with a tin roof. In his time the interior boasted a mangy billiard table, a library of mildewed novels, months-old copies of *Punch* magazine and the dusty skull of a sambar deer on one wall. The club bar was staffed with an Indian butler, and a punkah-wallah lay at the foot of the verandah pulling a rope with his heel to swing the punkah back and forth to create a cooling breeze. Members of Katha's British community whiled away interminable evenings with tepid gin-and-tonics and inane chatter about dogs, gramophones, tennis racquets and the infernal heat. One perennially favoured topic of conversation was the insolence of the Burmese. Older club members recalled with nostalgia the good old days of the colony, when you could send a misbehaving servant to the jail with a note reading, 'Please give the bearer fifteen lashes.' According to Orwell, the real seat of British power lay not in the commissioner's mansion or the police station, but in this sad, dusty little building.

In *Burmese Days*, the first scene in the club opens on a gathering of male club members. One of them has just read a notice posted on the board, which states that members must consider allowing an Asian member into the club, as was becoming the practice all over the country. When, in 1923, the British introduced diarchy, or joint rule whereby Burmese politicians could attend the country's parliament sessions, there was some pressure to open up the clubs to higher-ranking Burmese officials. Smaller clubs around Burma were forced to accept a Burmese member, but segregation remained in place in the big clubs in the cities of Rangoon and Mandalay. Even in 1930, after Orwell had left, the Burmese official who was appointed acting governor in place of the British governor who was away on sick leave was denied access to the Rangoon clubs. Whether it was a well-equipped compound in the capital or a one-room shack in the mountains, the club retained its status as the fortress within which the British inhabitants of Burma recreated for themselves the comforting, unshakeable mores of English society. Allowing an Asian to enter this citadel was therefore anathema to many members. Ellis, the volatile manager of a Katha-based timber firm in *Burmese Days*, takes great offence when he reads the deputy commissioner's notice: 'He's asking us to break all our rules and take a dear little nigger-boy into this Club . . . That *would* be a treat wouldn't it? Little pot-bellied niggers breathing garlic in your face over the bridge-table.'

In fact there were probably few Burmese who really wanted to enter the clubs. Htin Aung, the Burmese academic who witnessed Orwell beating a schoolboy at a Rangoon train station, recalled how his father became a district magistrate under the British government in the 1920s and was invited to join the local club. His father was forced to accept, but on the monthly occasions he visited the club, as a social duty, he never enjoyed it. *Burmese Days,* however, pivots around the machinations of one Burmese magistrate who schemes, plots and blackmails his way into the club, and of an Indian doctor who begs for the privilege of becoming a club member. The latter is Dr Veraswami, an Indian man with steel-rimmed spectacles and a badly fitting drill suit. (Veraswami's name was changed to 'Murkhaswami' for the first British publication of *Burmese Days,* thus losing the joke over his club nickname, 'Dr Very-slimy'. Incidentally, Veraswami is also the name of London's first Indian restaurant, spelt 'Veeraswamy', which opened for business in Piccadilly Circus around the time Orwell was working on his book and is still running today.)

Veraswami and John Flory are good friends, and Flory often visits the doctor for what the latter delightedly calls 'cultured conversation'. In these conversations, which always take place on the doctor's wide, dark verandah over a few bottles of beer, Orwell details his disillusionment with the Empire. By the time he was posted to Katha, Orwell had spent almost five years working in Burma and had formed strong opinions against colonialism that would endure throughout the rest of his life. Flory can't expound on his ideas at the club, and enjoys his visits with the doctor as he can then talk freely. The doctor, for his part, becomes agitated whenever Flory criticizes the Raj, and defends the British as great administrators who have built an efficient and unrivalled empire. Flory dismisses these administrators as mere moneymakers, declaring that they should drop Kipling's 'White Man's Burden' nonsense and stop living a lie (the lie being that the British are 'here to uplift our poor black brothers instead of to rob them'). One of

Orwell's earliest published pieces, written just a year after he returned to England and appearing in a French newspaper, was entitled 'How a Nation is Exploited: The British Empire in Burma'.
In it, Orwell described Burma as one of the richest countries in
the world, an earthly paradise full of natural resources which the
British administration had shamelessly robbed and pilfered.

Perhaps it is not surprising that *Burmese Days* is one Orwell
novel that the current regime hasn't banned: both the book and
the generals are rabidly anti-colonial. Present-day government
tracts on British colonialism echo Orwell's views, the only difference being the more vehement vocabulary used by the Burmese
regime. A collection I read was published by the Committee for
Propaganda and Agitation to Intensify Patriotism, and one
piece, which featured action-packed line drawings of warrior-like
Burmese fighting pirate-faced British soldiers, described how
Burma had been little more than a granary for the British Empire. The gist of the text was that the rapacious British imperial-
ists, who lived arrogantly capitalizing on the wealth they looted
from smaller nations, had wantonly plundered and exploited
Burma. They had filled their ships with Burmese rice, teak, oil
and gems, and had sailed their ill-gotten gains back to England
like pirates. In short, the shameless British lived in luxury on
property stolen from Burma.

This charge of voracious looting of Burma's natural resources
could just as easily be levelled at the current government's economic strategies, which it carries out for its own benefit at the expense of the Burmese people. As an elderly Burmese friend said
to me, 'The British may have sucked our blood, but these Burmese

generals are biting us to the bone!' Most historical accounts agree that the colonial government created an economy which did not favour the Burmese. Before the British annexed Burma, the country operated with an economy that was predominately barter-based. The British introduced currency, and opened the country to international trade. British authorities maintained control over all the main firms, and kept agricultural produce at government-controlled prices. Unable to compete with more sophisticated economic forces, many Burmese agriculturalists were squeezed off their land, and at one point in the 1930s almost half the land in the rice-growing provinces was owned by non-Burmans.

Still, Dr Veraswami persists in defending the Raj. The Burmese would be helpless without the British, he says. What do they know about building roads? Or extracting teak? If the British were not there to guide and protect and develop their resources, others would be in there ruining them. The British are selfless torch-bearers along the path of progress.

'Bosh, my dear doctor,' replies Flory. 'We teach the young men to drink whisky and play football, I admit, but precious little else.'

The doctor protests: what about the great tradition of British justice and the Pax Britannica?

'Pox Britannica, doctor, Pox Britannica is its proper name,' retorts Flory.

The British government in Burma provided only the semblance of democracy, Orwell argued in his article for the French newspaper. The true nature of the colony was despotic. The British built roads and irrigation systems (just as the generals are doing today), but they did so not for the benefit of the Burmese people, but in their own interests, to improve the infrastructure and therefore the profitability of the colony. The article went on to say that the British may have opened up a number of schools, and introduced Burma's first European-style university, but they provided an education sufficient only to produce messengers and low-grade civil servants, thus preventing the growth of any educated class which could rise up against them.

During the sessions at Veraswami's house, one of Flory's favourite targets is the club itself, and the excessive drinking which takes place within its walls. 'Of course,' says Flory, 'drink is what keeps the machine going. We should all go mad and kill one another in a week if it weren't for that. There's a subject for one of your uplift essayists, doctor. Booze as the cement of empire.'

The club building is still standing, but it has been turned into a government-owned co-operative. Where the garden used to be a riot of English flowers—larkspurs, hollyhocks and petunias—there are now large warehouses holding stores of rice, oil and sugar. The low tin roof of the club still hangs over a wooden verandah at the entrance, but the main room has been divided by a wall and is filled with desks and mismatched chairs. When I visited, there were only a handful of office workers scattered around the room. One was asleep at his desk, and another was busy unpacking a tiffin box of curries for lunch. The verandah at the back of the club, which had once overlooked the river, had been walled in to create another room. Looking out a window, I noticed that the river itself had changed its course. It was still possible to see its former path—its twists and turns and steep banks—in the shape of the lush green paddy fields which had replaced it.

Most colonial memoirs I read painted a jolly picture of life in Burma, making affectionate references to the butlers from Madras who prepared ice-cold shandy on river flotillas, ribald drinking songs around the club piano, shooting expeditions, dances. *Burmese Days* came as a surprise to some old Burma hands. Roger Beadon, Orwell's colleague at the Mandalay Police Training School, felt Orwell had 'rather let the side down'. Clyne Stewart, the burly principal of the training school, was reportedly livid and threatened to horsewhip Orwell if he ever saw him again. In the course of researching Orwell's time in Burma, I corresponded with a woman whose father and husband had worked as police officers in Burma in the early half of the twentieth century. She was upset by Orwell's jaundiced view of colonial society, and remembers a very different Burma where relationships between the British and the Burmese were on an equal level. She added that Orwell was unanimously disliked by his contemporary officers because he didn't fit in and did not seem to enjoy life in Burma—or, for that matter, anything at all.

In defence of his harsh portrayal of colonial society in *Burmese Days,* Orwell once wrote, 'I dare say it's unfair in some ways and inaccurate in some details, but much of it is simply reporting what I have seen.'

EACH DAY, as the sun begins to set across the river, a night market is set up along Katha's main street. It is a festive affair. Burmese ballads are played from the tea shops that spill out on to the pavements, and snack shops sell chopped pineapple and sticky rice steamed in bamboo. At one stall a man wraps handfuls of roasted peanuts in newspaper to sell to passers-by. Mobile betel-quid vendors park their lime-stained stalls on the street corners, and people drift up and down, chatting and snacking. An elderly man wearing a black blazer over his *longyi* sauntered smartly down the centre of the street tapping his wooden cane as if he were promenading along some Parisian boulevard. Two women giggled together as they coasted downhill on a bicycle, their waist-length hair streaming behind them in glossy black sheets.

As I walked down the street one evening, a tall Burmese man in his early twenties, with shoulder-length curly hair, approached me. 'Do you mind if I follow you?' he asked in English. He told me his name was Soe ('Soe what?' he joked), and that he had been watching me wander around town during the past few days. 'Do you know why I want to follow you?' he asked. I laughed and suggested he must be working for Military Intelligence if he was so interested in my activities. He laughed too, though I noted that he didn't deny my suggestion.

Soe told me he was trying to learn English, and wanted to practise with a native English speaker. Katha has no English teachers, and only a few tourists pass through the town each year, so he didn't have many other opportunities, he explained. He had been learning English by watching Hollywood movies rented from a video shop near his home. His English had an American lilt to it, and he used slightly out-of-date slang which gave me the peculiar impression that we were performing a bad film script. When I said he was welcome to join me, he said, 'Cool! Let's shake a leg.' And then he proffered a line perhaps once spoken by some gruff Humphrey Bogart-type character: 'Tell me something about yourself, lady. Go on. Shoot.'

I decided not to tell him anything about myself. Instead, I asked him why he was learning English. 'I dunno,' he said, shaking out his long hair. 'Sometimes I think I must have been an American in a past life—or maybe I will become one in a future life.'

'Why an American?' I asked.

'I just woke up one morning and felt like an American. I dunno how to explain it. It's just what I am: an American trapped in a Burmese body. Cool, huh?'

Throughout my travels across Burma I had met many young people who, like Soe, were eager to learn English. Whenever I was on my own in tea shops, at pagodas, sitting on trains, I was approached by people who wanted to practise their English. Generally we tried out simple conversational topics like what country I was from and how hot the weather was in Burma. When I asked them why they were learning English, they almost always gave me the same answer: because they wanted to leave the country. There were times when it seemed to me that everyone wanted to leave. I met trishaw drivers and tour guides who were busy plotting their escapes. In Mandalay I met a money-changer who showed me a photocopied map of the United States of America held together with sticky tape. He asked me if I could tell him any of the names of the American state capitals. 'Sure,' I said, looking at the map, next to which he had a list of the eleven names he had collected so far. To my shame, I could add only one more: Boise, Idaho. He told me he was trying to learn as much about America as possible, in preparation for his planned trip. He had been saving money for the past five years, and hoped to have enough in six or seven years' time.

If you are Burmese, there are two ways to leave the country.

The first option is to travel to the border of Thailand or India and cross over to the other side, where people wait endlessly, and for the most part hopelessly, in malaria-ridden refugee camps to gain asylum in another country, or for a better political climate that might make it possible for them to return to Burma. The younger brother of a friend of mine was planning to flee to the Burma–Thai border. When I spoke to him, he seemed to have no idea of the precarious life that might await him as a nameless refugee, and thought that if he could get to a Western embassy he would be rescued. 'If I could just tell them about my life,' he said, 'I know they would let me live in their country. All I have to do is inform them of the conditions we are forced to live under here and they would take pity on me. I know they would.'

The second option is even harder: to try to leave through official channels. Burmese people do not have passports and must apply through the government for temporary documents if they want to leave the country. Whenever I walked past the passport department in Rangoon I saw hoards of people scanning paper sheets stapled to wooden noticeboards to see if their name was on the list of people granted a permit. The process is expensive and time-consuming. The passport application can take anywhere from one month to a year, and there is no guarantee that, after paying the numerous bribes required, success will be forthcoming. Adding to the difficulty of leaving is the prohibition against Burmese nationals possessing foreign currency. In order to be granted permission to leave the country, they must produce evidence that someone abroad is willing to sponsor their trip financially.

I had seen the process at close hand when assisting Burmese friends who wanted to travel abroad to further their studies or to join academic conferences. One friend, who lives in Mandalay, had been accepted at an American university. It cost her the equivalent of $500 and four ten-day-long trips to Rangoon to get her passport. Once she had her passport in hand, she was given a one-month window in which to leave the country and had to return within a year, before the passport expired. Another friend paid the equivalent of $300 dollars to ensure that he would get his passport to travel to Thailand for a three-month training course. After waiting patiently for almost five months, he was told that his application had been refused. (He had once been a political prisoner.) Another friend was given, and could think of, no reason why his passport application was turned down. (He had never been imprisoned.)

As Soe and I strolled along the stalls of the night market, munching peanuts and talking, I asked if he was ever going to visit America. He told me that he entered the green-card lottery every year, sending off a return-addressed envelope to the American Embassy. But so far he had never had a reply. In any case, if he doesn't win some money, he explained, he could never afford such a trip. Though Soe had completed his secondary education, he hadn't been able to find a job and worked at his father's noodle factory. After midnight each night, the family started making Chinese wheat noodles to sell in the morning markets. By dawn, Soe was on his bicycle delivering the fresh noodles to stall-owners and vendors around Katha. 'Hey, it ain't so bad,' he said, shrugging his shoulders. 'I'll just hang out here for a while . . .'

Then, with a wonderfully hokey sense of timing, he launched into a slightly croaky rendition of 'Imagine' by John Lennon:

*Imagine there's no heaven,*
*It's easy if you try . . .*

The image of Soe sending off a letter to the American Embassy each year and never receiving a reply seemed to illustrate the tremendous sense of isolation that has enveloped Burma. Communications between Burma and other countries are frustratingly difficult. Often, when I tried to phone friends in Burma from abroad, the lines into the country were permanently engaged, and if I did get through I was inevitably cut off after a few minutes. The Burmese postal service is also notoriously unreliable, and letters and parcels are routinely rifled through. One man told me his aunt had sent him a box of chocolates from England, but when he opened the box there were only one or two pieces left, with a note written on customs-department notepaper saying that the rest had been eaten by rats. ('Rats indeed!' sneered my friend.) Email is available to those living in the bigger cities who can afford to pay for it, but all emails must pass through a central government server where they can be perused by MI, and emails going into and out of Burma are sometimes delayed for days. Though the Internet is available in Rangoon, its use is carefully monitored and only a specially selected number of web sites are accessible.

By the time Soe and I had done a full circle of the street, the market was already closing down. Fluorescent lights were unplugged from small generators, and carts were noisily rolled away down side streets. As Soe walked me back to the guest house, we compared our favourite bands and Hollywood actors. As with many people I had met in Burma, Soe's references seemed to come from a slightly different era, as if there were a time lag of decades between his home and mine. (His favourite band was The Beatles, and his favourite actor was Clint Eastwood.) When I had left Mandalay, for instance, I had asked some of my friends if there was anything I could bring with me the next time I visited. One pastor asked for a View-Master with biblical stories to use in his Sunday-school classes. The View-Master—a stereoscopic slide-viewer with images arranged around circular 'reels'—with biblical reels, I later learned, is now sold only as an antique. Another friend of mine had ticked the titles of some publications he wanted from an advertisement in a 1970 edition of *Reader's Digest* magazine. Among his selection were *Great Stories of the World— Love, Intrigue, Mystery, Sacrifice, Fun, Faith, Courage* and *How to Live with Life—100 authors—Genuine Help and Advice*. All his choices are long out of print.

At the entrance to my hotel, Soe held his hand up like a gun, pulled the trigger with his middle finger, and said, 'See you later, alligator.'

WHILE I WAS in Katha I went to visit a woman who is the guardian of one of Burma's many secret histories. Tin Tin Lay lives in an old house down one of the lanes that twist through the centre of town. The house is built of dark-stained teak, and the walls are made with floor-to-ceiling shutters with slats that can be tilted open to allow a breeze. The day I visited her the house was shuttered up against the cool weather. When I tapped on the front door it was opened almost immediately by an elegant woman wearing a lavishly embroidered *tamein* and a white-lace top. Her black hair was tied into a severe bun at the nape of her neck. I introduced myself and told her the name of a mutual friend who had suggested I drop in on her during my visit to Katha. She shook my hand with a gracious, almost regal, manner, and told me she would talk to me as long as I promised never *ever* to mention her name.

'We historians must keep our mouths tightly shut,' she said as she bolted the door and motioned me to a seat. 'We are scared. As Burmese people, we are not free to talk about what we want. We are not free to walk where we want. We are not even free to die: we must die according to their wishes.' She handed me a plump and slightly bruised banana. 'Eat!' she commanded.

Tin Tin Lay used to work as a history professor in Rangoon University, and when she retired she returned home to her native town, Katha, with her husband and her two sons. She now sat down opposite me and asked, 'What is it you want to know?'

Before the Second World War, Burma was one of the richest

countries in the region. Any economist comparing it with other countries in Asia would have thought it safe to wager that it would develop one of the region's most successful economies. Since then, civil wars have raged across Burma's border areas, taking an unknown toll on lives and natural resources, and the military regime has outlasted almost all other dictatorships around the world. How, I wanted to know, had the fertile ground of *Burmese Days* evolved so quickly into the wasteland of *Nineteen Eighty-Four*?

Tin Tin Lay blames all Burma's woes on a streak of authoritarianism that she believes runs through Burmese society. Before the British arrived in Burma the country was ruled by an absolute monarchy. 'We Burmese spent eight centuries living under these all-powerful monarchs,' she said. 'A Burmese king could kill you or destroy you or arrest you whenever he wanted.' As a result, she argued, the Burmese have become conditioned to authoritarian rule. 'We are trained to listen to our elders,' she said. 'We are trained to obey.' In other words, the Burmese have a psychological receptiveness to authoritarian government.

I had heard this controversial theory before. It was set out in a famous essay published in the early 1960s by the late Maung Maung Gyi, who had a doctorate from Yale University. He wrote about the despotic nature of Burmese kings, who were traditionally extolled as *Thet-oo Hsanbaing Mintayagyi*, which means 'The Great Owner of Life, Head and Hair of His Subjects', or a more succinct title could be used: *Bawa-Shin Min-Taya*, meaning 'The Arbiter of Existence'. Because there was no consistent law of primogeniture, the history of Burmese kingdoms is drenched in bloodshed. The great ruler King Anawyatha, who introduced

Buddhism throughout Burma, murdered his potential challengers on the advice of his soothsayers. The revered King Alaungpaya was noted for his supernatural powers, and was said to possess a sword that could fly through the air and slice off the heads of those who opposed him. The large number of rivals and challengers to the throne led to brutal massacres not only of the challengers themselves, but also of their families. The people lived at the whim of these great Arbiters of Existence; whole villages could be turned into slave markets, or be burned to cinders for harbouring dissenters. The result, wrote Maung Maung Gyi, can be seen in a Burmese proverb that says there are four things in life which cannot be trusted: a thief, the bough of a tree, a woman and a ruler. The Burmese thought-pattern had become adapted to the idea of a government as something oppressive and evil. The Burmese came to believe that misrule was an inevitability of governance. This psychological legacy has taught them that it is futile to stand up against a bad ruler, no matter how bad things get.

It is a theory that Tin Tin Lay would never be able discuss in public, unless she wanted to provoke the ire of the military junta (not to mention the many Burmese who would disagree with her). 'These views are unpopular—I know they are,' she told me. 'But there is a truth to them. Look at us. Here we are, suffering. Suffering under our own people. Year after year we are made poorer. Year after year we become more downtrodden. The government runs free, robbing, looting and raping us. Why?' She repeated her question, more sharply: 'Why?'

I suggested a more accepted explanation of how authoritarianism was able to take root in Burma: it was the fault of the

British. When the British took over Burma, they destroyed all the country's traditional institutions of governance—the monarchy, the monkhood, the central administration. They deported the king, who was the linchpin of the country's administration and religious systems, keeping him until his death under careful guard in exile in India. They replaced the traditional ruling systems with a ready-trained bureaucracy from India. And they practised a system of divide and rule among the ethnic minorities. This system was unsustainable without the British, and, when it crumpled in on itself after they left, the Burmese army stepped in to quell the ensuing chaos.

Tin Tin Lay looked at me with absolute disdain. I looked for somewhere to put my banana skin. Failing to find a suitable spot, I placed it delicately on top of a pile of notes that covered the small table between us.

'The British', she said, 'brought us democracy. It was the first time we had tasted it. We had never even heard of it before the British came, and we were not ready for it. I am ashamed of the Burmese people. I am ashamed of Burma and I am sad for the Burmese. We are so very, very ignorant. We are always looking for someone to blame, so we blame the British.'

It is easy to see why the current government would not be a big fan of Tin Tin Lay's take on Burmese history. 'They do not like to hear about democratic ideas,' she said. 'They do not like to hear about history, about the facts. They are interested only in nationalism and patriotism. There is no history in Burma any more. You can look in the school books and the libraries. You will not find it. We are a country without a history—without a truthful history.'

When our conversation came to an end, Tin Tin Lay glided leglessly beneath her *tamein* to the door. She undid the bolt, thanked me warmly for our spirited discussion, and asked me not to visit her again.

O N A SINGLE NIGHT some 2,500 years ago, King Pasenadi, the ruler of an ancient kingdom in northern India called Kotola, had sixteen bad dreams. They were vivid and disturbing depictions of strange worlds with two-headed horses, rocks that floated, wild wolves pissing into golden bowls, and cows kneeling down in the mud to suck milk from their own newborn calves. King Pasenadi described these visions to the Brahmin advisers in his court, and asked them what the dreams could mean. The Brahmins diagnosed doom and gloom for the kingdom, and prescribed a mass slaughter of the king's animals to appease the forces of evil. The king's wife, however, was unconvinced that the animal sacrifices were necessary, and she persuaded the king to ask the Buddha's advice. The Buddha was able to put the king's mind at rest. He listened to each of the dreams and told the king not to worry: these visions were prophecies that would not come true until after the king's reign. They spoke, said the Buddha, of a future time when rulers would become wicked and consumed by greed and power. Many Burmese believe that the king's sixteen dreams foretold the story of present-day Burma.

Around the time that Ne Win and his army took control, in 1962, paintings of King Pasenadi's dreams began appearing on the walls of pagoda compounds all over Burma, commissioned by locals. The Buddha's interpretations of King Pasenadi's dreams read like a karmic blueprint for Burma's troubles. In the king's eighth dream, for instance, people carried water to an enormous water jar. The jar was already full to overflowing, but the people kept pouring more water in. There were many smaller jars that needed filling, but they were ignored. The water from the large jar spilled on to the ground, while the smaller jars were left empty. The Buddha explained that a future ruler would force his people to work for him at the expense of their own livelihood. The people would be made to harvest the land for him, filling the ruler's granaries with rice while their own stores remained empty. (King Pasenadi's dreams have also been used against British rule: I once saw a painting of this dream which depicted a British colonial officer bullying a *longyi*-clad farmer into handing over his produce.)

In the king's fifteenth dream, a hideous and ungainly crow led a trail of mandarin ducks, each one pristine and elegant with golden, chestnut and royal-blue feathers. According to the Buddha, this dream foretold a time when the unworthy would take control over the noble. While the ignorant ruled the roost, the truly worthy people would be forced to kowtow to their demands in order to survive.

The Burmese landscape, both mental and physical, has long been loaded with prophecies, and Orwell's trilogy is only one among many texts in which you can read the future or the past in Burma. The most poetic and mysterious of Burma's prophetic arts are the *dabaung*. From the time of the kings, the *dabaung* have offered prophecies in the form of poems or rhymes. They do not come from the mouths of wise men or fortune-tellers, but are

sung by children, madmen and, sometimes, dramatic perform-
ers. No one knows exactly where the *dabaung* come from: they
simply appear in a ditty that children are singing as they play in
the street, or a verse that a nonsensical madman mutters to himself. In olden times, when the king wanted to know what was going to happen in the kingdom, he would send his advisers out
into the bazaars to listen for *dabaung,* which characteristically surface before great events take place. One *dabaung* warned a king
not to march against the army of neighbouring Siam. He ignored
it and was defeated. Another *dabaung* predicted that the royal dynasty to which the Burmese king Thibaw belonged would be the
last of its kind in Burma. Thibaw's dynasty came to an ignomin-
ious end when the British took over the country. In 1901, when
the Burmese author Kyaw Hla interpreted various ditties and
signs he saw around Burma as predicting the fall of Queen Victoria, he was promptly arrested by British authorities for trying to
incite rebellion against their rule. And there was a *dabaung* that
was fulfilled just a few years ago:

> *Two tooth temples are similar;*
> *People beggared; army fissured.*

This *dabaung* is said to refer to two pagodas, one in Mandalay and
one in Rangoon, that were recently built to house copied relics of
the Buddha's tooth. The *dabaung* warned that, when the construction of these two pagodas was completed, the Burmese
people would be impoverished and the army would split. In 1997,
around the time when the pagodas were completed, there were

serious power reshuffles within the military and the ruling SLORC reappeared in a new incarnation, as the State Peace and Development Council (SPDC).

I often felt that the fantastic rumours which rippled around the country were present-day descendants of the *dabaung*. Sometimes the rumours seemed to take on an element of collective wishful thinking. One man told me, over a couple of whisky-and-sodas, that the Karenni army was about to take control of Rangoon. Yet I had read in the Bangkok newspapers that the Karenni army, battered and broken by the might of the *Tatmadaw*, had recently signed a ceasefire agreement. 'They have new bombs,' said the man, shaking the ice in his drink—'incredible bombs that explode horizontally and destroy everything in the near vicinity. And guns, they have guns, too. Many, many guns, given to them by the American army and international NGOs. It's only a matter of months before the Karenni liberate all of Burma.'

These rumours and prophecies load the air in Burma with a sense of magic and foreboding: there is always an unnerving feeling that something is just about to happen. I had a scholar friend in Mandalay who promised an imminent uprising or the death of a general every time I met him. He was in a permanent state of anticipation. 'I am ready,' he told me. 'I am ready to help my people, to suffer for my people.' One time I met him when he had just taken the overnight train from Mandalay to Rangoon. He had dark bags under his eyes and I asked him why he was so tired. Was it a bad journey?

'No, not at all,' he replied. 'But I had to be prepared, so I sat with my bag in my lap the entire journey, waiting.'

'Waiting for what?'

'For anything,' he said. 'In Burma, anything can happen.'

If there was a fire in the neighbourhood, a slight earthquake, a visible comet, or any other slightly out-of-the-ordinary event my friend would prophecy the fall of the government. In Burmese, such visions are called *nameit,* or omens. A gecko that falls off the ceiling in front of you or a dog that barks as you are leaving the house is each a *nameit* that bode ill. My friend explained that he did not know whether the *nameit* he saw predicted good things or bad things. All he knew was that something was going to happen, soon. 'Stick around, if you want to see some fireworks,' he would say with a slow, knowing nod.

Nothing ever did happen—at least not on the scale my friend predicted. But, if there were never any nationwide fireworks, I got the sense that they took place all the time on a personal level. And these individual fireworks, these small internal implosions, no one could predict or control. In *Nineteen Eighty-Four,* Winston Smith struggles to control his rage: 'He had an almost overwhelming temptation to shout a string of filthy words at the top of his voice. Or to bang his head against the wall, to kick over the table, and hurl the inkpot through the window . . .' I knew a tour guide who was working in Rangoon. He loved Burma, he told me when I first met him some five years ago, and whatever state the government was in he would never want to leave his country. 'This is my home. It is where my family is and where my heart is,' he said. Still, we used to sit in tea shops and have long debates about human rights—he was a big fan of Abraham Lincoln, and admired the American president's abolition of slavery and his commitment to a 'government of the people, by the people, for the people'. In recent years, however, I noticed that the guide had begun to develop a nervous tick—a slight twitch beneath his right eye that made him look as if he was always winking at me. Each time we met the twitch became worse, until at our most recent meeting I saw that it had enveloped half of his face. It was as if whatever mask he had created was beginning to crack. In *Nineteen Eighty-Four* there was a word for this: 'facecrime'. At our most recent meeting, the tour guide begged me to help him leave Burma. 'I cannot survive here any more,' he said. 'I know that if I have to stay I will end up in prison.'

In King Pasenadi's last dream, the king saw goats chasing leopards and devouring them. The leopards were fleeing in terror, forced to hide trembling in thickets. The Buddha interpreted the dream as foretelling a time when unrighteous men would come to power and steal from the people what rightfully belonged to them. When the people pleaded with the leaders for their rights, the rulers would have them tortured and threaten to chop off their hands and their feet. The terrified people would be forced to agree with these new leaders and either live cowering within their land or flee.

T HE CHESS-PLAYER I had met at the Golden Banyan Tree Tea Shop never told me his name or what he did, but I made a habit of going to the tea shop in the late afternoons to see if he was there. One afternoon I found him sitting by himself gazing at the river. He looked up at me and smiled brightly. 'Sit! Sit!' he said. He ordered me a cup of tea, remembering that I liked it *paw kya*, or strong and not too sweet, and apologized for leaving so abruptly on our last meeting.

'That's OK,' I said, 'I'm sure you're busy, and I don't want to take up too much of your time.'

'Time?' he asked with a look of mock surprise. 'Time is the one thing we in Burma have a lot of. We are forced to spend our days quite listlessly. After all, what is there to do?'

He picked up a cake with pumpkin filling from a small selection on the table, unwrapped it, and handed it to me. He hadn't left abruptly because he was busy, he explained, but because he felt uncomfortable about having touched on the subject of Burmese politics with me. 'When I am with my friends in public we talk about football and the lottery,' he said. 'It is dangerous for us to say more. We have learned not to say things in the open. In private, of course, we say many things. But in public we just joke around.' As he unwrapped a slice of cake for himself, he said in an unanswerable declaration about Burma, 'Ah! What kind of country!'

We did end up talking about dangerous things as we pondered how change might come to Burma. 'Change has to come from outside. The world must pinch Burma harder,' said my companion, referring to the sanctions that have been imposed on the country by various Western governments. 'Give any money to these generals and it is like watching a poisonous plant grow.' Ever since the military's brutal suppression of demonstrators in the protests of 1988, trade embargoes of varying degrees have been enforced by the European Union and the United States. Aung San Suu Kyi has called for more complete economic sanctions to be imposed on Burma, in order to pressure the generals further. Activists in the West have launched boycott campaigns against foreign companies doing business in Burma which have led to a number of firms pulling out (Carlsberg, Triumph and Ralph Lauren, among others). Tour agencies such as Abercombie & Kent and Intrepid have also discontinued tours to Burma. The idea is not dissimilar to Ne Win's *hpyat lay byat* strategy with the ethnic insurgents—to cut off the regime's source of income and, in effect, starve it into submission. The regime, hungry for foreign cash, reacts sporadically to this international pressure, occasionally releasing political prisoners like bargaining chips or allowing Aung San Suu Kyi and her party, the NLD, more freedom to operate. But other Asian countries such as Thailand, Singapore and, more substantially, China have chosen not to ostracize Burma and continue to provide aid and investment. The jury is still out on what effect sanctions can have when the generals are propped up by a heavyweight country like China, not to mention an informal economy of drugs and money-laundering.

I asked my companion if he thought that change might come from within Burma. 'How?' he demanded. 'We cannot do anything from inside. The control is so tight. The MI are everywhere. They are in the tea shops, in the markets, even the beggars are listening to us talk.' He shook his head. 'Even the beggars!'

While we were talking, a group of young men sat down at a table next to ours. One of them wore a grey-and-aquamarine windbreaker emblazoned with the words 'Katha USDA'. The chess-player glanced briefly at them and slapped his thigh. 'Ha!' he declared. 'That's all!' And he stood up and walked briskly off down the street.

I stayed in the tea shop and watched a woman washing her laundry by the river. She pulled a dry *longyi* from her basket, dunked it into the water, and swirled it around. Then she sprinkled it with washing powder and slapped it up and down against a rock, each whack sending out a small explosion of bubbles and froth. Another woman stood waist-deep in the river washing her hair. A small plastic tub containing her soap and toothbrush floated next to her. Occasionally the tub would drift off and she would have to swim after it. Further up on the riverbank, a group of young boys had gathered around an injured crow and were poking the bird with sticks as it hopped and squawked and made futile attempts to fly off with its one tattered wing.

Winston Smith's great hope for change in the world of *Nineteen Eighty-Four* lies with his dream of an underground movement that is secretly plotting to overthrow the Party:

Some days he believed in it, some days not. There was no evidence, only fleeting glimpses that might mean anything or nothing: snatches of overheard conversation, faint scribbles on lavatory walls—once, even, when two strangers met, a small movement of the hand which had looked as though it might be a signal of recognition. It was all guesswork: very likely he had imagined everything.

Then, one day, a leading party member called O'Brien finds some pretext to invite Smith round to his lodgings, and Smith knows he has stumbled into the hitherto elusive Brotherhood.

In O'Brien's home, Smith swears into the underground, promising to give his life, to commit murder, to cheat, to forge, to blackmail, anything, to weaken the power of the Party. O'Brien describes a highly secretive organization in which there is no way to publicly recognize another member, no code or secret handshake. Each activist is given instructions through a handful of contacts that are frequently changed. When members of the Brotherhood are caught by the Thought Police, as each one inevitably will be, the most the organization can do to help them is to slip a razor blade into the prison so they can slit their own wrists. 'You will work for a while, you will be caught, you will confess, and then you will die. Those are the only results you will ever see,' O'Brien tells Smith.

Like Smith, I never saw and rarely heard evidence of an underground movement in Burma. But an underground is said to exist, and I met a former member who now lives in exile in Thailand. He was involved in the protests during 1988, and when he learned that the Military Intelligence had plans to arrest him in the ensuing crackdown he ran. Instead of fleeing the country, as many thousands of students did, he went underground, spending some eight years trying to mobilize action against the government and engage people in politics. He described to me the immense difficulty of creating a space, be it mental or physical, which exists outside the government's control.

The first hurdle is simply to connect with people. Unauthorized gatherings are prohibited and, beyond those run by the government, no social, religious or academic organizations are allowed. With constant surveillance and the ever present threat of prison, the underground network must be 100-per-cent trustworthy.

Once networks are formed, the next problem is how to act. In 1996, when Burma's underground was at its strongest, it was able to organize demonstrations that sometimes numbered up to 3,000 students, but it is now almost impossible to convince people to demonstrate when the reprisals are so great. In recent years a number of individuals have stood in solitary protest against the government. In November 2001 Dr Salai Tun Than, a retired university rector in his seventies, put on his academic gown, stood in front of Rangoon City Hall, and called for the unconditional release of all political prisoners. He was arrested and sentenced to seven years' imprisonment. Not long afterwards a former army sergeant handcuffed himself to an electricity pole near the NLD headquarters in Rangoon and announced, 'The *Tatmadaw* is for the country; the country is not for the *Tatmadaw*.' He, too, was swiftly arrested. And there have been others who demonstrated and are now imprisoned, among them two nuns and, arrested on a separate occasion, a couple of law students.

For the underground, leafleting is a safer method of conveying political ideas. Dissidents secretly print leaflets containing articles about Burmese politics, or sometimes just educational articles about social issues that would not pass the censors. The leaflets are folded up into tiny parcels and sealed with sellotape (so the contents cannot be immediately revealed). Distributors target certain intersections which students walk along during breaks between classes or lectures, and leave the scene as quickly as possible. 'It is difficult to have any sense of achievement with these methods, because you get trapped in a vicious circle,' said the former activist. 'You distribute pamphlets, you organize hit-and-run demonstrations, you get arrested, you are severely tortured, and when you are eventually released you begin work again distributing pamphlets.'

If a member of the underground is arrested, all his or her contacts must go on the run, hiding out in safe houses or monasteries, occasionally becoming ordained as monks or nuns. The dissident I spoke with told me that when the local authorities made sporadic door-to-door checks he had to climb up into the rafters of a house, or crawl into the water tank. One day a colleague of his was arrested and revealed his whereabouts. He escaped just fifteen minutes before the MI arrived, and fled over the border to Thailand. For the eight years he worked in the underground he never met with his family, as it would have been too dangerous. After he left Burma he learned that MI officers had told his family that, if they could convince him to surrender, the government would allow him to live a normal life and finish school. He also heard from another friend that the MI had directives to shoot him on sight.

'There are only four ways in which a ruling group can fall from power,' writes Orwell in *Nineteen Eighty-Four*:

Either it is conquered from without, or it governs so ineffi-
ciently that the masses are stirred to revolt, or it allows a
strong and discontented Middle group to come into being,
or it loses its own self-confidence and willingness to gov-
ern. These causes do not operate singly, and as a rule
all four of them are present in some degree. A ruling class
which could guard against all of them would remain in
power permanently.

N OT FAR from the old club in Katha there is a neighbourhood
of small houses packed close together and linked by a series
of winding dirt tracks. I walked along them one afternoon, winding my way up the hill until I found what I was looking for.
Poking above the palm-thatch roofs was a chimney with a few
desultory weeds growing from it. I walked through the narrow
gaps between the houses and came to a large clearing. There was
nothing in the clearing but a solitary, pale-orange chimney stack.
Halfway up the stack, five weathered wooden planks stuck out in
all directions like signposts, and on each side of its base were the
remains of brick fireplaces. Around the edge of the clearing I
found the foundations of a large house, and on one side entrance
steps leading up to a flat grassy patch. In *Burmese Days* this patch
of grass was a sitting room decorated with ornamental tables and
brassware trinkets from India. Orwell wrote that the room
smelled of chintz and dying flowers.

If I am reading Orwell's map correctly, this is all that remains
of the Lackersteen house. The Lackersteens are aunt and uncle

to Elizabeth, the woman whom Flory tries and fails miserably to marry. Mr Lackersteen, the manager of a local timber firm, is a parody of the gin-swilling empire-builder; he spends most of his time in forest camps, ordering bottles of whisky from the club and having young Burmese girls brought to his tent. Mrs Lackersteen is a classic memsahib, the title used for wives of British officials in the Raj. (In *Burmese Days* Orwell defines the memsahib as 'yellow and thin, scandalmongering over cocktails, making kit-kit with the servants, living twenty years in the country without learning a word of the language'.)

Like Flory, Orwell was surrounded during his time in Burma by people with whom he felt he had nothing in common and to whom he could not fully reveal himself. When Flory describes the constraints of colonial society, he could almost be musing on Oceania in *Nineteen Eighty-Four*:

> It is a world in which every word and every thought is censored . . . even friendship can hardly exist when every white man is a cog in the wheels of despotism. Free speech is unthinkable. All other kinds of freedom are permitted. You are free to be a drunkard, an idler, a coward, a backbiter, a fornicator; but you are not free to think for yourself.

In *The Road to Wigan Pier* Orwell describes his meeting another colonial servant on a train ride to Mandalay. The two spent half an hour testing each other's views, having a 'safe' conversation, before they realized they both had the same feelings towards the Empire. They then sat up in their bunks drinking beer as the train jolted along through the pitch-black night and 'damned the British Empire—damned it from the inside, intelligently and intimately. It did us both good. But we had been speaking forbidden things, and in the haggard morning light when the train crawled into Mandalay, we parted as guiltily as any adulterous couple.'

If Orwell felt isolated from the European community in Burma, he probably felt just as isolated from the Burmese. In the year he left the country, tensions between the two races were heightening and a number of Europeans were murdered. In the jungles south of Mandalay, a British forestry worker was killed by elephant handlers while logging in the jungle. In Ma-u-Bin, the town I had visited in the Delta, a French Catholic priest was hacked to bits with a *dah,* or Burmese sword. Down south, in the port town of Mergui, a Chinese pork-seller mistook a German man for the British sanitary inspector who had put him out of business and promptly killed him. A British assistant at a rubber syndicate in Victoria Point, the southernmost tip of Burma, was murdered while cycling home one evening. Newspapers reported these deaths as individual occurrences, unconnected with any larger political discontent with British rule. But this unprecedented wave of attacks must have unsettled the country's white community, and the resulting paranoia is echoed in *Burmese Days.* When a forester called Maxwell is sawn apart by *dah*-wielding Burmese, fear spreads quickly through the club members and throws Memsahib Lackersteen into a fit: 'We shall all be murdered in our beds,' she wails.

Most memoirs written by policemen who had been based in

Burma make at least some mention of the severe isolation which could plague officers far from their homes and families in solitary postings where they were sometimes the only European for miles around. To understand what it was like, one policeman recommended reading 'The Man Who Loved Islands', a short story by D. H. Lawrence. It is a strange and haunting tale about a man who starts a farm on an island, building a perfect miniature community with a housekeeper, a mason, a carpenter and a number of farmhands. His staff become dissatisfied at being cut off on the island, and one by one they leave. He sells the island and, with just two faithful staff, moves to a smaller one. When things begin to go wrong there, he departs for an even smaller island, where he builds a hut and lives in utter solitude, slowly losing track of the days of the week and the rest of the world.

'To talk, simply to talk!' bemoans Flory in *Burmese Days*. 'It sounds so little, and how much it is! When you have existed to the brink of middle age in bitter loneliness, among people to whom your true opinion on every subject on earth is blasphemy, the need to talk is the greatest of all needs.'

As I sat at the foot of the chimney, soaking up the blue skies and warm sunshine, a herd of biscuit-coloured goats with black-tipped ears rounded the corner. They were followed by an old man who led a baby goat, still unsure on its legs, tied to a string. He seemed unsurprised to see me sitting there. I asked him if he remembered the old house.

'Yes, I remember this house,' he said. 'It used be packed full of handsome furniture. It was a very grand house once.'

As he walked on, leading his herd around the side of the clearing, one of his goats skipped up the front steps and began tugging at the grass that grew around the base of the chimney.

In June 1927 Orwell was granted six months' home leave and sailed back to England. His family were on holiday in Cornwall when he returned, and he joined them there. His sister noticed 'a great change' in her newly returned brother—not just physically, but in his character. His hair was darker, he had grown a moustache, and he had become, to her mind, rather untidy—throwing his cigarette butts and used matches on to the floor and expecting other people to sweep them up. He had, she speculated, become too used to having servants. Sometime during that holiday, Orwell announced to his family that he had decided not to return to Burma and that he was going to give up his job as an imperial policeman and become a writer. According to his sister, the family were horrified that he would throw away a respectable career in the colonies for such an unpromising future.

The few snippets of autobiography that Orwell left behind indicate that his time in Burma was a major turning point in his life, marking his transformation from a snobbish public-school boy to a writer with a social conscience who would seek out the underdogs of society and try to tell their stories. Orwell's hatred towards colonialism, nurtured in the heat and solitude, grew like a hothouse flower. He wrote that he felt guilty about his role in the great despotic machine of empire and became haunted by the 'faces of prisoners in the dock, of men waiting in the condemned cells, of subordinates I bullied and aged peasants I had snubbed, of servants and coolies I had hit with my stick in moments of rage'. One of Orwell's most famous essays, 'A Hanging', describes walking a convicted criminal to the gallows in a Burmese prison. The key moment in the piece is when the condemned man steps aside to avoid getting his feet wet in a puddle and Orwell realizes that this nameless victim is a living human being just like himself: 'He and we were a party of men walking together, seeing, hearing, feeling, understanding the same world; and in two minutes, with a sudden snap, one of us would be gone—one mind less, one world less.' This essay, first published in 1931, is still used today in campaigns against capital punishment.

Tormented by these Burmese ghosts, Orwell began to look more closely at his own country and saw that England also had its oppressed and nameless masses in the form of the working class. The working class, he wrote, became for him the symbolic victims of the injustice he had seen in Burma. He felt compelled to enter the world of London's homeless and the destitute of Paris (and would, a few years later, describe his experiences there in his book *Down and Out in Paris and London*): 'I wanted to submerge myself, to get right down among the oppressed, to be one of them and on their side against the tyrants.'

*Down and Out in Paris and London,* which appeared in 1933, was Orwell's first published book, and it was not until some six years after he had left Burma that he completed *Burmese Days*. But one old colonial hand who was posted to Katha, and remembers playing three-handed bridge there with his wife and Orwell, claims that Orwell had already started writing *Burmese Days* while he was in the Imperial Police Force. Orwell's early character sketches for John Flory were indeed written on Government of Burma writing paper. I liked the idea of Orwell coming home from the Katha club each night to sit in his house and secretly scribble out his frustrations by the light of a kerosene lamp, just like Winston Smith writing his hidden diary in *Nineteen Eighty-Four*.

On Orwell's sketch map of Katha, the town ends abruptly with a few strokes of the pen and the word 'jungle'. I walked along the single road that led out to the edge of town. On either side of the road were neat two-storey houses: some constructed with blackened wood, others built of faded timber beams and brick walls smoothed over with plaster the colour of egg custard. The gardens were filled with trees, and bougainvillea hung down from the verandahs. On each front porch there was an earthenware jar of water with plastic cups so that passers-by could take a drink. A woman holding a child by each hand strolled by with an enormous cabbage balanced on her head. Two elderly women sat on the front steps of their wooden house smoking cheroots that seemed to me as thick as rolling pins. Every so often a truck thundered down the road, piled high with logs. Mostly, however, the traffic consisted of trishaws and pony carts painted in the bright reds, blues and yellows of a child's colouring book.

When the houses gave way to paddy fields I saw that Orwell's jungle was long gone. As I stood at the edge of Katha, watching a young boy on the back of a buffalo urge the beast through the muddy fields, a man cycled up to me. I couldn't remember seeing him before and he wore no uniform, but I assumed he must be MI. 'You should go back into town now,' he said.

I nodded wearily, and turned round to walk back. The man cycled slowly behind me, weaving his battered Chinese bicycle in great figures of eight until I was safely back within the limits of Katha.

SOON RAN out of things I could do in Katha. The historian had asked me not to visit her again, because she did not want to attract any more attention to herself, and, though I went back to the Golden Banyan Tree Tea Shop a couple of times, I never saw my chess-playing friend again. Every morning the guest house owner asked me when I was going to leave. He told me that the MI came to the guest house two or three times a day while I was out to ask him if he had managed to get any information about who I was and why I was wandering around Katha on my own. More than a few times, while I walked around town following Orwell's sketch map, I had noticed that I was being followed. And there were a number of strangers, like the long-haired Soe, who approached me in the street to quiz me. They may just have been friendly or innocently curious, but by then I saw everyone as a potential informer. One evening, while I wandered through the night market, a broad-shouldered man began walking beside me. He was smartly dressed in a blue-and-pink-checked *longyi,* and had a black beret perched jauntily atop his head. He wanted to know my name and occupation, and where I had come from, and what I was doing in Katha. I noticed, beneath the long folds of his *longyi,* he was wearing canvas army boots. He followed me along the stalls of the market, repeating his questions until I turned into my guest house.

On my last night in Katha I lay tucked up against the mountain chill beneath layers of thick blankets, listening to the doves cooing in the rafters of the house and the steady rush of the river outside my window. Someone in one of the cubicles further down the corridor turned on a radio. Though the reception was quite poor, every so often the name 'Aung San Suu Kyi' leaped out from the garbled monologue. I had a short-wave radio with me, and tried to tune into the BBC World Service. By opening the window and holding the radio so the aerial stuck out I was able to hear the weak and distant voice of an English newsreader. But the words were hard to decipher, and after a few moments they vanished in a sudden roar of static and crackle.

Every novel that Orwell wrote ends in defeat. The main character attempts to fight the system, but, just when you think the obstacles have been surmounted, he or she loses the battle. In *The Clergyman's Daughter,* Dorothy makes a brief bid for freedom from the constraints of her domestic servitude, but ends up returning to a life of buying bacon for breakfast and making costumes for the church pageant. Gordon Comstock, the poet in *Keep the Aspidistra Flying,* declares war against the 'money god', but eventually succumbs to writing advertising jingles for cash. And much the same is true of all Orwell's heroes.

Winston Smith in *Nineteen Eighty-Four* discovers that the Brotherhood he has joined is just another shadow organization of the omniscient Party, and O'Brien turns out to be his chief interrogator. In prison, Smith is tortured until the last murmur of dissent has been squeezed out of him, and the final scene of the novel finds him a broken man sitting in the Chestnut Tree Café, crying gin-scented tears for his love of Big Brother. In *Burmese Days*, John Flory ends up dead on the floor of his bedroom in Katha. For all his anti-Empire talk with Dr Veraswami, he was never able to muster enough courage to nominate the doctor as a member of the club. Among the scraps of paper on which Orwell wrote the early drafts of *Burmese Days* there is an epitaph for Flory. The poem was not included in the book, and Orwell had imagined it carved into the bark of a peepul tree somewhere in Upper Burma. It ends with the cautionary lines:

> *Take the single gift I give*
> *and learn from me how not to live.*

I scoured the notes that Orwell had written for his final novella, 'A Smoking Room Story', hoping for evidence of a more admirable hero. Orwell's frame of mind when he was planning the book cannot have been good. He was in a sanatorium in the Cotswolds being treated for tuberculosis which he believed he had contracted in Burma. And there are frequent references in his final notebooks to the atom bomb, which had been dropped on Hiroshima only a few years back, which led to thoughts about how the world would undoubtedly soon be blown to pieces.

Orwell described 'A Smoking Room Story' to a friend as a study of characters rather than ideas. The main character in the book is Curly Johnson, a graceful youth with wavy black hair—perhaps Orwell's first handsome hero. Also, unlike Orwell's other heroes, Curly is socially adept, able to sing along at a party, dance elegantly, and 'shake the poker dice in just the right manner'. The story is set on a ship sailing from Burma back to England, and, though Curly can sing along with the rest of the crowd, he is cast as the loner on the boat. The plot is structured around his flashbacks to his life working on a plantation in a tiny outpost in Burma, and he remembers the miserable bachelor atmosphere of his house with its dust and squalor, its dripping roof, and its worn gramophone records. At the end of his life, Orwell's vitriol against the British empire was still sparklingly sharp, and the colonial characters are painted with derisive strokes. (One has a gorilla-like laugh; others are offended if you are still sober by eleven in the morning.)

Like *Burmese Days*, 'A Smoking Room Story' was intended to explore the spaces behind the façade of empire. Curly's life in Burma is mired in seediness: whores and whisky bottles are littered around his house, and one evening, when the servant produces a mother and daughter for his pleasure, he throws poker dice with his friend to see who will have which one. (The mother was the one they both wanted, given that her daughter was only twelve years old.) A Christian priest living at a mission in the outpost seems to offer Curly some sense of salvation, encouraging him to change his ways and to better himself through books in the Rangoon library. The notes only hint at the discovery which will shatter Curly's admiration of the priest. There is gossip about the clergyman's penchant for boys, a fleeting glimpse of a photograph of a young person in a blue *longyi* placed on a chest of drawers, and a mention that it is sometimes difficult to distinguish the sex of Burmese children as they all wear similar clothes.

There are no details about how the novel might end, and the only grain of hope to be found is in the title of the penultimate chapter, which is called 'The Opportunity'.

I LEFT KATHA early the next morning. There was no electricity in the guest house when my alarm clock went off at four o'clock, so I lit a candle to pack my bags, creeping as quietly as I could over the creaking floorboards.

The pre-dawn sky was a deep periwinkle blue. A thick mist had blown in off the river, and the streets were still dark and empty. I walked along the riverbank, past luminous stone lions that guarded a pagoda with their glowing red eyes. I turned the corner on to the main road and saw that a tea shop was already opening up. The shop was lit with kerosene lamps, and I could see the serving boys—wrapped up in shawls against the morning chill—wiping down the wooden tables, laying out tiny cups and flasks of clear tea, and filling cigarette-holders. As they moved around, their shadows danced larger than life against the pale cement walls. One of the older boys was standing at a table and busily sticking round balls of dough on to the red-hot sides of a charcoal stove to make *naan* bread. Another boy lifted the lid off a giant tin kettle that squatted heavily over an open fire and jumped back as a great cloud of steam escaped: the tea was just about to boil.

There is no bus station in Katha, and I found the bus parked in a street not far from the market. There was a large crowd around it, and baskets and sacks were being tied on to the roof and shoved beneath the seats. The bus was an old commuter vehicle from China, and the original floor had been ripped out to allow more room for storage. When I sat on my seat my legs dangled way above a makeshift wooden platform. The front windscreen was plastered with stickers, small posters and photographs of revered holy sites around Burma; among them were the golden hanging rock of Kyaik-tyo, said to have been put in place by a wizard king, and the solitary peak of Mount Popa, which rises from the central plains and is home to the nat spirits. There were jewel-encrusted Buddha images, owls folded out of banknotes, and spiralling Pali inscriptions. I sat next to an elderly man smoking a long cheroot. He wore a broad-brimmed felt hat, and had thrown a bright pink towel around his shoulders. Passengers filed on to the bus in a steady stream of anoraks, scarves and towels. Two soldiers carrying muskets with wooden stocks and roughly hewn iron fittings squeezed their way through the sacks of vegetables and the wandering chickens to check ID cards, and eventually settled into specially reserved seats at the front.

The conductor, who had been securing bags on the roof, gave a loud whoop as he swung through the open door, and the driver turned the ignition key. I noticed a cardboard box tucked beneath his seat which didn't bode well for a trouble-free journey: it was filled with spanners and oil-soaked tools in preparation for a breakdown. As the driver revved the engine, the conductor bellowed the bus's various destinations into the empty streets. A young man running breathlessly down the road appeared in the headlights, and the conductor grabbed his hand and pulled him on board as the bus jolted forward. The laughing man squeezed into a space by the door and joked loudly that he needed a new wife, because the one he had wasn't very good at waking him up. The old man next to me chuckled, and a few people clapped in response.

In a few short minutes we had left Katha behind us. Damp bamboo fronds brushed against the windows, and small pagodas loomed ghostly white above the paddy fields. A familiar feeling of excitement swept through the bus as we set off on our journey, careering along a dirt path into the darkness.

# EPILOGUE

O N 30 MAY 2003, not long after I left Burma, Aung San Suu Kyi disappeared. Just after dusk on that day, she and some 200 members of the NLD were travelling in cars and on motorbikes down a quiet one-lane road in northern Burma. Four or five trucks followed close behind them. In the darkness, the headlights of one of the vehicles picked out the robed figure of a monk standing in the road. The monk approached Aung San Suu Kyi's car and asked her to stop and address some villagers who had gathered to meet her. As one of her bodyguards stepped out of the car to talk to the monk, men brandishing sharpened bamboo stakes and iron bars poured out of the trucks that had been following the cavalcade. They began smashing the car windows and dragging people off motorcycles and beating them. The NLD members were unarmed and unable to defend themselves. The air was filled with cries for help, and blood splashed on to the road. Aung San Suu Kyi was last seen sitting in her car. The rear window had been shattered, and there was blood on her face and shirt.

The government issued a statement claiming that members of the NLD travelling with Aung San Suu Kyi had provoked a group of pro-government youth and a skirmish had resulted in which four people were killed and fifty injured. According to the statement, Aung San Suu Kyi was being kept in protective custody and, for her own safety, details of her exact whereabouts could not be released. Was she alive? Injured? There was no way of telling. Others were missing, too: nearly 20 senior NLD members and over 100 people who were part of the cavalcade had yet to return home.

As the weeks passed, I followed the confused and contradictory reports that seeped out of Burma. When the attack began, many people fled into the surrounding jungle and watched what happened. Afterwards, they did not dare go back to their homes, but hid in monasteries and safe houses across the country. Some escaped to neighbouring Thailand, and, as they did, a very different picture of events began to come into focus. Eyewitnesses estimated that some 70 NLD members had been beaten to death and that over 100 had been arrested. The attackers were members of the USDA, and included government soldiers dressed in civilian clothes. It is believed that the regime organized the attack to intimidate Aung San Suu Kyi and to frame her and the NLD as troublemakers intent on destabilizing the country. It also provided the generals with a convenient excuse to make Aung San Suu Kyi disappear. Just over a week later, a United Nations envoy flew to Burma and was able to obtain a meeting with her. He reported that she was in good health, but was unable to divulge her whereabouts. There was speculation that she was being kept in special quarters in Insein Prison. It was not until three months after the attack that she was returned to her home in Rangoon and was placed, yet again, under house arrest.

I had wanted to end this book on a more hopeful note. As I sat at my desk, I read newspapers and searched the Internet looking for any signs of good news from Burma. I never found any.

The latter months of 2003 were marked by violent anti-Muslim riots believed to have been instigated by the regime to detract attention from the events of 30 May. The following year, in May 2004, the generals hosted a national convention designed to give the impression that democratic process would be instilled in the Burmese constitution. The convention was a sham: hand-picked delegates were prohibited from debating the articles within the regime's proposed constitution and proceedings were effectively rendered null and void by the fact that NLD party leaders were not released from house arrest and therefore could not attend the convention. In October 2004 it was announced that the SPDC's second-in-command, Khin Nyunt, who is considered by some to hold the most moderate views among the senior generals, suddenly retired due to health reasons. The similar "retirement" of numerous ministers who had close ties to him and the dismantling of the Military Intelligence, which came under his jurisdiction, indicate that his resignation had nothing to do with health. Rather, it has been interpreted by Burma analysts as a consolidation of strength within the military government; with the removal of Khin Nyunt and all those loyal to him, the country's most senior general, Than Shwe, no longer has any potential rivals to his power.

While working on this book I referred constantly to George Orwell's novel *Nineteen Eighty-Four*. Whenever I looked at it, reading random paragraphs and sentences, I was astounded by how accurately Orwell's writing paralleled the fears and emotions of the Burmese people I had met. As long as the military remains in complete control of the country and refuses to allow any voices other than its own to be heard, Orwell's words will continue to resonate in Burma. Still, history has shown that regimes which rule against the will of the people cannot last, and it is hard to imagine the Burmese generals will be able to maintain their stranglehold forever. I look forward to the day when Orwell's unwitting prophecy will have been ridden out and the pages of my copy of *Nineteen Eighty-Four* can finally be closed.

# ACKNOWLEDGEMENTS

I N RESEARCHING THIS BOOK, the most useful collection of George Orwell's writing was *George Orwell: Complete Works*, edited by Peter Davison (Secker & Warburg, 1998). This twenty-volume edition contains everything extant that Orwell wrote, from misspelled letters to his mother while he was at boarding school to the notes he scribbled on his deathbed. To look at the original manuscripts and letters, I made good use of the George Orwell Archive at University College London, which also contains a comprehensive library of Orwell-related books. I used older biographies written about Orwell, such as *The Unknown Orwell* by Peter Stansky and William Abrahams (Constable, 1972) and *George Orwell: A Life* by Bernard Crick (Secker & Warburg, 1980), as well as more recent volumes like *Orwell: Wintry Conscience of a Generation* by Jeffrey Meyers (Norton, 2000) and *Orwell: The Life* by D. J. Taylor (Chatto & Windus, 2003). Other books relating to Orwell's life which proved useful in my research were Jacintha Buddicom's memoir of her childhood with Orwell, *Eric & Us: A Remembrance of George Orwell* (Frewin, 1974); *Orwell Remembered*, compiled by Audrey Coppard and Bernard Crick (BBC Books, 1984); and *Remembering Orwell*, edited by Stephen Wadhams (Penguin, 1984).

At the India Office Records in the British Library I found a wealth of information on British-ruled Burma. There I was able to plunder the colonial administration's yearly *Report on the Police Administration of Burma,* as well as various crime reports and district gazetteers. It is a testament to the sheer wealth and depth of the information stored at the India Office Records that one is still able to look up Orwell's results for the exams he took in 1922 to enter the Imperial Police Force and learn that, of all the applicants, he scored the lowest mark for mounting and dismounting his horse. The British Library also houses a number of unpublished manuscripts written by British police officers who worked in Burma around the same time as Orwell, namely 'A Burma Bobby', written under the pen-name A. Meer Nemo, and 'A Burma Patchwork' by C. Bruce Orr.

To learn more about how other Westerners experienced Burma during the 1920s, I read a number of travel books from the period: *Peacocks and Pagodas* by Paul Edmonds (George Routledge, 1924), *Into the East: Notes on Burma and Malaya* by Richard Curle (Macmillan, 1923), *A Holiday in Burma* by C. M. Leicester (A. Wheaton & Co., 1928) and *The Gentleman in the Parlour* by Somerset Maugham (William Heinemann, 1930), among others. Memoirs written by retired civil servants of the British administration which also provided useful information included *Into Hidden Burma* by Maurice Collis (Faber & Faber, 1953), *The Silken East: A Record of Life and Travel in Burma* by V. C. Scott O'Connor (Hutchinson, 1928), *Reverie of a Qu'hai and Other Stories* by J. K. Stanford (William Blackwood, 1951), *Peacock Dreams* by William Tydd (British Association for Cemeteries in South Asia, 1987) and

*Burma Retrospect and Other Sketches* by C. J. Richards (Herbert Curnow, 1951).

For news of events inside Burma today I used the daily compilation of up-to-date articles and reports from sources around the world, including SPDC government statements, provided by BurmaNet News at www.burmanet.org. Another useful source was *The Irrawaddy*, a magazine which offers monthly coverage of Burma issues and an online news service available at www.irrawaddy.org. The Assistance Association for Political Prisoners (AAPP) was particularly helpful to me in sourcing information about political prisoners and the events of 30 May 2003; its reports and publications can be read at www.aappb.net. Of the books that have been written on Burma's recent history, I found *Outrage: Burma's Struggle for Democracy* by Bertil Lintner (White Lotus, 1990) and *Living Silence: Burma under Military Rule* by Christina Fink (Zed, 2001) both indispensable.

I'd like to thank Deborah Henley, whose initial enthusiasm gave me the confidence to begin this project, as well as my agent, Jeffrey Simmons, and my editor, Caroline Knox. Albert Paravi Wongchirachai offered moral support, and it was Sudaduang Puengrow's efficient back-up work that made it possible for me to spend months on end in Burma. Countless conversations with Sandy Barron and Nic Dunlop gave me the valuable opportunity to work through my thoughts. They both read my manuscript at various stages, as did Dominic Faulder; it is a much better book for all their suggestions, though any mistakes which may remain are, of course, my own. Most of all, however, I'd like to thank my parents, who patiently read each chapter as I finished it and provided me with seemingly infinite supplies of encouragement and advice.

These acknowledgements would be several pages longer if I were able to name the people in Burma who helped me without putting them at risk. I'd like to thank those who gave me their time and trusted me with their stories, as well as the many friends who helped me with logistics—introducing me to writers or former political prisoners—and also those who gave me wise counsel over endless cups of tea. A few friends of mine in Burma read the finished manuscript and offered invaluable suggestions; it saddens me that I am not able to acknowledge them by name.